MIRROR ON MIRROR

Harvard Studies in Comparative Literature

Founded by William Henry Schofield

33

MIRROR ON MIRROR

TRANSLATION

IMITATION

PARODY

Reuben Brower

HARVARD UNIVERSITY PRESS

Cambridge, Massachusetts

1974

To
DUDLEY FITTS
(1903–1968)
and
ROLFE HUMPHRIES
(1894–1969)
Poet Translators

Fortunati ambo! si quid
mea carmina possunt . . .

PREFACE

... to hold, as 'twere, the mirror up to nature ... —Shakespeare

Mirror on mirror mirrored is all the show ... —Yeats

The title and the subtitle of this collection of essays are intended to
suggest both the variety of literary arts that go under the name of
translation and their relationship to the so-called creative arts.
Hamlet's advice to the players is a statement of the classical and
Aristotelian position: all art, *poiesis*, including literature, is mimetic,
aiming in some degree to give us a faithful version of nature, of
anything and everything that is. Although the bleak line from Yeats
may suggest that the translator is an imitator of an imitation, we
need not follow Plato's example and exile all translators from the
republic of letters. Perhaps the main theme running through the
chapters of this book is that by exploring the work of the poet translators, we can learn something about the nature and the "making"
of poetry. It is also my hope that these essays, like those by other
writers in my earlier collection, *On Translation*, may add a little to
our increasing knowledge of the process and theory of translation.

I began *On Translation* at the suggestion of Harry Levin, Irving
Babbitt Professor of Comparative Literature at Harvard University,
and I am again indebted to him for his generous interest in arranging
for publication of the present volume. I am happy to thank Professor
Walter Kaiser, chairman of the Department of Comparative Literature, for many kindnesses during the time I was preparing these
essays for the press. For editorial services of various kinds I owe
a special debt to Miss Deirdre Carson.

RAB

Beech Hill
Northport, Maine

CONTENTS

MIRROR ON MIRROR

1

INTRODUCTION: TRANSLATION AS PARODY

It may be that every translator carries a parodist within him, mocking his most sublime and solemn efforts. For who could produce a better parody than the sedulous ape, the "added artificer"? After translating hundreds or thousands of lines of Virgil or Homer, what a temptation to smile in church, what a relief to let out the mocking other self, who honestly acknowledges that, try as he will, his best is only a parody or near-parody of the unattainable original. To say this or something like it is not to suggest that most translations are parodies, nor is it aimed at confusing genres or blurring definitions already sufficiently hazy. My purpose rather is to underline relationships and a common direction between the "makings" of the translator and the parodist, and to show further that translation like poetry is not limited to a single easily isolated activity. Poets not ordinarily thought of as translators can often be detected in the act of translating, imitating, and parodying other writers: Shakespeare and T. S. Eliot are obvious examples. Many successful translators in the past have been, and many now living are, poets: Chapman, Pope, Robert Lowell, Richmond Lattimore, Robert Fitzgerald are among the names that come to mind.

Within the broad range of acts of the imagination that we call "poetry," there is a scale of varying but related activities that we call "translation." A better general term for this scale than translation might be "version," since translation, because of its use in teaching foreign languages, carries for many an overtone of "literal." (What "literal" means in this connection is often not at all clear. To the teacher asking for the obvious literal meaning, the thoughtful student

1

might answer, "To which of 'me' in my many roles are you putting your question? 'Obvious' to me as *what?*")

A few of the many degrees on a scale of versions might be named here—from the most exact rendering of vocabulary and idiom to freer yet responsible translation, to full imaginative re-making ("imitation"), to versions where no particular original is continuously referred to, to allusion, continuous or sporadic, to radical translation, where a writer draws from a foreign writer or tradition the nucleus or donnée for a wholly independent work. "Radical translation" of a critical text or texts may entail rendering in completely new terms basic concepts from an alien writer.

Dryden was the first critic to set up such a scale, with three types of translation, to which he gave names still useful for roughly classifying the many kinds of action of the translator:

> First, that of metaphrase, or turning an author word by word, and line by line, from one language into another . . . The second way is that of paraphrase, or translation with latitude, where the author is kept in view by the translator, so as never to be lost, but his words are not so strictly followed as his sense, and that too is admitted to be amplified, but not altered . . . The third way is imitation, where the translator (if now he has not lost that name) assumes the liberty not only to vary from the words and sense, but to forsake them both as he sees occasion; and taking only some general hints from the original, to run division on the ground-work, as he pleases.
>
> Preface to *Ovid's Epistles*, 1680

But Dryden also illustrates how hard it is for the poet-translator to keep his various theoretical roles apart in practice. Although Dryden speaks scornfully of metaphrase and imitation, he can often be caught slipping into both of these inferior modes. When he gives us "polished elephant" (ivory) for Virgil's *secto elephanto,* or "pains of lab'ring oxen" (crops!) for *boum labores,* he is so metaphrastical as to be incomprehensible to anyone not familiar with the Latin text. Even in his *Aeneis,* where he aims at responsible paraphrase, he moves easily —sometimes to good effect, sometimes disastrously—into passages of imitation in which he freely adapts Virgil to the political, social, and sexual mores of Restoration England.[1] This freedom leads now and then to crudities of the kind that we might expect from Dryden's comments on Aeneas' desertion of Dido:

---

1. The latent anti-heroic, if not satirical, impulse in Dryden's translation of Virgil was first brought to my attention in a seminar report by Michael West.

2

Introduction

'tis true, [Virgil] colours the falsehood of *Aeneas* by an express command from *Jupiter*, to forsake the Queen, who had oblig'd him: but he knew the *Romans* were to be his Readers, and them he brib'd, perhaps at the expence of his Heroe's honesty, but he gain'd his Cause however; as Pleading before Corrupt Judges. They were content to see their Founder False to Love, for still he had the advantage of the Amour: It was their Enemy whom he forsook, and she might have forsaken him, if he had not got the start of her: she had already forgotten her Vows to her *Sichaeus;* and *varium & mutabile semper femina,* is the sharpest Satire in the fewest words that ever was made on Womankind; for both the Adjectives are Neuter, and *Animal* must be understood, to make them Grammar. *Virgil* does well to put those words into the mouth of *Mercury.*

The Dedication of the Aeneis

A translation of the *Aeneid* in this tone would pass beyond parody to travesty, the debasing of high style by having heroic characters talk the "low" language of moderns. It was Dryden, Charles Whibley says, who "marshalled" the Grub Street translators "to the fray":

> "A Translator," wrote the master, "that would write with any force or spirit of an Original, must never dwell on the words of an author." So lightly did they dwell upon their authors' words, that, in many specimens, it is not easy to distinguish between translation and burlesque.
>
> Cambridge History of English Literature, IX, 269

Not only does imitation in the seventeenth-century modernizing manner lead to parody; literalism also may. Dryden's "polished elephant" is exact enough, but comical, a candidate for a Bellocian bestiary. How close the relation was between parody and faithfulness to Latin idiom can be seen when Dryden transfers one of his Virgilian "metaphrases" to the context of satire. "Shook the honors," *decussit honorem* (for shaking locks of hair)—sheer nonsense in English—turns up in *Mac Flecknoe* with surprising effect:

> The *Syre* then shook the honours of his head,
> And from his brows damps of oblivion shed
> Full on the filial dulness.

When Dryden introduced the same phrase in his translation of the *Metamorphoses,* in a serious prophetic speech and without any justification in the original, can we be sure that he was not doing so with a knowing smile to his knowing reader: "You and I realize that this is slightly ridiculous in English, but we also appreciate the daring of using it deftly and getting by with it." This smile of amused recognition shared by reader and writer is the mark of all parody, nor is it necessarily directed against the author being parodied.

Accepting Dwight Macdonald's point that parody "concentrates on the style and thought of the original,"[2] we may grant further (as Macdonald presumably would not) that parody is basically a genuine poetic activity barely distinguishable in its elementary form from the apprentice art of a poet modeling himself on an older poet, as young Shakespeare practiced Marlovian rhythms and turns of style or as Wordsworth began by writing Thomsonian descriptive verse (some of it very nearly a parody of his model). Dr. Johnson's definition makes it clear that the characteristic action of parody is not inherently comic: "A kind of writing, in which the words of an author or his thoughts are taken, and by a slight change adapted to some new purpose." In illustration he quotes Pope on the *Dunciad:* "The imitations of the ancients are added together with some of the parodies and allusions to the most excellent moderns." Pope also applied the term in this serious sense to his Imitations of Horace, poems that assume familiarity with the Latin text and appreciation of the play of the version against the original. In the best of Pope's and Dryden's mock heroic poetry, the parodic style simulates the heroic so nicely as to barely break the epic decorum.

"Play" is a key word for the parodist and the translator, as for the poet. "And then to play!" says Frost—and in no joking context, "The play's the thing . . . All virtue in 'as if.'" "Play against" is equally important, not in the obvious destructive sense, but in the sense of creative embrace and rivalry, bringing out in sharp relief the style and total form of the original. This is apparently one of the meanings of *para-* ("along beside," "against") in the Greek *paroidia,* the dark original of the modern word. Aristophanes was a master of parody of "style and thought"; but even when we know the originals of his parodic lines, the point is not always clear, and the precise blend of admiration and criticism is almost impossible to assess. In the mock-Euripidean lyrics of *The Frogs,* Aristophanes' attitude is obvious, and where he stands in relation to Euripides' moral and philosophical innovations is plainer still. But though the tremendous style of Aeschylus is blasted in a series of farcical verbal and stage tricks, he

---

2. *Parodies: An Anthology from Chaucer to Beerbohm—and After* (New York, 1960), Appendix, "Some Notes on Parody," p. 559. Macdonald's brief comments are among the few helpful observations on the subject. The "bibliography" of parody is slight in every respect.

emerges as a hero, the upholder of the conservative ideal in literature, morals, and politics.

For the present discussion, the mixture of attitudes, like the play with and against the original, is the relevant point. On a scale of versions, both parodist and translator may share similar impurities of motive. If the parodist's mixed motives are rarely discoverable or demonstrable, the impression made on the reader of a particular translation is also often fairly ambiguous. "But," the restless reader of this essay must be saying, "no translator sets out to parody (in the critical sense) the author he has chosen to translate, in a work publicly offered as a translation (except as a joke)." We shall be completely at ease with this defense only if we are content with a fairly simple view of human motivation and intention as deliberate and conscious, or if we disregard the history of translations, especially of the Classics, with which these essays are mainly concerned.

A glance at the group of unconscious parodies in Macdonald's anthology is enough to give one pause as to the intentions of the most serious writers. Some demon or other self must have been at work when Wordsworth wrote

> —Hast thou then survived—
> Mild Offspring of infirm humanity,
> Meek Infant! among all forlornest things
> The most forlorn—one life of that bright star,
> The second glory of the Heavens?—Thou hast . . .
> *Address to my Infant Daughter, Dora*

And what of the uneasy apostrophe to the butterfly in the first version of the poem of that title—a tribute and a tone that might do for the author of the *Decline and Fall:*

> Much converse do I find in thee,
> Historian of my infancy!

As an instance of mixed motives in an avowed parodist, consider Housman's often reprinted *Fragment of a Greek Tragedy:*

> *Chorus:* O suitably-attired-in-leather boots
> Head of a traveller, wherefore seeking whom
> Whence by what way how purposed art thou come
> To this well-nightingaled vicinity?

Every idiom in these and the following lines, it has been said, can be matched by a corresponding one in a Greek play, but what was

5

Housman doing besides showing off his learning, in committing this outrage on his beloved (?) Classical texts? (Housman's attitude toward the Latin poets he so minutely and expertly edited is ambivalent, if not spiteful—the ultimate scholarly revenge on Classicists and the Classics.) Is Housman also expressing in his *Fragment*—for readers of Greek only—begrudging admiration for a language and a style so preposterous and so baffling, yet solemnly beautiful? Perhaps Housman was expecting from his professional audience something like the response of seventeenth-century readers to Dryden's daring literalisms. Or was his real target the (hated) translators of Greek plays. Whatever the motive, the "style" of the *Fragment* is a good example of what attending too closely to the author's words may produce. Pope sensibly refused to translate regularly and *au pied de la lettre* the epithets for Homer's heroes, since in the English context they may become misleading or absurd. In the last generation, Pound exploited the latent irony of literalism by going a step further and punning on the sound of the actual Greek words:

> O bright Apollo,
> τίν' ἄνδρα, τίν' ἥρωα, τίνα θεόν,
> What god, man, or hero
> Shall I place a tin wreath upon!

Dryden's advice to translators against "dwelling too much on the words of an author," though abused by his Grub Street contemporaries and occasionally by Dryden himself, is still of value, at least if the translator wants to be numbered among the poets and not among the parodists. But parody may result from erring in either direction, by being too close or by being too grandly free. Cowley, as a later chapter will show, was well aware that word-for-word versions of Pindar would sound like the disconnected ravings of a madman; but his own "inspired" versions often read like contrived mania. Cowley is in fact a good example of how a translator's native and hidden allegiances reveal themselves in parodic gestures: his comments on Pindar's lack of connection suggest that the poet who anticipates the "true" wit of the next century may have had little feeling for the connections, the "concord" within the apparent discord of Metaphysical wit. Conscious endorsement of the new wit, with its deliberate cultivation of Fancy, and extravagant indulgence in the old wit are two sides of the same coin.

In our own time, the pitfalls in translation of the old exactness, with unintended parodic effect, are illustrated in Nabokov's *Eugene Onegin*. By pushing the doctrine of perfect accuracy to its illogical conclusion, Nabokov has produced one of the curiosities of literature,

6

a deadly serious version of *Pale Fire*. He seems to be one of those, in Doctor Johnson's words, who think that "not to write prose is certainly to write poetry." The risks involved in enjoying the new freedom, while maintaining the highest standards of modern scholarship, may be seen in the serviceable and popular New English Bible.

The eminent Biblical scholars and "Literary Advisers" who cooperatively produced this translation can hardly be charged with a secret inclination to parody. (A parodist might have been more alert to the liabilities of a version of the Bible in present-day English.) The Joint Committee that supervised the translation described their work in advance as "a new translation, not a revision of the A.V. or R.V., having as its object to render the original into contemporary English, and avoiding all archaic words and forms of expression . . ."[3] The Committee also laid down the rule that "Hebraisms and other un-English expressions shall be avoided: freedom shall be employed in altering the construction of the original where that is considered necessary to make the meaning intelligible in English." The lapses in the New English Bible are not those of the seventeenth-century translators, who occasionally adhere too closely to Greek and Hebrew idioms. The lapses in the New text, though relatively infrequent, are perfect examples of committee English, of joint cooperative editing by Biblical and Literary Panels working without a deeply shared sense of style. The very fact that a separate Literary Panel was felt to be necessary is indicative of the conditions under which the twentieth-century version was made, of the "dissociation" between Biblical or linguistic science and literary culture. Here is the main source of effects inclining toward parody and of the failure to achieve an assured rhythm and firm control of tone. But the loss of a shared sense of style is more than a mere literary failure. By not allowing themselves the "comfortable ambiguity" of the older translators who were more faithful to the structure and diction of the Greek, and by deliberately "*not* aim[ing] at preserving hallowed associations,"[4] the translators of the New Bible have diminished the mystery and the humanity of a sacred book. Divinity like poetry depends for its power in some degree on being imperfectly understood. A particular mystery is why that earlier committee of forty-some scholar-divines, who worked in six "companies" on the King James version, did not produce the colorless uniformity of committee prose. To explain that mystery, it would be necessary to explore the history of the culture within which they worshiped and wrote. One thing is clear: they had a firm conviction of the sacredness of the Book and of their task. For

3. Quoted in *About the New English Bible*, comp. Geoffrey Hunt (Oxford, Cambridge, 1970), p. 21.
4. *Ibid.*, p. 23.

them translating was worshiping, as we can feel when we reread the eloquent[5] sentences from their preface beginning "It is a fearfull thing to fall into the hands of the living God." We may contrast with this the pallid and conventional reference to "the providence of Almighty God" in the Introduction to the New Testament in the twentieth-century version.

The Jacobean translators were fortunate in another respect: they had before them older versions in a distinct "Biblical" style ("already a little archaistic"),[6] and in cadences that they adopted and imitated in working up their revised text. From reading the older versions— from living them in church, in prayer, in daily quotation—they had acquired a feeling for a style that Englishmen had come to think of as sacred. Like the traditional oral style of the Homeric poems, idiom and cadences consecrated a way of life and faith and its sustaining beliefs. It was not, fortunately, a too sacred style, as the consciously "gross" vocabulary of Tyndale proves, but a style that could easily embrace material as well as spiritual fact, violence and sexual passion as well as the ways of righteousness and Christian love.

An example of the kind of lapse or anticlimax favored by the new conditions of translation turns up early in the gospel according to St. Matthew (not, it should be noted, the first book to be translated for this edition). After telling us, in almost the very words ("to" for "unto") of the Authorized Version, that "an angel of the Lord appeared to him [Joseph] in a dream,"[7] the story ends with this jarring sentence: "He took Mary home to be his wife, but had no intercourse with her until her son was born." To be told that "had no intercourse with" is the literal meaning for οὐκ ἐγίνωσκεν ("did not know") is hardly a defense. ("*Which* literal?" is again the natural question to ask.) The gospel narrator is made to use a "modern" (or is it?) expression that no husband or wife would use of their intimate life, and no human twentieth-century narrator would use in the present context. (The Greek idiom for "with child" is physically exact: ἐν γαστρὶ ἔχουσα, "having [a child] in her womb"). The natural modern idiom is "to sleep with": "He slept no more with his wife until . . ." "Had no intercourse" introduces the tone of the doctor's office or the

5. "The one passage that touches eloquence," Douglas Bush: *English Literature in the Earlier Seventeenth Century,* 2nd ed., rev. (Oxford, 1962), "Translations," p. 67.

6. *The Cambridge History of the Bible: The West from the Reformation to the Present Day* (Cambridge, 1963), p. 167.

7. This and later quotations of the N.E.B. are from the *New English Bible* (Oxford, Cambridge, 1970). This volume includes the revised edition of the N.E.B. *New Testament* of 1961. Passages cited below, to which mild exception is taken, are unchanged from the first edition. Being Hebrewless, I have limited my examples to the *New Testament.* It is my impression that there are fewer lapses in the *Old Testament.*

report of a social worker, Kinsey questionnaire in hand. The awkward lapse from a world where angels ascend and descend to speak with men into the chill clinical twentieth century occurs, we may suppose, because the translator felt that his idiom was more up-to-date than the Hebrew and Greek euphemism, which was apparently too obscure for twentieth-century readers. Yet this meaning of "know" is fairly common in Shakespeare, and it still has some currency, if we may judge by the title of a recent film. Two of the funnier exchanges in *Henry IV*, one between Falstaff and Mistress Quickly, the other between Pistol and Doll Tearsheet, depend on the Hebraic-Elizabethan usage; but modern audiences seem to get the point easily enough.

It may be said that in general the lapses in this translation show how hard it is for scholarly translators to catch the living idiom of modern English. While avoiding archaisms and ambiguities, the translators fall into the language of dictionaries and cliché narrative, or into idioms alien to the particular context. A random list of examples will enforce the point and perhaps entertain readers agile in spotting the "cultures" associated with particular speech mannerisms. Here are a number from Matthew (italics added): '*Pass no judgement,* and you will not be judged.' (7.1); 'Always *treat* others as you would like them to *treat* you . . .' (7.12); *perished* in the water (8.32); 'I did not come to *invite* virtuous people . . .' (9.13, here and often in N.T. for "call"); 'and I will give you *relief.*' (11.29); 'You vipers' *brood!*' (12.34, for "generation," "offspring"); 'So they *fell foul* of him . . .' (13.57); When Jesus had finished this *discourse* . . . (19.1); *fulfilment was given* to the prophetic utterance . . . (27.9); This story . . . is *current in Jewish circles* to this day. (28.15). Here are a few examples from later books of the N.T.: 'I have come *accredited by* my Father . . .' (John 5.43, for "in the name of"); 'the *true issue in this trial* . . .' (Acts 23.6, for "I am being tried on the question of"); I may *dole out* all I possess . . . (I Corinthians 13.3, for A.V. "I bestow all my goods to feed *the poor*" [A.V. italics]); Love is never boastful, *nor conceited* (*ibid.* 4, for A.V. "not puffed up"); When I was a child, *my speech, my outlook,* and *my thoughts* were all childish . . . (*ibid.* 11, for A.V. "When I was a child, I spake as a child, I understood as a child, I thought as a child . . .). In the last example the A.V. reproduces the verb forms and repetitions of the Greek—the New version is a good illustration of how the loss of rhythm and ritual repetition entails a loss of emotional and experiential depth. In the new economical version with its flat abstractions we can no longer *live* the memorable words of St. Paul.

As the examples from Dryden and Cowley indicate, there was a peculiar strain of ambiguity running through translations of the

Classics from the sixteenth through the eighteenth centuries. One explanation may be persisting memories of classroom boredom, since overemphasis on the classical languages was both the glory and the bane of the Renaissance grammar-school curriculum. Not the brightest of Shakespeare's knights laments that he has not "bestowed that time in the tongues I have in fencing, dancing, and bear-baiting. O! had I but followed the arts!" Holofernes, schoolmaster and "artsman," is an example of what following the arts was like in the schools of Shakespeare's youth. *Love's Labor's Lost,* the comedy in which Shakespeare dazzles us with numerous parodies, is one of his many works revealing the mingled contempt and admiration of his generation for ancient myth and literature. *Venus and Adonis* is filled with more—and less—successful attempts to imitate the wit of Ovid, a poet whose verses and style Shakespeare recalls in plays early and late. The ups and downs of tone in the narrative defy expectation and analysis:

> Over one arm the lusty courser's rein,
> Under her other was the tender boy,
> Who blushed and pouted in a dull disdain
> With leaden appetite, unapt to toy;
> > She red and hot as coals of glowing fire,
> > He red for shame, but frosty in desire.

> 31-36

Lusty comedy? Would-be titillation? Ovidian parody, or overserious imitation? (Others abide our question . . .)

Most of Shakespeare's reworkings of classical themes and texts (often read in translation) are what Dryden would call imitations, where the poet "taking only some general hints from the original . . . run[s] division on the groundwork, as he pleases." The whole range of versions can be illustrated in the poems and plays, from punning literalism to free translation, to parody and the faintest whiff of allusion. *Troilus and Cressida,* as the endless jar of critics has shown, is the great example of Shakespearean freedom in "translating" the ancient world and its literature, while leaving us with multiple possibilities for interpreting motive and effect. The Pyrrhus narrative in the players' scene of *Hamlet* has interesting if ambiguous implications when viewed within the context of the play; taken by itself, it bears an even more baffling relationship to Elizabethan versions of Seneca. Modern readers of Studley's *Agamemnon* find it hard to decide whether the translator and his audience were smiling or feeling solemnly classical when they heard lines like the following:

With bellowings, and yellinges lowde, the shores do grunt and grone,
The craggy clyves and roaring rocks do howle in hollow stone . . .

The most notorious of Elizabethan translations, the "riff-raff roaring" *Aeneid* of Stanyhurst, is to us a travesty (though with some remarkable Joycean mangling of English)—but to the author and his
public? Less boisterous translators like Surrey and North occasionally
jar us by inept syntax and anticlimactic shifts of tone. Chapman, in
his translations as in his plays, is one of the masters of self-parody,
and yet there is no translator of the *Iliad* of more noble mind, none
who can give us a more immediate experience of heroic glory and
terror, or of high moral drama, no translator who renders more con-
vincingly the physical energy and the violent passions of the Homeric
hero. But then we come on lines that throw off the most sympathetic
of readers:

Paris to Hector: "It is not any spleene
Against the Towne (as you conceive) that makes me so unseene,
But sorrow for it, which to ease and by discourse digest
(Within my selfe) I live so close; and yet, since men might wrest
My sad retreat like you, my wife (with her advice) inclinde
This my addression to the field, which was mine owne free minde
As well as th' instance of her words: for, though the foyle were
    mine,
Conquest brings forth her wreaths by turnes."
                                        VI. 366-373

The sixteenth and seventeenth centuries offered plenty of these
styles of excess that lend themselves to parody and self-parody. But
Seneca in Latin was "Senecan" before the Elizabethans stuffed their
version of his style with alliterative bombast from a dying tradition.
The *Thyestes* of Seneca is to us Grand Guignol comic, but the Elizabethans loved it, as they loved the witty excesses of Ovid and the
heroic rhetoric of Lucan and Virgil. They might well say after Ovid,
"ingenio periimus!" Had their knowledge of Greek been greater, they
almost surely would have been drawn to Pindar, and especially to
Aeschylus, as Marlowe may have been. Among the more instructive
paradoxes of literary history is that the century of moderation initiated by Dryden should have had a taste for both Horace *and* Pindar
(or what they regarded as Pindar). In later chapters we may note
how neoclassical translators sometimes managed to give Pindar and
Aeschylus a Horatian turn, thus managing to live in the best of possible literary worlds. The more sober geniuses of Greek and Roman lit-

erature—Sophocles, Menander, Horace, Lucretius—have not favored the destructive parodist.

The style of *Paradise Lost* is among the great styles of excess, one irresistibly attractive to Dryden, who used it admirably for serious parody and for his special type of heroic satire. The "Miltonic-heroic," a blend of Milton's own style with other strands of the English heroic tradition from Spenser, Chapman, and the mob of seventeenth- and early eighteenth-century translators and imitators, was ready for extinction when Pope miraculously revived it—and for the last time in serious poetry—in his *Iliad*. Neither the Restoration nor the reigns of Anne and the first two Georges could offer many examples of heroic nobility for a practicing epic poet. Marlborough, though a great general and one of the decisive figures in English and European history, was hardly a hero in the line of Achilles and Hector. As for George II—

> Oh! could I mount on the Maeonian wing,
> Your arms, your Actions, your Repose to sing!

Hints of parody and even burlesque creep into Pope's *Iliad*, and Dryden translates Homer in a vein not far from Cotton's *Virgil Travestie*:

> At *Vulcan's* homley Mirth his Mother smil'd,
> And smiling took the Cup the Clown had fill'd.
> The Reconciler Bowl, went round the Board,
> Which empty'd, the rude Skinker still restored.
> Loud fits of Laughter seiz'd the Guests, to see
> The limping God so deft at his new Ministry.
> *The First Book of Homer's Iliad,* 800–805

Dryden's leaning toward parody, especially in later years, is confirmed by the unexpected confession in his Preface to the *Fables* of a preference for Homer over Virgil: "This vehemence of [Homer in narrative], I confess, is more suitable to my Temper: and therefore I have translated his First Book with greater Pleasure than any Part of Virgil."

In his *Aeneis*, where Dryden usually maintains a more Roman decorum, the style in descriptive passages has, like Pope's in his *Iliad*, strong affinities with the pictorial manner of Rubens and the late baroque illustrators of the splendid first editions of their two translations. Rubens, with his Shakespearean genius for blending nobility with Ovidian sensuousness and fun, was capable of parody, but whether conscious or unconscious we cannot always be sure. When the Apollo Belvedere is set down, "quoted" with almost pedantic literalness, in the lively company of the gods on Olympus, is this an example of Renaissance piety or an amusing allusion to be appreciated by the artist and his cultivated friends? Whatever the answer, it is certain that many of Rubens' paintings contain parodies (in Dr. Johnson's sense) of ancient sculpture. We may be surprised to discover, thanks to Wolfgang Stechow, that the original of the virgin protected by St. George in a painting of that subject was a Roman statue of *Leda Caressed by the Swan.* Our surprise is lessened if we are familiar with the Renaissance view of Leda as "innocent victim," the Leda we know best from Yeats's visionary lyric. The apparently solemn engravers of Rubens' paintings often produce versions that approach burlesque. Dryden's and Pope's taste in the visual arts as reflected in their translations of Virgil and Homer was, like their taste in heroic poetry, backward-looking in relation to the purer classicism represented by seventeenth-century French painters and critics. Hogarth, who was highly ambivalent in his attitude toward heroic history painting, gave the final blow to the older style in England by allusive parody and imitation in his own satirical "histories" of harlots and men and women of fashion. Years after he had finished with serious versions of ancient epic, Pope did much the same thing for both literary and pictorial heroics:

> What? like Sir Richard, rumbling, rough and fierce,
> With ARMS, and GEORGE? and BRUNSWICK crowd the verse?
> Rend with tremendous Sound your ears asunder,
> With gun, Drum, Trumpet, Blunderbuss & Thunder?
> Or nobly wild, with Budgell's Fire and Force,
> Paint Angels trembling round his *falling Horse?*
> *The First Satire of the Second Book of Horace*
> *Imitated* (1733), 23–28

We may return now from history to our scale of versions, in particular to the relation between parody and translation. To translate poetry into poetry has been the aim of Chapman (and Denham) and of the best poet translators, from the Elizabethans to Dryden and Pope, to Lattimore, Fitts and Fitzgerald, Robert Lowell, and Richard Wilbur. But though there are subtle areas where no one can distinguish between writing a poem and doing a translation, the fact that "doing" seems the better word for the second process indicates some felt distinction. "Imitation," as used by Pope, and more recently by Robert Lowell, points to the same difference. The free versions of Pasternak, Blok, and Borges made by recent poet translators stand apart, if only at a slight distance, from their "own" poems. To acknowledge the distinction is not to imply that poetic translation is uncreative, produced mechanically without imagination. But however

13

free the version, a difference remains: between the act of "making" a version or "doing" a translation falls the shadow of another text. There are of course as many kinds of relation between poet translator and original as there are poets. Lattimore thinks of the other language as target, and aims quite consciously to impart to English readers some flavor of that otherness. (Browning aims so closely that he misses.) By contrast, there are poets who translate Russian poetry without knowing Russian, as the Elizabethans translated Greek literature from versions in Latin and French. Still, at least the shadow of a shadow is there; the mirror held up to nature is held up to the reading or the memory of reading a printed text in a language usually not the writer's first or even second language. Part of the excitement of doing a translation is the feeling of foreignness, even of the obscurity, of the haunting original. It might be claimed that the more ghostly-mysterious the text seems, the nearer the translator's process approaches free poetic creation. Gray, who remembered everything he had learned, comes off less well than Collins, who made beautiful mistakes, as in his "Freudian" transformation of the *Oedipus at Colonus:*

> Wrapt in thy cloudy Veil th' Incestuous Queen
>> Sigh'd the sad Call her Son and Husband hear'd,
> When once alone it broke the silent Scene,
>> And He the Wretch of Thebes no more appear'd.

But though a poet may draw on every conceivable kind of experience, including mistakes and poems and fragments of poems he remembers accurately, he is not, we suppose, conscious of another poem and its language (or he *is* making a version). It is the other whole poem that attracts the poet translator, that it exists not as idea or inciting nucleus that may "grow" a poem as he writes, but that it is there, completely "done," and to be rendered. Though the translator may or may not aim at echoing the idiom of the original, he is, we may believe, troubled by it, if only by its impenetrability or mere strangeness of sound.

In this great or slight overbalance of attention to another poem and its language and style, the translator, the maker of versions, and the parodist come together. It is ordinarily some excess, some oddity of style, including the oddity of extreme simplicity, as in Wordsworth and Ambrose Philips, that attracts the writer of parodies. He aims at a dislocation of attention toward the manner of the performance, like the jar we feel at catching our own gesture in a mirror when we thought we were fully intent on what we were doing. The parodist like the mannerist in painting is the most self-

14

conscious of artists. The opposite is true of the mature poet who has found himself and his style—unless his aim is parody. A young poet is liable to such extreme self-consciousness, and he may practice parody quite consciously, as Pope and Shakespeare did, or unconsciously, as Dryden did in his youthful metaphysical efforts, or Yeats in his early "folk" ballads and Verlainesque lyrics. Some scholarly translators of little independent talent have a way of parodying the manner, not of the original, but of some fashionable poet or style of a generation earlier, as Gilbert Murray echoed Swinburne and F. L. Lucas blended Tennyson and Housman. Pound and Eliot offered new temptations to the generation following their own. "Make It New" is good advice if followed as Pound exemplified it in his best early work. But "new" has too often been taken as "up-to-date," "twentieth-century." The B.B.C. modernisms of C. Day Lewis' *Aeneid* are already beginning to look awkwardly deliberate and funny. The excellent translations of Aristophanes by William Arrowsmith suffer at times from self-conscious salaciousness. His Petronius, which excited my generation, seems to the new generation to sacrifice the literary artifice of the original. It may be that no writer now over thirty can write with anything like Aristophanes' natural earthiness and purity. Perhaps no one can. The dark violence and bitterness of Juvenal fares better, notably in the version by Robert Lowell. But the rhetorical grandeur that Dryden commands in his translations of Juvenal and Lucretius, and the somber moral seriousness of Dr. Johnson's *Vanity of Human Wishes,* are perhaps irrecoverable in the twentieth century, if ever again.

Perhaps the moral of this progress along the scale of versions is the not altogether unexpected one after the mention of Johnson's great poem: the more surely a version can stand independently as a poem, the less risk there is of some shade of parody, of the reader's being overdistracted by a literary manner that seems amusing just because we do notice it and often at the wrong moment. Shakespeare as usual is the great example: he extended the life of ancient Rome, of Plutarchan biography, and of Ovidian metamorphosis in works that belong to the history of allusion and radical translation (the ultimate steps on our scale) *and* of poetry—*Antony and Cleopatra, Coriolanus,* and *The Tempest.* The allusion to Horace running through Pope's mature conversational poems, especially those not described as "imitations," has done more for the continuing life of the Horatian tradition in English than all the more accurate versions since Ben Jonson's metaphrase of the *Ars Poetica.* (Much the same thing could be said of Jonson's own casually Horatian poems addressed to his friends.) But the history of versions, like the history of poetry, is always turning up surprises, and twentieth-century American translators have produced more than their share. Among the most untranslatable of great writers in the West have been the *grands classiques* of the seventeenth century. Racine has long resisted translation into English, and he hardly seems amenable to parody (although Dryden comes near it in his pseudo-Racinian dramas). But Robert Lowell has recently made a free version of *Phèdre* that reads aloud wonderfully well. The passion of the woman of myth, so perfectly "contained" in Racine's noble alexandrines, can be felt again in this version; we know her *faiblesse,* if not her (untranslatable) *gloire.* Richard Wilbur, by a happy compromise between translation and imitation, has given Molière a life in verse on the American and English stage. He has done this by renewing the couplet, which according to the critics had died as a stage vehicle with Dryden. But it was Dryden who argued that rhymed verse, if not "natural" on the stage, nevertheless "causes delight"—and it does once more, in this fine American version.

2

VISUAL AND VERBAL TRANSLATION OF MYTH: NEPTUNE IN VIRGIL, RUBENS, DRYDEN

Although we commonly speak of "*the* Oedipus myth" or "*the* Hercules myth," and though anthropologists refer to mythical "archetypes" or "structures," it can be said that there are no myths, only versions. To put it another way, there are only texts for interpretation, whether the text is written or oral, a piece of behavior—a dance or a cockfight—a drawing or painting, a sculptured stone, or a terracotta pot. The principal texts I have chosen for exploration here are two of them verbal, the third a painting (with some related examples in other visual media). My primary concerns in exploring each text will be with how the "same" myth—the universalizing "the" seems unavoidable— is transformed when rendered in words or in line and color and what parallels and contrasts can be observed between these different events in expression.

The present essay began in a rather casual encounter between an interest in translation and an interest in paintings of the seventeenth and eighteenth century, particularly of classical subjects. While making some comparisons between Dryden's *Aeneid* and Virgil's, I happened to remember the beautiful picture by Rubens in the Fogg Museum, *Quos ego*—, or "Neptune Calming the Tempest," which is based presumably on a well-known scene in the first book of the *Aeneid*. From that encounter, and later visions and revisions, comes this venture into the notoriously beguiling study of a "Parallel Betwixt Poetry and Painting."

Reprinted from *Daedalus* (Winter 1972).

17

In Virgil's poem, it will be remembered, Neptune rises from the sea to calm the storm in which Aeneas was shipwrecked on his voyage from Troy. Aeolus, king of the winds, acting on Juno's orders, had loosed violent gales from the south, east, and west. Neptune breaks off his denunciation of the winds, *"quos ego—,"* "whom I—," in order to smooth the waves, scatter the clouds, and bring back the sun. He then rides off driving his horses and chariot beneath a cloudless sky. A glance at Rubens' picture (see figure 1) will show that the painting is strikingly like and unlike the narrative. Dryden's translation, though reasonably true to the speech and actions of the original, has revised the myth in ways that can be better understood once we are more familiar with Rubens' painting and the transformation that has taken place there. The painting, which I refer to henceforth as the "sketch," is a beautifully executed modello for a large work, a sketch in no pejorative sense.[1] Many questions besides the primary one concerning the transformation of a myth will arise as we explore our various texts. What is the mythical action "like" in each version?

Figure 1. Rubens, *Quos ego—,* "Neptune Calming the Tempest," Fogg Art Museum. Courtesy of the Fogg Art Museum, Harvard University, Alpheus Hyatt Fund.

1. Leo van Puyvelde, *Les esquisses de Rubens* (Bâle, 1940), p. 57. "L'exécution . . . est aussi poussée que dans un petit tableau de chevalet."

What does each version tell us about the mythical thinking or imagination of the author? What does it tell us about the world in which the translation grew? And since all three artists are rendering an event in nature, what is the experience of nature that comes through to us in the Virgilian narrative, the translation, and the picture?

Translations, in whatever medium, can be best understood not only in relation to an original text but in light of the "conditions of expression" within which they were created. Dryden's version is in rhymed pentameters, because that was held to be the proper measure for heroic poetry. Rubens' sketch has a pictorial rhythm common to many baroque paintings of mythological and religious subjects. Two conditions that affected Dryden and Rubens with almost equal force are the Renaissance and seventeenth-century doctrine and practice of "imitation" and the complex of literary and pictorial traditions variously referred to as "heroic" or "historical." The most important sense of imitation for the present study is not the exact copying of classical vocabulary or motifs, but that dynamic process of "assimilation," as Gombrich calls it,[2] by which a Renaissance artist remakes in his own terms what he has lovingly learned in active commerce with masterpieces of the past. Though Dryden spoke scornfully of modernizing imitation in contrast with translation, he indicates in *The Dedication of the Aeneis* that his aim has been imitation in a sense common to many of his contemporaries: "Yet I may presume to say . . . that taking all the Materials of this divine Author, I have endeavour'd to make Virgil speak such English, as he wou'd himself have spoken, if he had been born in *England,* and in this present Age."[3] Earlier in the same essay he shows that he recognized the close parallel between creative imitation in poetry and in painting:

> By reading *Homer, Virgil* was taught to imitate his Invention: That is, to imitate like him; which is no more, than if a Painter studied *Raphael,* that he might learn to design after his manner. And thus I might imitate *Virgil,* if I were capable of writing an Heroick Poem, and yet the Invention be my own: But I shou'd endeavour to avoid a servile Copying.[4]

2. E. H. Gombrich, "The Style *All'Antica:* Imitation and Assimilation," *Acts of the XX International Congress of the History of Art* (Princeton, 1963), II, 31. For this reference and other bibliographical information and for valuable advice in the preparation of this essay, I am indebted to John Abel Pinto. See his *Related Aspects of Roman Architectural Design,* unpublished honors thesis, Department of Fine Arts, Harvard College, 1970, pp. 52–53.
3. James Kinsley, ed., *The Poems of John Dryden* (Oxford, 1958), III, 1055. All quotations of Dryden's *Aeneis* are from this volume.
4. *Ibid.,* p. 1036.

We can sharpen our perception of what Dryden and Rubens "saw" in Virgil by considering briefly how the Greek Neptune, Poseidon, was presented in Homer and in one or two examples from the Greek arts of a later period. As Cedric Whitman has noted,[5] we have no certain illustrations of Homer's text from the Geometric vases more or less contemporary with the *Iliad* and the *Odyssey*, though there are paintings of episodes from the Trojan story not included in the Homeric poems. The contrast drawn by Whitman between Minoan and Geometric art is most helpful for understanding Homer's representation of his gods, and of Poseidon in particular:

> For the one, reality lies in the actual appearance; for the other, it lies in action and inner nature, and there can be no question as to which view is nearer to Homer's. Homer almost never describes anyone's actual appearance. His method is strictly dramatic, emphasizing always deed, motive, and consequence.[6]

To all who are familiar with the vivid images of Greek vase painting and sculpture it may be surprising to discover how little we are made to *see* the gods of Homer. We have, it is true, impressions of Athena's dazzling brightness and of the shining eyes of Zeus. But though we are told how Poseidon took three giant strides from Samos to Aigai, the point is not the visual image it may suggest to the modern reader, but the action as testimony of things not seen, of *numen*, divine power. In general, we see the Homeric gods doing and suffering, not "looking." For if the heroes of the *Iliad* are "godlike," the gods are like heroes. While Zeus sleeps, Poseidon defends the Danai, leading them to battle with the usual heroic cry, *iomen*, "let us go forward!" (XIV. 374). He comes to the rescue of one warrior, Antilochus; he is angry because of the death of another, Amphimachus, and enters the battle to avenge him: "A god, he strode through mortals' struggle" (XIII.238). We hear in prophecy how he will lead the way "with trident in hand" (XII.27) in destroying the Greek Wall. This is the sole mention of the trident in the *Iliad*, the phrase implying that Poseidon is using it as an instrument, as he does later in the *Odyssey*, when angered at Ajax, son of Oïleus, "taking the trident in his mighty hands, he struck the rock on Gyrai, and split it off" (IV.506–507). But if the actions and emotions are manlike, the scale is gigantic. Poseidon speaks with the voice of "nine or ten thousand men" (*Iliad* XIV.135)—though this reminds us of Achilles'

5. Cedric Whitman, *Homer and the Heroic Tradition* (Cambridge, Mass., 1958), p. 95.
6. *Ibid.*, pp. 89–90.

colossal shout at the trench. The epithets commonly used of Poseidon similarly imply action on a huge scale: He is *gaioxos ennosigaios*, one "who encircles the earth and shakes it." He is also *kyanochaites*, "dark (blue)-haired," an epithet also used of the mane of horses, and perhaps suggesting the color of the sea. (Both connotations are appropriate since Poseidon is also closely associated with horses.) It is worth noting that he is not grey-haired, no old man of the sea. Zeus is in fact older and more powerful. But though Poseidon acknowledges Zeus's superior strength, he reminds him that they are both equal in honor, and that as the lot gave Hades the underworld, and Zeus the heavens, so his share was the "grey sea." He adds that the earth and "broad Olympus" are common property of all three, thus emphasizing both his Olympian character and his role as earth-god (XV.190–195). He is the great earth-shaker when he steps down to Aigai, an episode that anticipates in part the scene in Virgil:

He took three long strides forward, and in the fourth came to his goal,
Aigai, where his glorious house was built in the waters'
depth, glittering with gold, imperishable forever.
Going there he harnessed under his chariot his bronze-shod horses,
flying-footed, with long manes streaming of gold; and he put on
clothing of gold about his own body, and took up the golden
lash, carefully compacted, and climbed up into his chariot
and drove it across the waves. And about him the sea beasts came up
from their deep places and played in his path, and acknowledged
    their master,
and the sea stood apart before him, rejoicing. The horses winged on
delicately, and the bronze axle beneath was not wetted.

XIII.20–30[7]

There is visual splendor in these lines, but gold, it should be remembered, is not merely something beautiful to the eye, but a sign of kingliness and divinity, of the "unperishing." Equally notable is the matter-of-fact character of the narrative. The horses are "bronze-shod," as elsewhere in Homer; the lash is "well-made," and the language of harnessing, mounting, and driving is standard and formulaic; the chariot, *diphros*, is no different from those used by Homeric warriors. Miracle enters with: [Poseidon] "drove it across the waves" and "the bronze axle beneath was not wetted." But "miracle" as I have used it is a term of the Enlightenment, of a world governed by laws of nature, whereas in Homer the marvelous "occurs as it

7. Translation by Richmond Lattimore, *The Iliad of Homer* (Chicago, 1951).

occurs," and it is recorded in the same tone in which "real" events are recorded. As there is no distinctly physical world, so there is no distinctly spiritual one. The "will of Zeus" is not *la sua volontade,* but what Zeus quite simply wants and intends. Magic is present very often in other actions of Poseidon. He takes the form of many persons; he strikes a man with his staff and it fills him with courage; he bewitches one hero with his eyes and makes the spear stroke of another useless. These and similar actions of many gods are "just the things gods do," and the resultant effects on mortals might well have taken place without divine intervention. To say that a god caused or occasioned the behavior is not to rationalize it away, but to make the commonplace mysteriously wonderful. (As it is: how does a man suddenly become brave? why does the spear miss its mark?)

It may be said that when the Greeks represented their gods definitively in painted and sculpted images, they ran the risk of making the wonderful commonplace. The unnamable god of the Hebrews rightly forbade graven images: he was a *spiritual* divinity in a sense that Christians and Platonists well understand. It is the human that is glorified in Greek sculpture as in the Homeric poems. None of Homer's gods can compare in heroic dignity with Achilles and Hector. The well-known bronze in Athens (see figure 2), whether of Poseidon[8]

Figure 2. Poseidon/Zeus, ca. 470–350 B.C. National Museum, Athens.

8. The identification as a statue of Poseidon is accepted by Gisela M. A. Richter, *A Handbook of Greek Art* (London, 1959), p. 89.

or of Zeus, is majestic in stance and noble in facial expression. The impression of contained, arrested motion, as often in Greek sculpture, is the "thing"—the effortless ease of the athlete, of a *man*, not of a divinity in the Judeo-Christian sense. (A "god" yes, but not God.) The heroic character of the figure comes out if it is compared with a Hellenistic counterpart[9]—in the overripe, sensuous handling of muscles, the melodramatic pose, the turbulent locks of hair, the absence of an implied inner life.

We can see what happens when the heroic vagueness of Homer is translated into clearly outlined figures by looking at the Poseidon of the Amphitrite Painter[10] in the Boston Museum (figure 3). Here Poseidon is shown as a slender young man in the act of attacking Polybotes, whom he has already wounded. The god, bearded, his long hair crowned with a wreath, seems about to run his trident into the

Figure 3. Poseidon and Polybotes, Attic red-figured Kantharos, Museum of Fine Arts, Boston. Courtesy of the Museum of Fine Arts, Boston.

9. A bronze statue of Poseidon, the Louvre, *ibid.*, p. 190.
10. For this example, the one below by the Troilus painter, and for most helpful suggestions, I am indebted to Emily D. T. Vermuele, Samuel Zemurray, Jr., and Doris Zemurray Stone Radcliffe Professor, Harvard University. For the vase by the Amphitrite Painter, see L. D. Caskey and J. D. Beazley, *Attic Vase Paintings in the Museum of Fine Arts* (Boston, 1963), pt. III, no. 152. 98.932, pp. 52–53, pl. LXXXV.2.

giant's side (as he actually does in another version, in the Louvre).[11] Over Poseidon's left arm a "small wrap" falls in elegant motionless folds from beneath a pillowy mass, "the island of Nisyros (which he snapped off with his trident from the island of Cos)," and which he is about to "bring down on his opponent."[12] "What man, what god is this?" His glance is alert and amused, and his slight figure—David to Polybotes' Goliath—looks more like the quick-devising Odysseus than the great god of the *Iliad*. If Homer's Poseidon were accurately rendered, he would be of Brobdignagian proportions. A more serious version of the same scene, by the Troilus Painter,[13] shows the god going after the giant with a more violent if less well-aimed forward thrust. Both these figures, like many representations of gods on Greek vases, are barely distinguishable in size or type from the heroes or the young men leaving for wars. Their divinity is marked principally by their icons, the trident, the club of Hercules, the helmet of Athena, the drinking cup of Dionysos.

To jump from these fifth-century forms to Virgil's scene is to have a curious sensation of moving both backward and forward in time—a characteristic response to a poem that is at once a recall of the Homeric world and a prophecy of Rome's Augustan age. Postponing consideration of this mixture of impulses and motifs, let us concentrate first on picture, on scene and gesture in Virgil's account of how Neptune calmed the storm:

Interea magno misceri murmure pontum
emissamque hiemem sensit Neptunus et imis   125
stagna refusa vadis, graviter commotus; et alto
prospiciens summa placidum caput extulit unda.
disiectam Aeneae toto videt aequore classem,
fluctibus oppressos Troas caelique ruina.
nec latuere doli fratrem Iunonis et irae.   130
Eurum ad se Zephyrumque vocat, dehinc talia fatur:
"Tantane vos generis tenuit fiducia vestri?
iam caelum terramque meo sine numine, venti,
miscere et tantas audetis tollere moles?
quos ego—! sed motos praestat componere fluctus.   135
post mihi non simili poena commissa luetis.

---

11. *Catalogue des vases peints de la Bibliothèque Nationale* (Paris, 1902), II, 429, no. 573.
12. Caskey and Beazley, *Attic Vase Painting*, p. 53, n. 10.
13. J. D. Beazley, *Attic Red-Figure Vase-Painters*, 2nd ed., II (Oxford, 1963), 1643, 10 bis. For photographs of this vase, now in Williamstown, Mass., see *Masterpieces of Greek Vase Painting*, catalogue of André Emmerich Gallery, Inc. (New York, 1964), no. 24.

maturate fugam regique haec dicite vestro:
non illi imperium pelagi saevumque tridentem,
sed mihi sorte datum. tenet ille immania saxa,
vestras, Eure, domos; illa se iactet in aula   140
Aeolus et clauso ventorum carcere regnet."
　　Sic ait et dicto citius tumida aequora placat
collectasque fugat nubes solemque reducit.
Cymothoe simul et Triton adnixus acuto
detrudunt navis scopulo; levat ipse tridenti   145
et vastas aperit syrtis et temperat aequor
atque rotis summas levibus perlabitur undas.
ac veluti magno in populo cum saepe coorta est
seditio saevitque animis ignobile vulgus;
iamque faces et saxa volant, furor arma ministrat;   150
tum, pietate gravem ac meritis si forte virum quem
conspexere, silent arrectisque auribus astant;
ille regit dictis animos et pectora mulcet:
sic cunctus pelagi cecidit fragor, aequora postquam
prospiciens genitor caeloque invectus aperto   155
flectit equos curruque volans dat lora secundo.

Aeneid I.124–156[14]

To read this narrative properly demands, in Henry James's phrase, "a sharper survey of the elements of Appearance" than any similar episode in Homer—Poseidon's journey in the *Iliad,* or the shipwreck of Odysseus. Virgil asks us much more often to attend to the seen thing, the picture in words, as in the memorable lines just before this passage:

apparent rari nantes in gurgite vasto,
arma virum tabulaeque et Troia gaza per undas.
118–119

Here and there are seen swimmers in the vast gulf,
arms of men, and planks, and Troy's wealth on the waves.

The first impression in the Neptune narrative is of the sea's confusion, *magno misceri murmure pontum,* the storm that the god "sees," *sensit.* Next, the waters sucked up from the lowest depths, *imis/stagna refusa vadis,* the phrase neatly placed between *Neptunus* and *graviter commotus,* "mightily stirred," so that we take the parti-

14. Text of F. A. Hirtzel, ed., *P. Vergili Maronis Opera* (Oxford, 1900). On Dryden's use of the text edited by Ruaeus, see J. McG. Bottkol, "Dryden's Latin Scholarship," *Modern Philology,* 40 (1943), 243–245.

ciple as describing the sea's "wild commotion" and the god's anger. (Note here and throughout the importance of descriptive adjectives —aural, visual, emotive.) Then follows the unforgettable contrast: the god "looking forth," *prospiciens*, raises his "*calm* head," *placidum caput*, from the sea's surface. "He sees," and we see, "the scattered, broken fleet," *disectam classem*. We hear of his "divine power," *numine*, and glimpse again the confusion of earth, sky, and masses of water (133–134). "Sooner done than said," the god "calms the swollen waters," *tumida aequora placat;* "he chases the clouds away and brings back the sun" (143). "The nymph Cymothoe and Triton, working together, *adnixus*, shove, *detrudunt*, the ships from the sharp rock, *acuto scopulo*." In a series of swift action verbs—like Homer's in describing Poseidon's destruction of the wall—the god "himself with his trident lifts the ships, lays open the vast sandbanks, soothes the water, and on light wheels goes gliding over the very top of the waves" (145–147). At the end Neptune is seen guiding horses and chariot with the reins, moving away against a clear sky, *caeloque invectus aperto*—one final brilliant image of light, reviving by contrast the clouds and "the black night brooding on the sea," *ponto nox incubat atra* (89), when the storm struck.

The increased emphasis in Virgil on appearance and scene, as compared with similar passages in the *Iliad*, is proof of an interest in the natural setting for its own sake rare in Greek poetry. Yet if we think of the phrase Wordsworth once used of Virgil in a disparaging contrast with Dryden, "his *eye* upon his object,"[15] we must feel that Virgil had *his* eye on much more than the event in nature. The storm is being "done up," given scenic value in a kind of mythological drama. It is surprising that so much of the simple anthropomorphism of Homer has survived: down-to-earth human actions and feelings— using the trident as a lever to heave up ships, the passionate anger of the god. But there is also some loss of the immediately magical and the divinely mysterious, some imminent separation between icon and intended religious significance. The presence of the looming Roman *fatum* is more *felt*, as everywhere on the *Aeneid*, than the imported Olympians. As often happens in translations, a retraction in one area is matched by a gain in another area of experience slighted or vaguely implied in the original. The Neptune of the *Aeneid*, this scene notwithstanding, is much less of a dramatic character than Poseidon in the *Iliad*. In nearly every episode in which Poseidon appears, he is vigorously carrying out his role as ally of the Greeks in the long

15. Ernest de Selincourt, ed., *The Early Letters of William and Dorothy Wordsworth* (Oxford, 1935), p. 541, cited in L. Proudfoot, *Dryden's "Aeneid" and Its Seventeenth Century Predecessors* (Manchester, 1960), p. 196.

drama of the Trojan war, and his will be the final act, when with Apollo he destroys the wall of the Achaeans. The gain in Virgil comes through dynamic assimilation: Virgil turns Poseidon into something new, a *literary* symbol, which bears a part, as recent critics have shown, in the imaginative order of the whole poem. The order is not Homer's, but the creation of a very different kind of poet, a poet of symbolic and lyric narration.

Before considering how Virgil's form of "proceeding" is reflected in his transformation of the Poseidon myth, let us look briefly at Neptune's speech to the winds and the related simile of the man whose wise words put a stop to an incipient uprising, *seditio* (148–153). Even when Neptune sounds most like the Greek god—as when Poseidon reminds Zeus that the three brothers born of Kronos and Rhea each got an equal share of honor "when the lots were shaken" (XV. 190)—the rhetoric, the accent, and the implications are very different. Poseidon's rhetoric is familial, though saved from vulgarity by the formulaic style, but Neptune has been through a course in Roman forensics, and the tone is reminiscent of Cicero to the followers of Catiline—shrewd, but senatorial. The aposiopesis, "*quos ego—*," is the master stroke of an accomplished orator: the terrors of the incompleted sentence are more fearsome than anything he might merely *say*. Instead of a "lot," we hear of *imperium* (almost "sphere of influence"), a term reeking of Roman power and law, of the Augustan world constitution, the peculiar political achievement that Virgil's poem is celebrating. In an admirable passage, Victor Pöschl reminds us of the surprising force and extension of meaning and of the links with a larger imaginative design through Virgil's use of a political simile for "the subjection of the storm." In so doing, Virgil was "highlighting a very important sphere of the poem (namely that of the historical world)." "The connecting symbol becomes an expression of the symbolic relation between nature and politics, myth and history, which is at the heart of the *Aeneid*." In speaking of Virgil, we may refer rightly to an "order of Nature" under divine law, implying a sophisticated notion, an *idea,* of which there are only faint hints in the poetry of Homer. But we also feel that the Neptune-Aeolus myth has a new function in Virgil as a poetic symbol for the storm, locally for the actual storm, and in the larger economy of the poem for the "wave breaking against Roman destiny."[16] Or, as Brooks Otis points out in his analysis of *Aeneid* I, "the contrast [in the simile] between the *vir pietate gravis ac meritis* [the man revered for 'piety' and his services], and the *ignobile vulgus* [the common herd] armed

16. Victor Pöschl, *The Art of Vergil*, trans. G. Seligson (Ann Arbor, 1962), pp. 22, 23, 24.

by *furor* reveals at a stroke the human meaning of the storm."[17] In Otis' view, the storm and its calming becomes an instance of the dominant moral and thematic pattern of the *Aeneid*, the opposition of *pietas* and *furor*, enacted in countless events throughout the poem. A use of myth so easily open to thematic interpretation comes close to allegory. Though many readers will agree that Virgil does not quite cross the line between the two modes, they may at the same time feel that we are too often distracted, so to speak, from men or gods in action, from drama, to something beyond, to large values and concerns—the history and destiny of Rome, the moral and religious ideal of "piety," the dream of a harmony attainable among personal, political, divine, and natural realms of experience.

If we now recall Virgil's action-picture and turn to Rubens' sketch (figure 1), what do we see, disregarding for the moment the historical occasion of this adaptation of the original? What strikes the viewer above all is violent motion—in the waves, the horses, and the wind-tossed clouds—seen against the mellow golden light at the horizon and opening in the distant sky. The center and director of this movement is Neptune, who is stepping forward and upward in his chariot-shell, his piercing look following the line of that marvelous gesture of command toward the departing winds and the returning light. The streaming hair and beard, the twisting torso, the whole body "works" with the emotion implied in glance and gesture. The mighty right arm and the trident-thrust (exactly on the line of the forward bending knee), symbolize, like the outstretched left arm and pointing finger, power and intention—no question here of anything so practical as raising ships or splitting rocks or wounding a giant adversary. Yet the trident is no mere identifying icon or stage prop as in its decorative use by many artists, including Rubens himself on occasion. The grandly serious look, the body's total gesture, are alone sufficient: no further evidence of things seen or unseen is necessary, as in Homer and in Virgil. We are nearer to something like the imagined gesture of *Fiat lux*.

As we should expect, the pictorial element has been much enhanced. The buxom nymphs, in lighter tones of brown and pink, with faint sea-blue touches on the hair, blend below into sea-green waves, as if to blend mythical figure and its origin. The winds appear as half-seen faces and forms emerging from cloud-wind streaks, figures and clouds alike done in a range of fused colors from grey and slate blue to brownish and pinkish tones. The chariot-shell—no literal

17. Brooks Otis, *Virgil: A Study in Civilized Poetry* (Oxford, 1963), p. 230 et passim.

Homeric or Roman war chariot—has produced a kind of wheel with incomplete spokes sprouting "naturally" from the shell whorl. No wheels as in Virgil move lightly over the water: this wheel, such as it is, is involved in the hazy watery motion. The horses are sea horses, hippocampi, legs entangled in panic violence, vivid expressions of the sea's turbulence. These creatures could hardly be driven, nor does this god think of driving, though one nymph pulls—ineffectually— on a "pink bridle."[18] Rubens' scene is not least pictorial in over-all composition, in the manner in which violent motion is ordered and contained: the central and echoing diagonal thrusts, of which Jacob Rosenberg speaks so eloquently, the balancing of light and dark in human and animal figures, in ship and sail forms, in areas of sea and sky, the posing of definite and less definite outlines—color, line, and light so harmonized that all actors, animate and inanimate, seem to be caught up in the total natural and supernatural event.

How composition works in the two media of picture and poetry is particularly significant for defining the different reinterpretations of the Poseidon myth. "Words move in time only." In Virgil the action-picture is enmeshed in other narrative and nonnarrative contexts of metaphor, theme, and history. The painter has only one instant, at the most the brief time while the eye moves, as in viewing Rubens' sketch, from left to right, upward and downward within the frame. The shift from poem to painting is all the more striking when the artist has chosen for his moment a speech, an effective piece of rhetoric compared to another piece of rhetoric.

What happens, then, in Rubens' translation? No "calm head" rises from the water; Virgil's anticipation of the calm to come is rendered here immediately in the outstretched hand pointing toward the smoother sea and the brighter light. What was storm and darkness *before* in Virgil is in the picture storm and coming brightness here and now. Virgil's contrasts are compressed with a much more shock-ing effect. The overwhelming violence of the horses and waves in the foreground is countered directly above by the lovely arc of sails as the favoring breeze fills them. At one point the compactness of poetry is equaled or surpassed in picture: Virgil's *graviter commotus*, simul-taneously the sea's and the god's disturbance, is rendered in Rubens' sketch by Neptune's figure moving in harmony with waves, horses, clouds, and other deities. "Consider," Burckhardt says of Rubens' rare lapses into theatricality, "how seldom his figures are shown in loud, emotional speech, how they never rant, how his hands, with all their

18. Jacob Rosenberg, "Rubens' Sketch for Wrath of Neptune," *Bulletin of the Fogg Museum of Art,* 10 (1943), i, 14. My seeing of this detail and of much else in the sketch is indebted to Rosenberg's beautiful study.

29

abundance of beautiful gesture, never gesticulate."[19] In *Quos ego*—
the whole body speaks, language is gesture, drama compressed to the
uttermost. And with what result?—an increase in the sense of
miracle, of spiritual—the word is now inevitable—power. Virgil's
speech, noble as it is, makes the god himself proclaim his power,
meo numine; and his invective is uncomfortably like scolding, as it is
in Homer. To compare the marvelous act to the feat of an orator
is to run the risk of bringing miracle down to political reality (a risk
Virgil willingly embraced).

In Rubens we are brought closer to the unexplained wonders of
Homer, but with the matter of fact "doings" left out. Hence Rubens'
drama and his god are more deeply serious, splendidly and ineffably
godlike. The compression and the immediacy enforce the implication
of a purely spiritual power, paradoxically "out of the blood" of this
warmly living god. But he is not the dark-haired youthful god of
Homer or of the "Landing of Marie de Médicis,"[20] who puts his hand
to the great ship, bringing it against the pier. The head of the *Quos
ego*— Neptune, white-haired and bearded, with his intent eye, can
scarcely be disassociated from images of God himself. We find much
the same head and expression in many religious pictures by Rubens,
of God in the coronation of the Virgin and in the Trinity, of saints
and Old Testament patriarchs (and sometimes of elder pagan deities
indistinguishable from saints and holy men of the Judaeo-Christian
tradition). The contemporary audience, well educated in religious
art, would have seen and felt this association more instinctively than
we do. The ease and frequency with which Rubens transforms pagan
figures and motifs into Christian ones, and occasionally, Christian
into pagan, has often been noted, most recently in Wolfgang
Stechow's *Rubens and the Classical Tradition.*[21]

It is commonly assumed that Rubens had seen the *Quos ego*— of
Marcantonio Raimondi (ca. 1480–1527/37), based on a drawing by
Raphael (figure 4).[22] A look at the engraving will reinforce what I

19. Jacob Burckhardt, *Recollections of Rubens,* ed. H. Gerson, trans.
Mary Hottinger (London, 1950), p. 73; Burckhardt's chief example is
"Queen Tomyris receiving the head of the slain Cyrus," in the Boston
Museum.
20. Photograph in Adolf Rosenberg, *Klassiker der Kunst* (Leipzig, 1905),
p. 239.
21. Wolfgang Stechow, *Rubens and the Classical Tradition,* Martin
Classical Lectures (Cambridge, Mass., 1968), p. 47, and examples in chap.
3, "Transformation." Note the example of "Mary Magdalene transformed
into a *Pudicitia*," p. 58.
22. The attribution of the original design to Raphael, often mentioned,
appears in Adam Bartsch, *Le peintre graveur* (Vienna, 1803–1821), XIV,
264–269 and Henri Delaborde. *Marc-Antoine Raimondi* (Paris, 1888), p.
146. "Elle [Marcantonio's engraving] semble avoir été faite pour servir de
frontispice à une édition de l'Enéide," p. 146.

Figure 4. Marcantonio Raimondi, *Quos ego—*, "Neptune Quelling the Storm," Fogg Art Museum. Courtesy of the Fogg Art Museum, Harvard University, Gray Collection.

have been saying about the "spiritual" in Rubens' sketch and show the difference between more or less literal illustration or visual translation and live reworking of a poetic text. (The splendid quality of the original, the richness and warmth of contrast, and the almost excessive clarity of line are largely lost in the photograph.) Marcantonio has chosen the exact moment when the god, rising from the sea, launches his verbal attack on the winds. His lips are parted in speech, and he pulls hard on the horses' rein. Ships are seen wrecked or sinking, and a slightly earlier event is introduced—Aeneas "stretching his palms to the stars," *duplicis tendens ad sidera palmas* (I.93). No one will be tempted to use "spiritual" of this snub-nosed well-muscled strongman. The figure as a whole is less dramatically expressive than Rubens': for example, the right arm thrusting the elegant trident downward (not forward) seems comparatively weak. The hippocampi, with their oddly elongated necks and snouts, comically equine expressions, and inextricably entangled fish-tails, seem to belong to a more prehistoric age than Rubens'. The all-too human faces of the slightly sullen wind-cherubs may have given Rubens a hint for his beautifully vague cloud beings, but they are curious substitutes for Virgil's revolutionary "mob" (as Michael Putnam calls them).[23] Though well composed, the engraving has little of Rubens' composition in emotional and imaginative depth, or in subtle echoings and blendings of line and color.

But, as readers familiar with Rubens' sketch must be saying, the painter had other and more complex intentions than the engraver. The sketch was a model for a huge painting on an architectural stage erected to welcome Ferdinand Cardinal Infante of Spain on his entrance into Antwerp, April 17, 1635. Ferdinand, brother of Philip IV, had journeyed from Barcelona to serve as governor of the Netherlands in succession to Isabella, Rubens' patron and friend. Antwerp had commissioned Rubens to design a series of magnificent triumphal arches and stages to adorn Ferdinand's progress through the city.[24] Though assistants executed most of the paintings, Rubens gave the finishing touches to the large *Quos ego*—, if he did not do the whole picture (as some accounts suggest). Before the painting (now in Dresden) was turned over to the Cardinal in 1637, Rubens "again repainted" it along with the companion piece on the meeting

23. "Throughout his account of the winds and their doings, Virgil treats them metaphorically either as horses or as a foolish mob, part beast, part brutish man, easily misled into wreaking havoc." Michael Putnam, *The Poetry of the Aeneid* (Cambridge, Mass., 1965), p. 11. If the equine character of the winds was recognized by Rubens and his contemporaries, the sea horses also may have been regarded as embodiments of the winds.
24. Max Rooses, *L'oeuvre de P. P. Rubens* (Antwerp, 1886–1892), III, 292–293.

at Nordlingen between Ferdinand of Spain and Ferdinand of Hungary.[25] The event that lay behind sketch and picture was, according to a contemporary narrative, somewhat less disastrous than the shipwreck of Aeneas. Ferdinand's fleet, having sailed from Barcelona, arrived safely at Caduquès (now a semibohemian resort on the Costa Brava). "Après le temps se changea avec des tramontanes et vents contraires" it proved impossible to continue the voyage for "thirteen whole days": Then came the morning when "the sea grew calm, and with the wind [from the south] in the stern, they parted at mid-day, and the weather was so constant and favorable, that on the next morning they began to make out the coast of France."[26] At a distance of three years and many miles, this princely contretemps became to the eye of imagination the glorious event of Rubens' sketch, in which Virgil's simile was in effect reversed, the historical reality now being compared to the storm and calm of myth. In Rubens' adaptation of the Virgilian moment, the ships are seen quite unharmed, the dark-hued clouds moving through and above them, and the spectral wind-face to the far right, Boreas (the wind unfavorable for sailing toward France), is pursued by southern and western winds that fill the sails of the splendid vessels now getting under way. In Virgil, it will be remembered, *all* the winds are loosed by Aeolus, and Neptune directs his wrath especially against the Southeast and West, Eurus and Zephyrus.

We are beginning to see meanings in Rubens' work that would not be apparent apart from three "translations" that his sketch underwent: the large painting by the master and his pupils, the engraving (figure 5) by a colleague, T. van Thulden, and the verbal explanation by Gevaerts, which accompanied the engraving in the *Pompa Introitus* . . . *Ferdinandi*,[27] a splendid folio memorializing and interpreting all the works of art and the various celebrations of the Cardinal Infante's entrance into Antwerp. The first shock comes when we see the Dresden version, inferior in nearly every respect to the sketch, though less obvious in its outlines and less abrupt in its transitions than the engraving. Since the commentary is based on the engraving, we may consider a few changes from the sketch, along with Gevaerts' interpretations. In general, we may say that everything has become terribly definite, with a loss in the effect of a hazy and mysterious mythical-natural sea change. The wind-faces have taken on the

25. *Ibid.*, p. 298; Rooses cites evidence that the whole picture was originally executed by Rubens. J. Rosenberg, "Rubens' Sketch," p. 14, says "retouched, but not executed by Rubens."

26. *Le voyage du Prince Don Fernande infant d'Espagne*, trans. from Spanish of Diego de Aedo y Gallart (Antwerp, 1635), pp. 19–20.

27. C. Gevartius, *Pompa Introitus honori serenissimi principis Ferdinandi Austriaci Hispaniarum Infantis* (Antwerp, 1641), pp. 19–20.

Figure 5. T. van Thulden, engraving after Rubens, *Quos ego—*, from C. Gevartius, *Pompa Introitus honori serenissimi principis Ferdinandi Austriaci Hispaniarum Infantis* (Antwerp, 1641), Houghton Library. By permission of the Harvard College Library.

solidity of Marcantonio's cherubs, and Boreas is now an aged swimmer with fin-like wings and hands and legs like twisted forms of half-baked pastry, *brachiis in pennas desinentibus & serpentinis pedibus*, Gevaerts says. The whorl of the shell blending easily into the wheel has disappeared, and one nymph hangs heavily on a spoke, turning it, we are told, with the help of her sisters. The suggestion of rationalizing in Rubens is crudely exposed: *Quâ re vortex marinus denotatur, qui in gyrum actus ipsam promouet. NYMPHAS autem quasi LYMPHAS, notum est.*[28] "(By [their turning of the wheel] is signified the sea's whirlpool, which being driven in a circle, carries it [the shell] forward. It is well known that we speak of 'Nymphas' as it were for 'Lymphas' [waters].)" In Rubens' sketch all three nymphs are caught up in the dramatic and visual movement, one looking forward with arm outstretched, the second pointing ahead

28. *Ibid.*, p. 16. The form of shell-wheel may be traditional, perhaps from early illustrations of Ovid. See below, pp. 36–37.

and glancing back to engage the attention of her sister, who is also looking toward the god. In the engraving, the inert turner faces forward, the next nymph turns away, and the third looks coyly out at the viewer. The god's gesture has lost its full effect, since as Jacob Rosenberg notes, his hand comes uncomfortably close to the serpentine legs of Boreas. (Neptune's hair and beard no longer stream in the wind.) Parts, including the too accurately equipped "triremes," shatter the blended life of the whole.

Gevaerts' commentary brings some interesting support and some surprising increments to our earlier reading of the sketch. The inscription on the title page of the *Pompa Introitus* is a bald adaptation of the Virgilian prophecy, *Aeneid* VI.851, 853:

> Tu regere imperio Belgas Germane, memento:
> Parcere subjectis et depellare superbos.

Later in the commentary, the great triumphal arch for Ferdinand[29] is compared with the "Arch of Titus Augustus." In another scene, the temple of Janus is adorned with sculptures of Peace and War, and Gevaerts offers an appropriate quotation (VII.601–605) that echoes Jupiter's words in *Aeneid* I.291–296, on the closing of the temple and the binding of *Furor* (a thematic echo[30] of Neptune's action in the storm scene). In the whirl of quotations from Latin and Greek authors, it is curious that Gevaerts never cites or refers to the "*quos ego—*" passage. When describing a Neptune on another stage, Gevaerts quotes in Greek the Homeric epithets for Poseidon and comments on them with appreciation of the god's role as earth-shaker. Neptune "bears the trident, since he strikes and lashes the earth with his waves."[31] Gevaerts' interest in historical evidence, *historica fide*, helps us appreciate what he and the people of Antwerp saw most vividly in Rubens' scene. An inscription below the engraving begins with *Neptuno sternente fretum*, "Neptune calming the sea," but most of the five lines are spent in praising the "noble cargo" and the ship that brought it safely over "the Tyrrhenian waters." One suspects that Rubens or his associates reread his sketch in a way to fit this more obvious emphasis, one more to the taste of a seaport town.

What then was Rubens doing in the sketch as compared with the engraved version? Something much more complexly organized, and more subtly related to local history, to contemporary and older artistic, literary, and religious traditions. Both versions are very much of

29. Plate before p. 109.
30. Otis, *Virgil*, p. 230.
31. Gevartius, *Pompa Introitus*, p. 149.

their time, but the sketch is more profoundly baroque than the painting in many features we have noted—the focus on the "moment," the strong contrasts and violent movement, the diagonal thrust, and above all in the dramatic expressiveness of Neptune's form and gesture. The effect of spontaneity in the whole is characteristic of Rubens' better sketches: "La forme surgit du pinceau en même temps qu'elle naît avec la pensée artistique dans l'esprit de l'artiste."[32] Behind the sketch lies a powerful mythical vision, Virgilian and Homeric and peculiarly Rubensian. If Rubens renews for us the moment of anger in the *Aeneid* and the change that followed, and if he suppresses some of the humbler actions of the god in both ancient versions, he also revives the religious mystery of divine action in Homer. He goes still further along the road toward a purely spiritual interpretation of mythical action and toward a more immediate and impressionistic expression of an event in nature, while not forgetting the human actor—a combination that allies him with Homer of the storm similes and the landscape painters of the later seventeenth and even the nineteenth centuries. There is in Rubens' sketch the oddest blend of precise observation, of rationalizing (as in the treatment of the chariot-shell), and of primitive mythical vision (as in the wind-faces): "The wheel survives the myths."

But as Svetlana Alpers reminds us in her splendid Introduction to the Torre de la Parada series,[33] Rubens' alliances with the past and the future are not easily defined. His treatment of the human body as dramatically expressive is at once in line with contemporary theory and related to practices of Hellenistic sculptors, whose work Rubens had so closely studied. If like Homer and "unlike Ovid, Rubens commanded a heroic style, which he could inform with a sense of real life without puncturing its ideality,"[34] he was also capable of entering into the Ovidian world of irreverence and comedy, as he did in creating the paintings for the Torre de la Parada. Here too he was working in an earlier tradition, that of the sixteenth-century illustrators of the *Metamorphoses*.[35] Looking through some of the volumes to which Mrs. Alpers refers, we come on plates that may account for some of the departures from Virgil's text in Marcantonio and in Rubens or his colleagues. In *La Métamorphose d'Ovide figurée* (1557), a "Fin du déluge" pictures Neptune in a shell driving two hippocampi. The verses below, based on Metamorphoses I.324–

32. Puyvelde, *Les esquisses de Rubens*, p. 28.
33. Svetlana Alpers, *The Decoration of the Torre de la Parada*, in *Corpus Rubenianum Ludwig Burchard*, IX (London and New York, 1971). My discussion here and later is much indebted to the "Conclusion," pp. 166–173.
34. *Ibid.*, pp. 167–168.
35. *Ibid.*, pp. 80–100.

344, tell how the clouds give way to "Aquilon, leur ennemi contraire." In "Vénus et Pluton," Pluto comes from the underworld in a shell-like chariot drawn by horses. In the *Metamorphoseon Libri XV* (1582), a very animated Neptune rides on a lively and amusing hippocampus[36] —a version also illustrated by Gevaerts from ancient coins. This continental Ovidian tradition appears in England in Franz Cleyn's "engravings for Sandys's Ovid [1632], which . . . represent a parallel effort to Rubens' works" for the Torre de la Parada. "They share with Rubens an interest in the mythological narratives as human dramas."[37]

Cleyn also illustrated the Ogilby translation of Virgil (1654),[38] a volume well known to Dryden, who spoke scornfully of the translator, though on occasion borrowing from his fairly accurate if inept version. With an eye to costs, Dryden and his publisher took over Cleyn's illustrations for the *Virgil* of 1697. Dryden's visualization of figures from Greco-Roman mythology was almost certainly influenced by these Rubensian baroque engravings. Though Cleyn did not illustrate the *Quos ego*— episode, Ogilby's rationalizing notes on the passage— of a kind we have encountered in Gevaerts—are worth nothing. Aeolus is referred to as the "king of the Aeolian Islands," who, famed for his ability to foretell "the change of Winds, . . . therefore was thought to have power over" the stormy weather. On the same page we are told that "the physical ground of all, is this: Tempests are begotten by the Clouds, over which *Juno* presides, they being agitated by the Winds, of which Aeolus is Lord."[39] The note on Neptune's horses is even more illuminating: "Turnebus, and others understand here, *Hippocampi, Sea-Horses.*" Ogilby then quotes Statius as evidence that hippocampi have hooves in front but "trail off behind in the form of fish" (*postremi solvuntur in aequora pisces*).[40] While this fits Rubens' steeds, it does not fit Cleyn's illustration for the Neptune scene of Book V (figure 6), where the god assures Venus that the Trojan ships may pass safely on, though "one [Palinurus] must give his life for many" (815). This plate, also used in Dryden's volume, gives a much lighter-hearted impression than the *Quos ego*— illustrations, in part since Neptune is here shown in a milder mood, soothing the fears of the goddess. His erect figure and gesture dominate the scene as in Rubens, and he strides forward with dignity and strength (in spite of an awkward twist of the right flank). Neptune is not

36. Page 52.
37. Alpers, *Decoration of the Torre de la Parada,* p. 93; "invented by Franz Cleyn and executed by Salomon Savery," p. 92.
38. John Ogilby, *The Works of Publius Virgilius Maro, Translated, Adorn'd with Sculpture, and Illustrated with Annotations* (London, 1654).
39. *Ibid.,* p. 168.
40. *Ibid.,* p. 171.

Tum Saturnius hæc
Fas omne est, Cytherea,
Vnde genus ducis merui
Compreſsi, & rabiem
Iungit equos curru, geni
Fræna feris manibuſque

domitor maris edidit alti:
meis te fidere regnis,
quoque: ſape furores
tantam cœlique, mariſque,
tor. ſpumantiaque addit
omnes effundit habenas. Eand.l.i

Henrico Dukeſon Arm:

Tabula merito votiua.

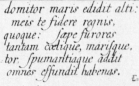

Figure 6. Franz Cleyn, "Neptune and Venus," from John Ogilby, *The Works of Publius Virgilius Maro* (London, 1654), Houghton Library. By permission of the Harvard College Library.

pointing with his trident, but in the act of launching it (at what?),[41] and he is holding the reins of four spirited and capering horses(?), with fin-like forefeet, though without fish tails. He is snub-nosed and crowned, his somewhat protrusive eye fixed on the goddess above. This Neptune is beneficent-looking, and seems to have the beginnings of a smile on his lips, parted perhaps in speech. From her bathlike triumphal car, Venus answers with a tender glance and a charmingly deferential gesture. The upper sky opens for her epiphany, as in Virgil, *fugiunt vasto aethere nimbi* (V.821). The god's shell (ending in a cheerful dolphin's head) has the most cunning and convincing wheel-whorl we have yet encountered. It apparently works as a paddle-wheel, something like the vortex in Gevaerts' note. (It may be of course that both Rubens' and Cleyn's chariots derive from a common original in illustrations of Ovid.) The lighter tone of Cleyn's scene is picked up—perhaps with a glance at Virgil's nereid band (825–826)—in three decorative mermaids gaily swimming, one with "locks blown forward in the gleam of eyes," another with a comic-book smile of flirtatious satisfaction. Not far off, a male swimmer (Palinurus?) half-emerges from the waves.

One slightly unsettling question before we turn to Dryden: was Rubens' sketch surely based on Virgil's *Quos ego*—? Not solely, as we have seen, but as the focal mythical image in a complex of historical allusions and many sorts of visual impressions. To strains noted earlier, we may now add one of Ovidian lightness—in the eager nymphs (for Virgil's lone Cymothoe) and in the lusty Triton blowing the way for the sea lord. This is Triton's usual function in both Virgil and Ovid, but not in *Aeneid* I, where with Cymothoe he is a vigorous helper in freeing ships from the rock. He is very prominent in the scene from *Metamorphoses* I (above), where Neptune "The wild waves calmes, his *trident laid aside*" (Sandys' translation). There is also that pink bridle held by the smiling nereid. A glint of Ovidian comedy—of Homeric and Shakespearean "relief"—enters the Renaissance *Fiat lux* of Rubens.

Dryden had access to Rubens' Olympian imagery through other channels than Cleyn's engravings, as Jean Hagstrum suggests in his interesting account of baroque pictorial elements in Dryden's odes.[42]

---

41. John Pinto has suggested a possible connection with Bernini's "Neptune and Triton," ca. 1620, where Neptune thrusts his trident downward, with great vigor, apparently toward the water of the fountain in which it was originally placed. See Howard Hibbard, *Bernini* (Baltimore: Penguin Books, 1965), pp. 39–43. Note, in relation to Cleyn's shell, "the trailing cloak that suddenly becomes a dolphin," p. 40 Cleyn's triton bears some resemblance to the rear view of the triton in Bernini's group, and possibly to the triton of the Piazza Barberini.

42. Jean Hagstrum, *The Sister Arts* (Chicago, 1958), pp. 197–208.

He could hardly have avoided seeing Rubens' apotheosis of James I on the ceiling of Whitehall, although "by 1687, humidity had already been fatal to it."[43] (It is appropriate that James II "authorized a complete restoration.") The passage on Rubens in the supplement to Dryden's translation of Dufresnoy's *De arte graphica* shows some acquaintance with criticism of Rubens,[44] if not surely direct knowledge of the paintings. More to the point is the remark in his own *Parallel of Poetry and Painting,* cited by Hagstrum, on the close correspondence between pictorial posture and epic description: "The posture of a poetic figure is . . . the description of [the] heroes in the performance of such or such an action."[45] Dryden follows this with a highly pictorial account of Aeneas' "posture" before killing Lausus. It should be noted that Dryden had interrupted his *Aeneis* to do the translation of Dufresnoy, and that these notions of pictorial rendering of heroic gestures were in his mind at the time he was translating Virgil.

How does Dryden's *Quos ego*— appear in the context of the literary and pictorial traditions we have been observing in Rubens and in various writers and artists, ancient and modern? It is still the most readable and energetic version in English:

> Mean time Imperial *Neptune* heard the Sound
> Of raging Billows breaking on the Ground:
> Displeas'd and fearing for his Wat'ry Reign,
> He reard his awful Head above the Main:
> Serene in Majesty, then rowl'd his Eyes   180
> Around the Space of Earth, and Seas, and Skies.
> He saw the *Trojan* Fleet dispers'd, distress'd
> By stormy Winds and wintry Heav'n oppress'd.
> Full well the God his Sister's envy knew,
> And what her Aims, and what her Arts pursue: 185
> He summon'd *Eurus* and the western Blast,
> And first an angry glance on both he cast:
> Then thus rebuk'd; Audacious Winds! from whence
> This bold Attempt, this Rebel Insolence?
> Is it for you to ravage Seas and Land,   190
> Unauthoriz'd by my supream Command?
> To raise such Mountains on the troubl'd Main?
> Whom I—But first 'tis fit, the Billows to restrain,
> And then you shall be taught obedience to my Reign.

43. Puyvelde, *Les esquisses de Rubens,* p. 287.
44. W. Scott and G. Saintsbury, eds., *John Dryden's Works* (Edinburgh, 1892), XVII, "The Judgement of Charles Alphonse Du Fresnoy," 503–504.
45. *Ibid.,* 318–319.

Hence, to your Lord my Royal Mandate bear,   195
The Realms of Ocean and the Fields of Air
Are mine, not his; by fatal Lot to me
The liquid Empire fell, and Trident of the Sea.
His Pow'r to hollow Caverns is confin'd,
There let him reign, the Jailor of the Wind: 200
With hoarse Commands his breathing Subjects call,
And boast and bluster in his empty Hall.
He spoke: and while he spoke, he smooth'd the Sea,
Dispell'd the Darkness, and restor'd the Day:
Cymothoe, Triton, and the Sea-green Train   205
Of beauteous Nymphs, the Daughters of the Main,
Clear from the Rocks the Vessels with their hands;⎤
The God himself with ready Trident stands,   ⎬
And opes the Deep, and spreads the moving sands;⎦
Then heaves them off the sholes: where e're he guides⎤ 210
His finny Coursers, and in Triumph rides,   ⎬
The Waves unruffle and the Sea subsides.   ⎦
As when in Tumults rise th' ignoble Crowd,
Mad are their Motions, and their Tongues are loud;
And Stones and Brands in ratling Vollies fly,   215
And all the Rustick Arms that Fury can supply:
If then some grave and Pious Man appear,
They hush their Noise, and lend a list'ning Ear;
He sooths with sober Words their angry Mood,
And quenches their innate Desire of Blood: 220
So when the Father of the Flood appears,
And o're the Seas his Sov'raign Trident rears,
Their Fury falls: He skims the liquid Plains,
High on his Chariot, and with loosen'd Reins,
Majestick moves along, and awful Peace maintains.   225

The large contrasts of Virgil's and Rubens' scene are there, though the analogy between god and orator is less salient in this much expanded version. The rhetorical tone, which has a counterpart in Virgil, is louder and more insistent throughout. Other stresses, emotive and visual, also have some basis in the original, but their character can be best understood in relation to sixteenth- and seventeenth-century pictorial styles. As in Rubens and the engravers, there is much violent movement and feeling, sharply contrasted with their opposites. There is also the continual emphasis on *seeing* Neptune in various poses and with various looks and implied emotions. "He *reared* his *awful* Head" ("awful" is Dryden's addition), yet he is also "Serene in Majesty" (179–180). "The god himself *with ready Trident*

41

stands" (208). Attention is directed first to the pose, then to the action. Again, "the Father of the Flood *appears* . . . and . . . his *Sov'raign Trident rears*"—sight and gesture without words are sufficient: "Their Fury falls" (221–223). Neptune is seen "High on his Chariot" (224) (as in all the pictorial versions).[46] He moves "with loosen'd Reins" (224–225), which is reasonably close to Virgil's text (note however the descriptive "with" and the participle for an active verb). But the final picture, "Majestick moves along," is nearer to Rubens: this god is no mere charioteer. One line, "And first an angry glance on both he cast" (187), though not in Virgil, is quite comparable to the strong look of Rubens' Neptune. The line and a half added by Dryden, "then rowl'd his Eyes/Around the Space of Earth, and Seas, and Skies" (180–181) suggests something of the scale of Rubens' scene; but the "rowling" eyes are baroque with a vengeance, more grotesque than those of Cleyn's engraving. Other pictorial elements not in Virgil are added: "and the Sea-green Train/Of beauteous Nymphs, the Daughters of the Main" (205–206)—which has the effect of dimming the precise if "low" acts that follow. Dryden does mention the "Chariot," but like the painters he brushes over the awkward business of a chariot race on the water. The wheels are not mentioned, and the "finny Coursers" recall the pictorial style and the rationalizing tendency of the seventeenth-century versions and their commentators. Stock poetic diction—note also "Wat'ry Reign" and "the liquid Plains"—elevated and vaguely visual, is the verbal equivalent of the heroic descriptive style in painting. The writer makes a gesture toward picture, without giving much evidence of having *seen* anything in particular.

What probably most strikes twentieth-century readers of Dryden's lines is the heightening of the imperial and the political themes, although there are analogies in the arbitrary gesture of Rubens' god and in the many references to the historical occasion, more blatant in the painting than in the sketch. As often, Dryden adopts a note in Virgil, heightens it, and loads it with local applications. The underlining of the imperial and royal character of Neptune appears from beginning to end of the passage: "Imperial *Neptune*," "Wat'ry Reign" and "obedience to my Reign," "Majesty" and "Majestick," "my supream Command," "your Lord," "my Royal Mandate," "sov'raign." Finally, the god is the ruler who "awful Peace maintains"—language that might suit the Supreme Deity of the next century. In the grand generalizing force of this phrase and in the insistent "my" emphasizing the royal prerogative, Dryden reflects Charles II's seriocomic obsession with the image of an absolute monarch, ruling by divine

46. Compare also *Paradise Lost*, II.1, "High on a Throne of Royal State."

right.[47] The scornful references to "th' ignoble Crowd" are more vulgar than Virgil's, and we hear the Tories' fear and mockery of "Rebel Insolence" and "Rustick Arms." The dignity and wisdom of Virgil's "grave and Pious Man," though the translation is literal to a fault, is brought down by the context to English political realities. To define the parallels and the differences between Dryden and Rubens in this area would require a separate monograph. "The subtle adaptation of the mythological scene" in Rubens, says Rosenberg, "to the actual life of the prince shows how earnestly the Baroque humanists and artists undertook to prove the Divine support of the sovereigns."[48] Rubens is doing more than this, as we have seen, in the commanding presence of a Godlike figure who reminds us of a spiritual order perceptible in Nature and superior to kings, though the allusion confers honor on them. In Dryden's version, as in his royal odes, the strain of the royal-divine rhetoric is all too evident, as it is for some viewers (though not for the writer) in the Marie de Médicis cycle, where myth happily eclipses history.

What finally can we say about Dryden's translation of myth in relation to Virgil, Rubens, and the other texts, verbal or visual, that we have surveyed? We can hardly suppose or expect that Dryden's mythological event will reveal the complex poetic, historical, and moral ordering of Virgil's poem. That cannot be if Virgil is to "speak such *English,* as he would himself have spoken, if he had been born in *England,* and in the present Age." Resonances are lost on which larger connections depend: "pious" is not *pius* and "Fury" is not *furor.* But it should be said that in spite of these inevitable losses, Dryden's *Aeneid* as a whole carries over much of Virgil's sense of history and "destiny." The political and rhetorical accent of Dryden's lines, which has some justification in Virgil, unfortunately also inclines his version toward the values and mores of the rising Tory party in the reigns of Charles II and his brother. That Dryden attempted to *picture* the action again starts from a Virgilian quality, though the style of his verbal "painting" derives from the baroque manner of Cleyn and more generally from the Rubens tradition as it reached not the most visual of English poets. Although the "postures" of Dryden's Neptune remind us of Rubens' god, they also remind us that Dryden did not take either his visual apparatus or the divine machinery very seriously. The tendency to emphasize the pose, not the act or the *numen,* to rationalize miracle by omission or soften it by veiled poetic diction, will find a point of arrival in the picturesque gods and

---

47. David Ogg, *England in the Reign of Charles II,* 2nd ed. (Oxford, 1956), 2nd ed. corrected, Oxford Paperbacks, 1963, "The Crown in Parliament," II, 450–454.
48. J. Rosenberg, "Rubens' Sketch," p. 9.

goddesses of decorative painters and landscapers of the eighteenth century in Italy and in England. Pope, who looked on Nature with more reverence and with a keener eye as painter and mythmaker, and who loved mythological allusions in landscape and garden, also saw their possible triviality and abuse:

> Here Amphitrite sails thro' myrtle bowers;
> There Gladiators fight, or die, in flowers;
> Un-water'd see the drooping sea-horse mourn,
> And swallows roost in Nilus' dusty Urn.

But if Ovidian irreverence, which anticipated the death of the gods, had its effect on the tradition that touched Dryden in the Cleyn engravings, if it also affected Rubens even in the noble mood of the *Quos ego*—, it did not prevent him from embracing other mythical modes and ways of seeing, even contradictory in impulse. He, too, quietly omits the more humble operations of Homer's Poseidon and Virgil's Neptune, and he subdues the literalism of "wind-men and -women," and of war chariots at sea and their human drivers. How Virgil regarded Neptune's "shovings" and "liftings" we cannot know, though at least one critic sees a "rough humor" in this and similar narratives in the *Aeneid*. What is most remarkable about Rubens is that he harmonizes both the deeper Virgilian and the Homeric visions. His *Quos ego*— bears a weight—perhaps too great a one—of historical and ideological reference: the heavens themselves, God and Nature, further the purposes of the king of Spain and his emissary. But if we return to the visual "thing," we see that without literalism, Rubens renews the Homeric vision of human figures and gestures dramatically expressing events both natural and supernatural.[49] In the way in which rushing lines, subtle harmonies of color and light, work to give a sense of how Powers are "begotten" from our sensations of the physical world, he takes us beyond Homer to where all myths begin:

> One's grand flights, one's Sunday baths,
> One's tootings at the weddings of the soul
> Occur as they occur. So bluish clouds
> Occurred above the empty house and the leaves
> Of the rhododendrons rattled their gold,
> As if someone lived there. Such floods of white

49. Alpers, *Decoration of the Torre de la Parada*, p. 173, notes that both Delacroix and Burckhardt "called Rubens the Homer of painters." See Burckhardt, *Recollections of Rubens*, p. 157.

Came bursting from the clouds. So the wind
Threw its contorted strength around the sky.

Could you have said the bluejay suddenly
Would swoop to earth? It is a wheel, the rays
Around the sun. The wheel survives the myths.

—Wallace Stevens, "The Sense of the Slight-of-hand Man"[50]

50. *The Collected Poems of Wallace Stevens* (New York, 1954), p. 222, quoted with permission of the publisher.

3

THE THEBAN EAGLE IN ENGLISH PLUMAGE

The most diligent and believing student will not find one glance of the Theban eagle in West and his colleagues, who have attempted to clothe the bird with English plumage. Perhaps he is the most untranslatable of poets, and though he was capable of a grand national music, yet did not write sentences, which alone are conveyed without loss of another tongue.— PREFATORY NOTE TO THOREAU'S TRANSLATIONS OF PINDAR.

The aim of this essay is not to damn unhappy translators but to draw attention to what makes Pindar's poetry almost unique and almost untranslatable—the metaphorical patterns of his odes. Let us first see what one of these patterns is like by making a fairly complete analysis of the First Pythian Ode. We shall then consider some English versions of Pindar, from the seventeenth century to the twentieth, to see what happens in translation to the beautiful and artful patterns of the original poems.

The First Pythian honors Hieron of Syracuse as founder of Aetna and his son Deinomenes, who is the king of the new city. In the course of the ode Pindar refers to Hieron's recent victory over the Carthaginians and Etruscans at Cyme and to Gelon's victory over the Carthaginians at Himera in 480. Beginning with the "quivering stroke" of χρυσέα φόρμιγξ, Pindar sings of the lyre's effect on men, gods, and the enemies of Zeus, especially Typhon, who rests beneath Mount Aetna. After praying for the new city and its founder, he tells how Hieron won his victory at Cyme, though, like Philoctetes, he was

Reprinted from *Classical Philology* 43 (1948).

The Theban Eagle in English Plumage

suffering from disease. He soon turns to sing of Deinomenes and to pray that the new Dorian city may ever be peaceful. Next he recalls the battles of Cyme and Himera along with the victories at Plataea and Salamis, which he had also honored with songs. In closing, he urges Hieron to say and do the right thing if he wants to enjoy a fair reputation now and after his death.

We may well wonder how the elements in this "eruption" can constitute anything like a unified work of art. Beyond the more obvious historical and mythological links, there must be some further mode of connection which makes us feel, as we certainly do, that the poem is a glowing imaginative whole. If we look closely at Pindar's language, we shall find a connecting pattern which is essentially poetic and Pindaric and through which the "extreme and scatt'ring" elements of the ode are linked in lively relation.

We first glimpse this pattern in a curious series of words which are closely related in meaning and etymology. Listen to them: l. 2, ἀκούει; l. 26, ἀκοῦσαι; l. 84, ἀκοά; l. 90, ἀκοάν; l. 99, εὖ ἀκούειν. (We should add to this group two other expressions: ll. 13–14, βοὰν ἀΐοντα; and l. 90, κλύειν). If a poet is concerned with what he talks about, Pindar seems to be concerned with "hearing." As the individual contexts show, Pindar's stress is on "what is heard" or on "sound," though his expressions never let us forget the active process of "hearing" and "making sounds." If we now read through the ode, we shall find a whole sequence of expressions for sounds or forms of utterance or closely related actions and things. There are at least thirty of them, from the φόρμιγξ of the first line to the φόρμιγγες of the last epode. Similar echoing pairs are fairly common: l. 3, ἀοιδοί and l. 94, ἀοιδοῖς; l. 38, εὐφώνοις; and l. 70, σύμφωνον; l. 42, περίγλωσσοι and l. 86, γλῶσσαν; l. 60, ὕμνον and l. 79, ὕμνον. Among these resounding words[1] we should note especially κελαδῆσαι, which means both "sing loudly" and "praise." It is one of a considerable group of expressions for "praise" and "glory": l. 31, κλεινός; l. 37, κλυτάν; l. 38, ὀνυμαστάν; l. 43, αἰνῆσαι; l. 66, κλέος. Both κλυτάν and ὀνυμαστάν are closely connected with the "sound" series: the poet prays that Aetna may be

... ἵπποις τε κλυτὰν
καὶ σὺν θαλίαις εὐφώνοις ὀνυμαστάν.

("glorious for crowns and horses, and famed for the music of her feasts"). We feel a further link between "glory" and "sounds heard" in the etymological connection of κλεινός, κλυτάν, and κλέος with κλύω. The joining of crowns with "glory" and "music" points to a minor

1. Most of them are quoted in the course of the essay.

47

chain of echoes, "flower and wreath": 1. 66, κλέος ἄνθησεν; ll. 49, 50, δρέπει πλούτου στεφάνωμ'; 1. 89, εὐανθεῖ ὀργᾷ; 1. 100, στέφανον.

From these rough groupings it is clear that the repetitions and echoes of sound and sense point to a large metaphorical structure in the poem. The central metaphor in this pattern is Sound—the sound of harmonious music and the sound of glorious deeds. The theme is not simply music[2] or harmony.[3] Nor is it true, as Norwood[4] suggests, that the lyre symbol united "all these events, hopes, and prayers." Though Norwood shows quite beautifully the continuity of the Sound metaphor, he is here, as elsewhere in his book, too eager to ascribe a unifying power to a single "visual object." Music, as symbolized in the lyre, is only one of several forms of sound through which Pindar envisages and *composes* his diverse interests, from love of his art to concern for Hieron's rule.

In the opening section of the poem we hear the lyre with its quivering (ἐλελιζομένα) and rushing (ῥιπαῖσι) and dartlike sounds (κῆλα). We are made to think also of μουσική, the art of Apollo and the Muses (Λατοίδα σοφίᾳ βαθυκόλπων τε Μοισᾶν). The more inclusive theme of Sound is introduced in the second line with ἀκούει, and the "sound of glorious deeds" appears in the next line in ἀγλαΐας, which is at once "brightness" and "victory" and the "songs of poets," the ἀοιδοί who are mentioned presently. So by the end of the first antistrophe we have almost all the elements which make up the harmony of the ode: the sound of the lyre, the sound of glorious deeds, and the poet's song.

In this opening section the complementary "quiet" theme appears: there is the sleep of the eagle (εὕδει) and the deep sleep of Ares (κώματι). Musical sound, we feel, brings peace and harmonious order, an implication which is later expressed in the prayers for the success of the new city (ll. 35–38; 67–73): the feasts of Aetna are to be εὐφώνοις and the peace a harmonious peace, σύμφωνον ἐς ἡσυχίαν.

But the Sound metaphor includes also inharmonious sound, which is associated with the enemies of Zeus and other disturbers of order. There is the "roar" (πατάγῳ) of Typhon's mountain, the "most dreadful streams he sends up, a marvel to hear" (ἀκοῦσαι). There is the barbaric cry, the ἀλαλατός of the Etruscans, and their lament for their lost ships (ναυσίστονον).

Pindar contrasts with these ugly noises the sound of the glory of the kings who rule the cities of Sicily. Immediately after describing

2. "Music" is the title of the Wade-Gery and Bowra translation of the ode (see n. 13 below).
3. See Basil L. Gildersleeve, *Pindar: The Olympian and Pythian Odes* (New York, 1885), notes to Pythia I, pp. 240–242.
4. Gilbert Norwood, *Pindar* (Berkeley, 1945), p. 102; for discussion of symbolism, see Lectures V, VI, VII.

The Theban Eagle in English Plumage

the mountain's fearful roar, he mentions Aetna's "glorious founder" (κλεινὸς οἰκιστήρ) and the herald's cry which announces his victory. Pindar, the ἀοιδός, sings of his desire to praise Hieron (αἰνῆσαι μενοινῶν), of his ὕμνον for the new king and of his ὕμνον for the victory at Himera, and of his songs for the victories at Salamis and Plataea.

The poet also keeps fresh the memory of less dramatic honors— the way of life of a good king. The last form of the Sound metaphor, the "sound of kingly reputation," appears in the closing section of the poem. The connection between the arts of the poet and the ruler is rather subtly suggested. Indeed, it is hard to know whether Pindar is talking to himself or to Hieron when he says: "If your utterance is just right, there is less blame." The closeness of the two arts is further implied by a curious echo: "Forge your *tongue* on the anvil of truth," he urges Hieron. The γλῶσσαν recalls the lines in which Pindar first speaks of his craft, when he tells of the gods who make men "wise and strong and golden-tongued" (περίγλωσσοι).

These closing lines are packed with wonderful resounding expressions—ἀκοά, the sound of a reputation which citizens cannot bear to hear; ἀκοὰν ἀδεῖαν κλύειν and εὖ ἀκούειν, the sweet sound of a wise ruler's reputation; αὔχημα δόξας, the boastful sound of good fame; ἐχθρὰ φάτις, the hateful talk which a tyrant hears; ἀοιδοῖς, φόρμιγγες, the music of poets' lyres; and παίδων ὀάροισι, the soft voices of singing youths. Back of the immediate references to Hieron and his rule rises the larger symphony of Sound, thanks to the resonances which many of these words have acquired in the earlier parts of the poem. The στέφανον of the last line shows at once this growth of meaning and Pindar's peculiar art. The crown is the lordly crown of wealth plucked like a flower (δρέπει πλούτου στεφάνωμ'). It is also the flower of glory (κλέος ἄνθησεν), the *heard* echo of great deeds. And, finally, the flower of glory is connected with the art of the ruler, who has just been told to rule εὐανθεῖ δ' ἐν ὀργᾷ παρμένων.

The Pindaric pattern which we have been describing is twofold: first, the sets of verbal echoes[5] (exact repetitions, etymological cognates, words parallel in meaning); and, second, the pattern of relations which make up the main metaphor. The various interests which excite Pindar—the power of music, the poet's art, the glory of heroes, the order of a Dorian city, the fear of barbarian disorder —enter into combination as so many forms of Sound. But this second pattern depends directly on the first. Pindar connects music and glory and order and royal tact by his art in using the Greek

5. "Echoes" is used here in the sense in which Bury uses the term: "For Pindar does not confine his 'responsions' to verses metrically corresponding —and Metzger has to some extent recognized this—but indicates the train of his thoughts by verbal echoes anywhere, independently of the metre." J. B. Bury, *The Nemean Odes of Pindar* (London, 1890), Intro., pp. xx–xxi.

49

language to make those curious chains of verbal echoes. We have
seen how he takes advantage of the likeness in forms and meanings
of ἀκούω and its derivatives, of the etymological links between κλέος
and κλύω, of the metaphors implicit in σύμφωνος and εὐανθής. The Pindaric harmony is inseparable from the notes that compose it.

If this is Pindar's way, it is easy to see why he has been the despair
of translators. Cowley, who in 1656 published his "Pindarique Odes"
expresses this despair and the impossibility of closely reproducing
Pindar's language: "If a man should undertake to translate *Pindar*
word for word, it would be thought that one *Mad man* had translated
another."[6] His versions, as we might expect, are very free, but they
do make us feel some of Cowley's excitement in discovering the poetry
of Pindar. Let us look at one of his translations, "The Second Olym-
pique," and see what happens to the metaphorical pattern of the
original. Pindar's Second Olympian, an ode to Theron of Agrigentum,
has for its main metaphor the idea of alternation in human affairs,
which is expressed most vividly in the figure of shifting streams.
There is a more or less closely related theme of the "flower and shoot,"
that is, the stock of a noble race. Cowley's version is happily not quite
what we might expect from his headnote: "The *Ode* (according to
the constant custom of the *Poet*) consists more in *Digression*, than
in the main *subject*."[7] "The main subject" does appear in Cowley's
poem, though in lines which give a rather sprightly version of the
original metaphor:

> . . . Fortunes favour and her *Spight*
> Rowl with alternative *Waves* like *Day* and *Night*.

But Pindar's optimism, being far less simple, is infused with the sense
of fated recurrence of evil and good. "Oblivion" does not destroy
"the very trace of foregone Ills," for *woe sleeps on:* θνάσκει παλίγκοτον
δαμασθέν. Characteristically, the adjective suggests by its etymology
that the woe returns, that it is barely checked. What is the central
metaphor for Pindar becomes, in fact, a "digression" for Cowley, and
he does not include in the rest of his translation a single one of the
five or six echoes of the main theme. Although his version of the
famous passage on the afterlife is full of incidental, rather Spen-
serian, beauties, the "flowery bindings" of Pindar's ἄνθεμα χρυσοῦ are
completely missing. This translation, like Cowley's original "Pindari-
ques," leaves us with the feeling that for him Pindar's poetry was
indeed an *"unnavigable Song."* Although in 1706 Congreve wrote

6. Abraham Cowley, *Poems*, ed. A. R. Waller (Cambridge, 1905), p. 155.
7. *Ibid.*, p. 157.

nobly of Pindar's "perpetual coherence" and "secret connexion"[8] of thought, poets and poetasters went on writing "Pindarick" odes in Cowley's "impetuous Dithyrambique" vein.

It is interesting by way of contrast to read some translations published in 1749,[9] made by a man who was full of scorn for Cowley and his imitators and who had a considerable knowledge of the Greek language and antiquities, Gilbert West. Readers of his version of the First Pythian may not hear the voice of Pindar, but they will find some nice passages in the just classical vein of Gray's "Elegy":

> Thus fresh, and fragrant, and immortal blooms
> The Virtue, Croesus, of thy gentle Mind.
>
> . . . .
>
> Him therefore nor in sweet Society
> The gen'rous Youth conversing ever name;
> Nor with the Harp's delightful Melody
> Mingle his odious inharmonious Fame.

As the last two lines suggest, West's version conveys some sense of Pindar's metaphor, the "harmony divine" of music. But closer comparison of West's language with Pindar's shows us why the total pattern of his poem is so un-Pindaric. Take, for example, a phrase which catches exactly the metaphor implied in the original, the translation of σύμφωνον ἐς ἡσυχίαν as "sweet Accord." But when we turn to West's translation of the parallel εὐφώνοις, we find only an eighteenth-century cliché, "heav'nly Lays," and so Pindar's "Accord" is lost. And if we note the context in which "sweet Accord" occurs, we can see another reason why in West a happy phrase may have so little of Pindar's force:

> And still in golden Chains of sweet Accord,
> And mutual Peace the friendly People bind.

The musical metaphor is contained within another metaphor, which is merely occasional and ornamental. But Pindar's metaphor is functional; the sensuous beauty it evokes in passing contributes to the growing order of his poem. Almost nowhere in West's version can we find any equivalent for Pindar's musical sequences of "hearings" and "soundings." We miss most in West's language what is most important in Pindar, the particular, physical experience of hearing

---

8. "A Discourse on the Pindarique Ode," *The Works of Mr. William Congreve*, 3 vols. (London, 1710), III, 1074.

9. Gilbert West, *Odes of Pindar . . . to Which is Prefixed a DISSERTATION on the OLYMPICK GAMES* (London, 1749).

or making sounds; so we find for ἀκούει, "attends"; for εὖ ἀκούειν, "The soul-exalting Praise of doing well." Pindar's words do not let us forget that what he is connecting is like sensations or actions as well as like words, but West's elegancies often conceal both kinds of pattern. As Dr. Johnson put it, "He is sometimes too paraphrastical."[10] He strews his verses with phrases such as "sounding chords," "heav'nly choir," "the subtle pow'rs of Verse and Harmony," etc. Unlike Pindar's less numerous, but more precise, echoes, they produce no musical design, only a kind of rhetorical rumble.

We are reminded of that "cumbrous splendor" which so disgusted Johnson in the Pindaric odes of Gray. *The Progress of Poesy* (1757), Gray's "First Pythian," should be a constant reminder that to imitate Pindar is even more risky than to translate him; for, in spite of the "pomp of the poetical machinery," the ode falls apart into a series of show passages which are connected mainly by chronology and Gray's learned footnotes. Although Gray borrows Pindar's musical metaphor, his language shows little Pindaric continuity; there are few signs that, like Pindar, he felt the music in each of the experiences he so artfully describes.

It is curious that a translation published in 1822 (by Abraham Moore)[11] should show the most evil effects of eighteenth-century poetic conventions, particularly of that abstractness which eliminates the sensuous particulars from poetry. Too often in Moore's version, personification calleth unto personification. For example, the balance of ἀκοὰν ἀδεῖαν κλύειν and εὖ ἀκούειν comes out as:

Fame's dulcet voice, . . .

and

Above
The goodliest gifts of Jove
Fortune the first, Fame claims the second, place;
The man whose grasp, whose filled embrace
Both Fame and Fortune holds, life's noblest crown has twined.

Clearly, in translating Pindar, one parallel will not do so well as another.

The nineteenth-century writer who it seems might have best shown

10. Samuel Johnson, *Lives of the English Poets*, ed. G. B. Hill, 3 vols. (Oxford, 1905), III, 33.
11. Reprinted in *The Odes of Pindar*, trans. Dawson W. Turner, Bohn's Classical Library (London, 1898).

English readers the harmony of Pindar was Thoreau.[12] Although he made a complete version of only one ode—the brief Fourteenth Olympian—Thoreau shows in this single translation that Pindar's poetic order may emerge if a translator will "leave the poet alone." One of the minor and beautiful symmetries in that poem is formed by the contrast between λιπαρᾶς Ἐρχομενοῦ, the home of the hero, and μελαντειχέα δόμον Φερσεφόνας, where the hero's father now rests in death. Thoreau's words bring out the full sharpness of this light and shadow. The strophe begins,

> O ye, who inhabit for your lot the seat of Cephisian
> Streams, yielding fair steeds, renowned Graces
> Ruling bright Orchomenos,
> Protectors of the ancient race of Minyae,
> Hear, when I pray.

This is matched in the antistrophe by

> Now to Persephone's
> Black-walled house go, Echo,
> Bearing to his father the famous news . . .

The transcendental editors who published these translations might well be forgiven their remarks about the attempts of "West and his colleagues."

Twentieth-century translators have at least one advantage over Thoreau and his contemporaries—the detailed knowledge of Pindar's art which has been gathered by the scholar-critics of the last two generations. They are fortunate, too, in writing at a time when the language of English poetry has been undergoing one of its major renewals. Two fairly recent translations of the First Pythian, one by Wade-Gery and Bowra (1928),[13] the other by Richmond Lattimore (1942),[14] show quite clearly both these advantages. The Wade-Gery and Bowra version is wonderfully free from the poetic clutter and classroom idiom which make so many scholarly translations unreadable. Although Pindar's echoes are seldom very closely reproduced, the main connections of metaphor stand out clearly: an English

<hr>

12. *The Writings of Henry David Thoreau*, Walden ed., 20 vols. (Boston, 1906), V, *Excursions and Poems*, "Translations from Pindar," pp. 375–392.
13. *Pindar: Pythian Odes*, trans. H. T. Wade-Gery and C. M. Bowra (London, 1928), pp. 79–87.
14. *Some Odes of Pindar*, trans. Richmond Lattimore, The Poet of the Month (Norfolk, Conn., 1942), pp. 5–9. These translations are included in *The Odes of Pindar*, trans. Richmond Lattimore (Chicago, 1947).

reader of this version can really see that music is one unifying theme of the poem. And, occasionally, as in the opening strophes, a Pindaric series is quite exactly followed:

> The light foot *hears* you . . .
> And things that God loves not
> *Hear* the voice of the maids of Pieria . . .
> A marvel and wonder to see it, a marvel even to *hear* . . .

These translators are no more able than others to find an English equivalent for the witty echo of εὐφώνοις and σύμφωνον; but they do not lose the "linked sweetness" of the original figure: "the music of her feasts" is answered by "peaceful concord."

Although Lattimore occasionally lapses into translator's English, he is often very adept at suggesting the chainlike sequences of Pindar's Sound pattern. Sometimes he does this by inventing parallels which are Pindaric, if not to be found in the original: for example, "shaken with music" (ἐλελιζομένα) and "shaken to hear" (ἀτύζονται βοὰν ἀίοντα), or "singing fulfilment" (ὕμνον τελέσαις) and "singing in season" (καιρὸν εἰ φθέγξαιο). As these examples show, Lattimore brings the reader very close to Pindar's active language of "hearing" and "sounding." And so he succeeds more nearly than the other translators in equaling Pindar's closing strophes with their many sounds of sweet speech and song. But I should add that Lattimore's "good repute" (εὖ ἀκούειν), like Bowra's "good name," is a reminder that English is not Greek and that translators new or old are not Pindars. As we have seen in comparing various versions, though a translator may seem to have grasped Pindar's main metaphor, he can never achieve the same closeness of relation throughout the whole poem, for that depends on a kind of verbal device which can rarely if ever be reproduced. To read these translations is to see more clearly that Pindar's odes, which "to the Dorian mode . . . rose like an exhalation," are the structures both of a genius and of the genius of a language.

4

POPE'S *ILIAD* FOR TWENTIETH-CENTURY READERS

For readers of literature the ancient world is not any one thing. Certainly it is not the carefully reconstructed past of a scientific historian; for the meaning of antiquity, Greek, Roman, or Biblical, is more than any historical "reality." Our commerce with all these early worlds has been enriched—a purist may say, distorted—by the writers and artists, particularly of the Renaissance, who have interpreted them in powerful and unforgettable expressions. Whatever Julius Caesar or Brutus may have been in fact, their significance for most of us has been permanently affected by Shakespeare's play. We accept Shakespeare's interpretation as clearly among the valid ones —unless, of course, we are provincial enough to suppose that the true meaning of the Roman past has been settled by the reigning school of ancient historians. The characters of the Bible have been similarly shaped for us by great versions in art and in literature. Who can think of Moses or David without a flitting image of Michelangelo's sculptures coming between him and his reading of the Old Testament? The tough and canny Israelite of the biblical story can hardly have been much like the Greco-Roman heroic youth that we see in Florence. Nor can the biblical hero have been exactly like the young man in Nicolas Poussin's *Triumph of David* (1630), who strides through a crowd of matrons and elders gathered before the portico of a great Roman temple.

The King James translation of the Bible is a prime example of a

Reprinted from *The "Iliad" of Homer,* trans. Alexander Pope, ed. Reuben A. Brower and W. H. Bond (New York, 1965).

work of literature that has imposed its vision of antiquity as the true and only one on readers of many generations. It is also an example of the fact that an earlier version of a great text may have values not to be replaced by a later one, though the later version may be linguistically and historically more accurate. The reader of the *New English Bible* will undoubtedly find fewer obscurities than in the older version, but he may feel, as I have suggested in the Introduction, that he is no longer reading a sacred book. Although the King James version is from one point of view so obviously dated, from another it is dateless. Like all true works of literature it is irreplaceable, and like Shakespeare's plays it is at once Elizabethan-Jacobean and contemporary with anyone who makes the effort to learn its language. Who would care to read *Antony and Cleopatra* in a translation produced by the authors of the new New Testament? Both the Jacobean Bible and Shakespeare's great Jacobean play point to the paradoxical conclusion that if a translation is to live, it must be thoroughly contemporary, a literary success in the style of its time and in a distinct style of its own.

Alexander Pope's *Iliad* is a triumph of exactly this sort. Since its appearance in the early eighteenth century (1715–20), scholars have kept saying with Richard Bentley that it is "not Homer," but readers have happily gone on reading. Despite the Romantic prejudice against Pope, his *Iliad* has continued to be reprinted, and to judge from the sheer number of editions published throughout a period of nearly two hundred and fifty years, it has been the most readable and most read of all English translations of Homer. We live in an age of excellent translations from Greek, many of them more accurate than Pope's in relation to the original language and to historical fact, but only a rash prophet would assert that they will have a longer literary life than Pope's *Iliad*. Like George Chapman's *Homer* and John Dryden's *Virgil*, Pope's *Iliad* goes to prove that the way for a writer to ensure a long life for his translations is to be a poet of a high, if not the highest, order.

The way for a twentieth-century reader to enjoy the works of these great translators is to give them the hearing they demand, not to complain that they are not Keats or Yeats, but to be alert to their special style and vision. Because of a considerable change in taste during the past forty years, we are today better prepared to read Pope's version than at any time since the Romantic revival. T. S. Eliot and Ezra Pound, who did a great deal to effect a change in attitude toward Dryden and Pope and other poets of wit, also did much to encourage the present generation of translators. The public for the new poetry has also been the public for the new versions of Homer and the Greek dramatists.

Pope's Iliad

What sort of a hearing does Pope expect? He offers one important hint as he concludes his comparison of Homer and Virgil in his admirable *Preface* to the *Iliad:* "Homer makes us Hearers, and Virgil leaves us Readers." Though Pope is talking here of Homer's power of engaging us in the action—as if "we were there"—he has just been praising the speeches of the *Iliad,* saying that "It is hardly credible in a Work of such length, how small a Number of Lines are employ'd in Narration." As his translation will show, Pope is looking for readers who have an appetite for speeches in the oratorical sense, for resounding declamations. He also expects his reader to have a painter's eye for effects of light and shade, color and movement, for over-all pictorial design. (In Jane Austen's *Northanger Abbey,* the heroine finds that she cannot see the views admired by her sophisticated friends, because she has not had lessons in drawing.)

One might offer the heretical advice that the best way to begin reading Pope's *Homer* is to go to the nearest museum or art library and look long and hard at mythological paintings and "Historical Pieces" by masters of the seventeenth and eighteenth centuries. Here we can find analogues to the visual world of the antique evoked by Pope's translation: grand figures of heroes, gods, and goddesses caught in sculptural poses of dramatic gesture and swift motion, the heroes and gods of magnificent physique, the goddesses voluptuously charming. We see these supernatural beings resting on billowy clouds, or moving in earthly paradises of dark and rich foliage, or posed against backgrounds of threatening rocks and seas or of pompous Roman architecture. The presiding genius of these paintings, from Flemish Rubens to the Venetian Giambattista Tiepolo, is Roman-Virgilian and Ovidian, not Greek and Homeric. When on rare occasions a subject is taken from Homer, the settings, costumes, and poses are usually more Roman than Greek.

In one of his greatest frescoes, *Achilles on the Seashore* (about 1757), Tiepolo paints a scene that might well be used to illustrate Pope. "Under the shadow of towering rocks," a critic writes, "Thetis and her Nereid companion gaze mournfully at the brooding hero; and the note of pagan sadness looks back to early Renaissance treatment of classical story." Here are the first few verses of the scene in Pope's translation:

> Not so his Loss the fierce Achilles bore;
> But sad retiring to the sounding Shore,
> O'er the wild Margin of the Deep he hung,
> That kindred Deep, from whence his Mother sprung.
> There, bath'd in Tears of Anger and Disdain,
> Thus loud lamented to the stormy Main.

The "sad retiring" hero, "the sounding Shore," and the "wild Margin of the Deep" are in feeling and pictorial effect closely related to Tiepolo's painting. The image a few lines later of the goddess rising as "the Waves divide" and her tender "exploring" of Achilles' sorrow are also matched in Tiepolo's fresco, where Thetis looks out from the hollow of a wave, gazing sadly toward her son.

But as Pope continues, he moves into a style that is neither elegiac nor pictorial:

> O Parent Goddess! since in early Bloom
> Thy son must fall, by too severe a Doom,
> Sure, to so short a Race of Glory born,
> Great Jove in Justice should this Span adorn:
> Honour and Fame at least the Thund'rer ow'd
> And ill he pays the Promise of a God;
> If yon proud Monarch thus thy Son defies,
> Obscures my Glories, and resumes my Prize.
> Far in the deep Recesses of the Main,
> Where aged Ocean holds his wat'ry Reign,
> The Goddess-Mother heard.
>
> 460–470

Achilles' address to his mother is in Pope's high oratorical manner, marked as usual with him by distinctly Roman touches in diction. "O Parent Goddess" reminds us of the way Virgil's Aeneas speaks to his mother (*O dea certe*), and "proud Monarch" together with "Jove" and the Latinate verbs "obscures" and "resumes" recall the imperial ruler of the *Aeneid*. Pope's original audience would have been reminded too of the Virgil they perhaps knew best, of Dryden's great translation. Two phrases in the last line and a half, "Goddess-Mother" and "wat'ry Reign," are in fact both used by Dryden in his *Aeneis*. Although eighteenth-century readers might not have remembered exactly where they had seen these expressions before, they would have felt, either from knowing Dryden or Milton or other narrative poets of the seventeenth century, that Pope was writing in the "truly heroick" way.

Pope would expect then some familiarity with this heroic style in poetry and in art, and he could also count on a considerable agreement as to what an epic, or "heroic poem," should properly be— assumptions very generally shared by Pope's literary public, though most unfamiliar today. What is meant by "heroic poetry" and by "Homer" has changed a good deal since 1715, and most decidedly during the past thirty or forty years. To understand better what Pope was trying to do, how his view of Homer helped and hindered him, we shall need at least a rough notion as to how we ourselves regard Homer and his world. We may discover that in some respects Pope was in a better position to translate the *Iliad* than even the most knowledgeable of recent translators. Because of his easy familiarity with the heroic tradition in classical and in English poetry, and because of attitudes then prevailing toward traditional poetic styles, he was able to create certain poetic equivalents for Homer's art that have not been surpassed in any English version.

Before turning to eighteenth- and twentieth-century views of the Homeric and the heroic, let us look briefly at a number of passages where Pope's heroic poetry is at its best. First hear Agamemnon, leader of all the Greeks, as he calls his soldiers to battle:

> Ye Greeks be Men! the Charge of Battel bear;
> Your brave Associates, and Your-selves revere!
> Let glorious Acts more glorious Acts inspire,
> And catch from Breast to Breast the noble Fire!
> On Valor's side the Odds of Combate lie,
> The Brave live glorious, or lamented die;
> The Wretch who trembles in the field of Fame,
> Meets Death, and worse than Death, Eternal Shame.
>
> V.651–658

By any view, this is the language of heroes, noble and eloquent speech with a confidence of accent matched only in the best of Shakespeare's history plays. Hear next the equally certain and convincing voice of a great god, Jove himself, as he threatens the Olympians and asserts his unshakeable will:

> But know, whoe'er Almighty Pow'r withstand!
> Unmatch'd our Force, unconquer'd is our Hand:
> Who shall the Sov'reign of the Skies controul?
> Not all the Gods that crown the starry Pole.
> Your Hearts shall tremble, if our Arms we take,
> And each immortal Nerve with Horror shake.
> For thus I speak, and what I speak shall stand;
> What pow'r soe'er provokes our lifted Hand,
> On this our Hill no more shall hold his Place,
> Cut off, and exil'd from th' Æthereal Race.
>
> VIII.560–569

We may recall the militant God of *Paradise Lost*, or perhaps rather Satan, especially because of the tough strength in

Mirror on Mirror

For thus I speak, and what I speak shall stand . . .

Or see the field of battle glorified by the act of a god:

> He [Nestor] spoke, and round him breath'd heroic Fires;
> Minerva seconds what the Sage inspires.
> The Mist of Darkness Jove around them threw,
> She clear'd, restoring all the war to view;
> A sudden Ray shot beaming o'er the Plain,
> And shew'd the Shores, the Navy, and the Main:
> Hector they saw, and all who fly, or fight,
> The Scene wide-opening to the Blaze of Light.
> First of the field, great Ajax strikes their Eyes,
> His port Majestick, and his ample Size:
> A pond'rous Mace, with Studs of Iron crown'd,
> Full twenty Cubits long, he swings around.
> Nor fights like others, fix'd to certain Stands,
> But looks a moving Tow'r above the Bands;
> High on the Decks, with vast gigantic Stride,
> The godlike Hero stalks from side to side.
> XV.806–821

For a contrast in scene and in feeling consider how Pope announces the coming death of Patroclus (the Greeks are trying to carry off the body of Cebriones, whom Patroclus has just killed):

> Now flaming from the Zenith, Sol had driv'n
> His fervid Orb thro' half the Vault of Heav'n;
> While on each Host with equal Tempest fell
> The show'ring Darts, and Numbers sunk to Hell.
> But when his Ev'ning Wheels o'erhung the Main,
> Glad Conquest rested on the Grecian Train.
> Then from amidst the Tumult and Alarms,
> They draw the conquer'd Corpse, and radiant Arms.
> Then rash Patroclus with new Fury glows,
> And breathing Slaughter, pours amid the Foes.
> Thrice on the Press like Mars himself he flew,
> And thrice three Heroes at each Onset slew.
> There ends thy Glory! there the Fates untwine
> The last, black Remnant of so bright a Line.
> XVI.938–951

In the final couplet Pope characteristically marks this prophetic moment by a beautiful and memorable image (his own invention, not Homer's). A little later he will bring out the historic sense of the actual death by rhythmic "pointing" and a portentous reflection:

> The Lance arrests him with a mortal Wound;
> He falls, Earth thunders, and his Arms resound.
> With him all Greece was sunk; that Moment all
> Her yet-surviving Heroes seem'd to fall.
>
> 989–992

In Achilles' prayer before he sends Patroclus out to meet this end we hear the voice of absolute heroic joy:

> Oh! would to all th' immortal Pow'rs above,
> Apollo, Pallas, and almighty Jove!
> That not one Trojan might be left alive,
> And not a Greek of all the Race survive;
> Might only we the vast Destruction shun,
> And only we destroy th' accursed Town!
>
> XVI.122–127

Finally, consider Pope's description of Achilles in one of the most splendid moments in the *Iliad,* when he strikes terror among the Trojans by his tremendous shout from the trench:

> The Hero rose;
> Her Aegis, Pallas o'er his Shoulders throws;
> Around his Brows a golden Cloud she spread;
> A Stream of Glory flam'd above his Head.
> As when from some beleaguer'd Town arise
> The Smokes high-curling to the shaded Skies;
> (Seen from some Island, o'er the Main afar,
> When Men distrest hang out the Sign of War)
> Soon as the Sun in Ocean hides his Rays,
> Thick on the Hills the flaming Beacons Blaze;
> With long-projected Beams the Seas are bright,
> And Heav'ns high Arch reflects the ruddy Light;
> So from Achilles' Head the Splendours rise,
> Reflecting Blaze on Blaze, against the Skies.
> Forth march'd the Chief, and distant from the Croud,
> High on the Rampart rais'd his Voice aloud;
> With her own Shout Minerva swells the Sound;
> Troy starts astonish'd, and the Shores rebound.
> As the loud Trumpet's brazen Mouth from far
> With shrilling Clangor sounds th' Alarm of War;

Struck from the Walls, the Echoes float on high,
And the round Bulwarks, and thick Tow'rs reply:
So high his Brazen Voice the Hero rear'd:
Hosts dropp'd their Arms, and trembled as they heard;
And back the Chariots roll, and Coursers bound,
And Steeds and Men lye mingled on the Ground.
Aghast they see the living Light'nings play,
And turn their Eye-balls from the flashing Ray.
Thrice from the Trench his dreadful Voice he rais'd;
And thrice they fled, confounded and amaz'd.

XVIII.241–270

"Splendid, certainly," the reader is saying, "but is it Homer?" A question to be asked, but not easily answered, since what Homer *is* "really" is still being debated, and since the views held by scholars and critics have been changing so rapidly of late. It was only in the mid-twenties and early thirties of this century that the oral composition of Homer's poems was clearly proved and accurately described. Only toward the end of World War II were the Achaeans, the Greeks of the Iliad, surely (more or less surely!) shown to be a Greek-speaking people. To speak more generally, our understanding of the world in which Homer's heroes lived and in which the *Iliad* was composed is continually being altered by the work of archaeologists, linguists, and literary critics. We can sketch here only a rough outline of the view of Homeric poetry that seems to be most commonly held today.

First, a word about the *Iliad* and history. The war of Troy—or something like it—did take place; the bare story of the expedition goes back to the destruction of a small city, the Seventh Troy on the same site, at a date somewhere around 1200 B.C. Archaeological finds indicate that this city was connected by trade with the Mycenaean civilization of the Greek mainland, the home of the Achaeans. Their leader, Agamemnon, lived in Mycenae, one of the great centers of this civilization; the sage, Nestor, lived in another, the city of Pylos. The Bronze-Age culture of these and other mainland cities—which was related to the older culture of Crete—had its last and greatest age in the two centuries preceding the fall of Troy (1400–1200 B.C.). The massive stone work of palaces and tombs, the royal ornaments of gold and silver that have been found at Mycenae, and the written records discovered there and elsewhere show that these cities were fairly impressive centers of military and commercial power. We must not think of the last great period of Mycenaean civilization as a golden age of peace and plenty, but rather as an era of warlike chieftains and their followers, who made frequent raids on one another and on the territories of various Mediterranean peoples, including the Hittites and the Egyptians. This period, the Heroic Age of the Greek world, is recalled, much altered by the deceptions of memory and imagination, in Homer's *Iliad*. There are only a few details in the poem that can be surely identified as Mycenaean, such as the body-covering shield of "great Ajax" and the boar's tusk helmet of the Cretan hero, Meriones.

Other archaeological features of the poem—casual references to iron weapons, the round shield, fighting in close "hoplite" formation—belong to the centuries that follow the downfall of Mycenae, anywhere from the eleventh to the eighth century B.C., a very dark period indeed. It is during this period that the geometric style of vase-painting, the first distinctly Greek style in art, emerges. The *Iliad* as we know it must have been composed in Ionia, on the coast of Asia Minor, toward the end of the eighth century; this is the time when Homer lived and sung.

Although the language of the *Iliad* is primarily Greek of the Ionic dialect, it shows a mixture of dialects of three other regions, and some touches of the much earlier Mycenaean Greek. The diction is enriched further by many archaisms and by obscure terms peculiar to Homer, some of them totally incomprehensible to the Greeks themselves. The language of the Homeric poems is thus a special poetic one, never spoken on land or sea. Perhaps the diction of Spenser in *The Shepherd's Calendar* or *The Fairy Queen* might give an English reader some sense of the peculiar character of Homeric Greek. The verse form, the dactyllic hexameter (six dactyls — ∪ ∪ or equivalent spondees — —) is governed by complex and strict conventions, to which there are a dazzling number of exceptions, which are in turn governed by rules of exception. The style is also marked by the repeated use of a great number of identical phrases and lines; a third of the lines in the *Iliad* recur elsewhere in the poem, some of them many times.

During the nineteenth century, studies of Homer's style and language made it increasingly clear that so special a style, with its set phrases, blended dialects, and elaborate metrics, could hardly have been the creation of one poet or even one generation of poets. From the mid-eighteenth century on, various critics had been saying or assuming that the poems or the separate lays from which they grew must have been orally composed by "folk" bards or singers. It was in the nineteen twenties of this century that a young American scholar, Milman Parry, following hints of German and French critics, proved conclusively that the Homeric poems were composed in a traditional oral style. Parry showed that the Homeric technique of "oral verse-making" was completely different from that of any written style and that, in the future, literary criticism of Homer must always bear this fact in mind. Although readers must always have noticed the many fixed phrases or formulas in Homer, no one had defined exactly their character and use. Parry pointed out that each formula expressed some given essential idea (for example, a man's name or an act of warfare) and that it filled one and only one metrical position in the verse (that is, the last part, after one of the regular pauses or caesuras). Moreover, for any one idea and position there was ordinarily only one or at the most two formulas available for the singer to use. For example, if in the first half of the line up to the caesura the singer had described some act of Hector, he had only one phrase with which to complete the line: "great Hector of the flashing helmet." There were an immense number of such phrases for various characters and actions, all ready-made for the singer to use—an obvious advantage to a poet who was making up his poem orally. It seems quite certain that only poets composing aloud would have invented such a style and have continued to use it, and to use it so extensively in a single poem. Most of the diction of the Homeric poems, if not all, is formulaic. In thinking of Homer, we have then to adjust ourselves to a way of making verse quite unlike that of a writer who constantly varies his idiom, adjusting each adjective and verb to fit a special context. The oral poet is working much of the time not with single words, but with the larger units of phrase, line, and theme.

But what sets traditional oral poetry apart especially is the attitude toward language and style that it imposes on the singer and his listeners. The singer uses the fixed phrase because it is convenient, and also because it is the true epic way of saying that particular thing. The listener too feels the special character of the singer's rhythm and diction, that it has been consecrated to the expression of the heroic way of life. So when he hears "cloud-gathering Zeus," he will hardly see a very precise image, since he has heard the phrase so often. But the formula is not without meaning, because it does name something peculiar to Zeus; no one else is described by this same epithet. As the phrase becomes familiar to the listener, he is left with some transient "great-cloudy-sky-god" impression, generalized, though not utterly without sensuous value. We do not meet this and similar epithets in isolation, but in context with many other epithets and action phrases: Zeus is also "of crooked counsels," and he is the god "who turns his shining eyes toward the scene of battle." These expressions, and many others for the qualities and actions of other gods and heroes, build up our "Zeus sense," our "Achilles sense," our impressions of all sorts of persons, events, and relations. Together they excite and define our living awareness of the character of the Homeric world. For a comparison, we might think of our response to an impressionistic painting: we do not consciously see the individual splotch or dot of color, but the total visual form, the glowing haystack or the sunlit field of grass and flowers.

What is the total configuration that the Homeric style composes? Something too complex to reduce to the formulas of literary criticism, although the large outlines are clear and distinct. The traditional language gives us above all a picture of the hero, of his characterizing acts and loyalties. Seen in his purest form, he is the man who fights skillfully in the front ranks, who faces death while clearly acknowledging its terrors, who lives for the moment of action, whether "he wins glory or gives it to others." He has the highest sense (*aidos*) of his obligation to live heroically, and the clearest awareness that his lot and the lot or fate of all men (*Moira*) cannot be changed and will be fulfilled. The hero fights for glory while he lives and for honor in the praises of men after he is dead. But his glory also includes substantial rewards here and now of wine, food, sheep, and farmland. The Homeric hero is an aristocrat enjoying his social and material prerogatives, not the knight of an other-worldly ideal seeking his true reward in heaven.

But the *Iliad* is not a poem about a hero without a face, or about a set of merely typical heroes; nor does it give the impression of having been composed by an archetypal poet-computer. There are few persons in literature that we remember more distinctly than Achilles and Hector or Helen and Paris, and though like all of Homer's characters they speak in the formulaic style, all have their personal dramatic voices. We are "Hearers" of men acting and suffering in a tragic drama that ranks with the greatest plays of Sophocles and Shakespeare. But no critic with an understanding of the traditional oral style has been very successful in describing this extraordinary literary achievement. By contrast, critics have pointed out considerable differences in conversational idiom, imagery, and psychological notation in the language of individual characters and scenes in plays by Shakespeare and the Greek tragedians. Yet it is here that Homer—whoever he was—comes in: a great dramatic poet and a master of the traditional style, who not unlike Shakespeare reworked the poems of earlier poets, who yet made something so new and so commanding that the *Iliad* as a whole could not be forgotten or lost. While singing the deeds of many heroes and working in traditional themes and episodes, Homer skillfully focused his poem on the wrath of Achilles: its rise in the opening episode and its fierce renewal in the embassy scene (Book IX); its slackening as Achilles sends Patroclus to fight in his place (XVI), the transformation after Patroclus' death of anger into violent grief and more violent revenge, and finally, in the meeting with Priam, the recognition of the tragic mystery of all heroic violence. Achilles has asserted the heroic values more fully than any other hero in the *Iliad*, he has fought more nearly alone, and by killing Hector, he has surely won the highest glory. But the irony of his success is underlined by the death of Patroclus, by the joylessness of his own triumph, and by the ever-present sense of his coming death: ("What he lives by, he dies by.") Achilles does not actually die in the *Iliad*, but he is dying from the very beginning of the poem:

> Sing the wrath—oh goddess—of Peleus' son Achilles
> The destroying [wrath] which brought the Achaeans
> ten thousand sufferings . . .

The second half of the first line, and in the second line both the first two words and the final phrase, are all formulaic. Very characteristic too is the grammatical and rhythmic pattern of this second line, with the enjambement or run-over of the participle followed by a relative clause. But to point out these conventional features is not to diminish the effect on ear and mind of having wrath-and-death struck as the keynote of the career of Achilles and of the thousands who suffered with him. These two opening lines, in their seemingly casual but formulaic and subtly balanced pattern, again illustrate the stylized character of Homeric poetry. Still other qualities of Homer's art and imagination will come out more clearly when we come to review the *Iliad* in Pope's version.

But first we need to have a notion of what Pope and his audience expected a heroic poem to be, what they regarded as Homeric. Two characteristics strike us as we read late seventeenth- and eighteenth-century critics of the epic and the poems they regarded as "heroick": their relative lack of the historical sense, and their willing acceptance of the ideal of a traditional style reserved exclusively for heroic poetry. The first separates them from most twentieth-century readers and critics; while the second brings them nearer to the Homeric singer and his original audience. Both characteristics are better understood in relation to the Renaissance theory of the heroic poem and the literary situation in which poets attempted to write one (see Chapter 7, "Dryden's Epic Manner and Virgil"). The notion of "the true heroick poem"—to us one of the curiosities of literature—seemed to the literary public of the seventeenth and eighteenth centuries exactly as valid as the theory of traditional oral composition seems to present-day writers on the epic. Its authority rested on the testimony of a long series of writers, mostly Italian and French, including some of the best poets and critics of the sixteenth and seventeenth centuries.

Pope's Iliad

From the sixteenth to the late eighteenth century, translators of Homer and Virgil like Chapman, Dryden, and Pope, and poets like Milton who undertook to write modern epics, were all more or less influenced by this fashionable and imposing critical theory.

By Pope's time the theory had very nearly become, in Swift's mocking phrase, "a receipt for an Heroick Poem." Contemporary critics tell us, for example, that the heroic poem must have an explicit moral purpose and unity of action, a perfect hero, a subject taken from the history of Christian times, and supernatural agents or machinery. The poet must not, however, take as his subject the central mysteries of the faith. As the requirements suggest, the model is more often the *Aeneid* than the *Iliad*, but the *Aeneid* Christianized and allegorically interpreted. The style considered appropriate to heroic themes was also more Virgilian than Homeric: the diction tends to be grand and Latinate, the tone and ordering of sentences rhetorical in the Roman sense of the term.

Because of the lack of a strict historical sense, critics could easily regard Homer and Virgil and Renaissance poets as contemporaries, or rather as almost outside time. But because of this deficiency by our standards and because of the common habit of imitating the ancients in school exercises and in original compositions, a poet of the early eighteenth century felt quite naturally that to write heroically was to write as other poets before him had written. Among writers and readers generally there was an assured acceptance of traditional styles that has not been possible in English poetry since the Romantic revolt. But this was a cheerful and loving acceptance, as the acceptance of the oral style must have been for the Homeric singer. As Parry once pointed out, the traditional diction of Homer represented something more than a fixed code in vocabulary and phrasing, it was "the work of a way of life which we may call the heroic . . . a term that can only be understood in the measure that one can think and feel as they did, for the heroic was to them no more or less than the statement of all that they would be or would do if they could." The traditional oral style was their way of epitomizing the whole outlook on life—the love of glory and clear-eyed facing of death, the paradoxical sense of absolute mastery combined with the acknowledgement of fated limits—that Hector, Achilles, and other heroes in the *Iliad* constantly express. They express it, because they are presented in a language that keeps reminding us of the heroic values and vision.

When Pope and his contemporaries used a fixed metaphor such as "the flames of fight" or "the fields of fame," they are not merely satisfying a neo-classical standard of correctness in style. For them, as for the Homeric singer and his listeners, to use these and similar phrases was to pay homage to a noble manner of life. Although English society in the eighteenth century was hardly heroic, the ancient aristocratic tradition was not quite dead. The noble lords knew, if with irony, what high manners and high virtues were, and on occasion they could exhibit them in speech and in action. There is the classic story recounted by Arnold of Lord Granville, who though near death insisted on tending to affairs of state, and who supported his resolve by reciting an appropriate speech from Homer. "I quote this story . . ." Arnold explains, "because it is interesting as exhibiting the English aristocracy at its very height of culture, lofty spirit, and greatness, towards the middle of the last century."

For Pope as for Granville, it was altogether natural to find in the language of an earlier poet the best expression of a modern attitude. In his original poems Pope often concentrates his richest and most precise meanings in a word or phrase echoed from Virgil or Homer, or from Dryden or Milton, or from any other writer who comes to mind. In the early eighteenth century the language of old authors did not belong to a dead historical past, in part because the boundaries were so uncertain between what we call the periods of Greek, Roman, Renaissance, and modern history. The boundaries between translation and original composition were correspondingly less precise. When Pope was translating Homer, he often found what Homer meant by consulting the English poets who had prolonged and renewed the heroic tradition in English poetry. For Pope and his generation there *was* a heroic language and style that they could accept and use. But since the style had been built up by writers who were thoroughly soaked in current theories of the heroic poem, their diction carried with it a Virgilian and late-Renaissance vision of Homer's world and Homeric attitudes. As the story of Granville also reminds us, this vision had a reality that was more than merely literary. The literary vision of antiquity was based on a living cultural tradition, in particular on a knowledge of the ancient languages that the modern reader may well envy: Lord Granville quoted his lines from Homer in Greek.

We can hardly expect Pope to have a twentieth-century scholar's knowledge of Mycenaean and other early Greek cultures. (It is well to remember that Homer and the Greeks of later centuries didn't have it either.) But the few relics of historical fact surviving in Homer are as discoverable in Pope's version as in the original. The learned commentator can point out the same references to Mycenaean shields and helmets, or to Greek hoplite formations, though the hints of the latter are much broader in Pope, thanks to his happy unawareness that this mode of fighting belongs to a much later period. But both the Preface and the Observations (or notes) show that he and his editorial assistants are reasonably alert to differences between the world of Homer and the modern period. Pope, like Swift, sides with the Ancients against the Moderns, but when he defends the simplicity and roughness of manners in the *Iliad* as an "authentick Picture of that ancient World," he is approaching the viewpoint of nineteenth- and twentieth-century historians. It is however one thing to see the differences and another to translate them into poetry, and it is easy enough to demonstrate that Pope's style is often more polite than Homer's, particularly in scenes of court life and gallantry. But on occasion, as in the comic scene of Book I where Vulcan serves the feasting gods, Pope renders Homer's beauty of impression and familiarity of fact more perfectly than a prosily exact scholar can:

> He [Vulcan] said, and to her Hands the Goblet heav'd,
> Which, with a Smile, the white-arm'd Queen receiv'd.
> Then to the rest he fill'd; and, in his Turn,
> Each to his Lips apply'd the nectar'd Urn.
> Vulcan with awkward Grace his Office plies,
> And unextinguish'd Laughter shakes the Skies.
> Thus the blest Gods the Genial Day prolong,
> In Feasts Ambrosial, and Celestial Song.
> Apollo tun'd the Lyre; the Muses round
> With Voice alternate aid the silver Sound.
> Meantime the radiant Sun, to mortal Sight
> Descending swift, roll'd down the rapid Light.
> Then to their starry Domes the Gods depart,
> The shining Monuments of Vulcan's Art:
> Jove on his Couch reclin'd his awful Head,
> And Juno slumber'd on the golden Bed.
>
> I.766–781

The two couplets beginning "Vulcan with awkward Grace . . ." indicate how Pope—quite consciously, we know—tries to find an equivalent for Homer's curiously mixed diction. Like some later translators, Pope thinks it right to use some words "of a venerable *Antique* Cast," both biblical and more or less archaic, but he nicely diminishes their pious associations by introducing Latinate or classical expressions, so adding at the same time another strand of antiquity and remoteness from common use. "Unextinguish'd," for example, is rigidly literal, but almost comically Latin. "Blest" might sound sufficiently sacred or biblical, if it weren't countered by the pagan "Genial," and "Celestial" is Christian "heavenly," but with a Latin resonance. The level is not too polite: "Laughter shakes the Skies" is vigorous enough for Dryden, though not clownish, like "rude skinker" in Dryden's own translation of the passage. Pope's "dialect" is not Homer's, but it does give an appropriate impression of a language artfully created for its special purpose. Everyone who reads a modern plain translation should read Pope once, if only to be reminded that Homer's style is, as Pope might say, a "designed" style. Homer's music is closer to Mozart than to the tune of a popular ballad.

Pope like Homer is not the untutored genius of the Folk. He is master of an art very remote from that of a traditional oral poet; like Virgil he is a self-conscious craftsman, selecting language to give his verse an aura of the antique and the heroic. But the conventions of his period favored the effort to achieve modes of expression and effects that were as he once said "parallel" to Homer's, "tho' not the same." Although he does not translate every single Homeric formula, nor attempt to use the same English words for each recurrence, his habitual poetic use of epithets is often more Homeric than that of any later poet-translator in English. Fixed phrases recur—as they do in Virgil or Milton, though much more frequently—and they tend to recur in the same part of the verse, usually at the close. Looking back at passages quoted earlier (pp. 57–59) we have for example: "the sounding Shore," "the stormy Main," the "wat'ry Reign," "the Field of Fame," and "th' Æthereal Race." (Hundreds of others can easily be found elsewhere in the translation.) Their convenience in rhyming couplets may seem painfully obvious, but it is a convenience very nearly in the full Homeric sense. Phrases of this sort are essential to heroic poetry as Pope understands it, they suit the characteristic rhythmic pattern of the couplet with its strong mid-line pauses, and they fit the balancing patterns of phrasing and thought that the rhythm all but demands.

Because these fixed phrases are used so often by Pope, we read them in a quite Homeric way as action-image units and as ornamentally heroic. As Parry says of Homer's epithets, they adorn not the local context, but the whole poem. "This," the reader of both Pope and Homer feels, "is how the heroic line and the heroic world are made." In many of the phrases Pope's eighteenth-century audience would also have recognized a Homeric or Virgilian or Miltonic parallel. As one critic has noted, Pope often uses these expressions with a bardlike lack of regard for the special context. "The stormy Main" does not mean that a storm is going on; nor is "the sounding Shore" any more noisy than usual. In the unchanging nature of Homer—and of the eighteenth-century epic—the Main is always sounding. Pope must have seen that the fixity of Homer's epithets implied a fixity in the scheme of things, an order that he naturally interpreted as the Great Show of Nature of seventeenth- and eight-

eenth-century philosophers. In comparison with later translators Pope
thus has a further advantage in the eternal return of his rhymes. As
in his original poems they lend added assurance that all is ordered for
the best in the best of imagined worlds. They do this simply by being
heard, and by recurring so often in company with familiar words and
orders of words, and with familiar kinds of meaning. Pope also had,
like Homer, the advantage of working in a recognized style, one
whose norms were accepted without question by his contemporaries.
They are more easily recoverable for readers of this century than for
those of the nineteenth century—recoverable, that is, for anyone who
has made the rediscovery of the poetry of Dryden, Samuel Johnson,
and Pope himself.

But Pope was first a poet, and only secondarily a translator, and in
his treatment of many epithets he deftly and beautifully adapts the
original phrase to its new setting or rejects it because it does not tone
in well with the local dramatic and emotional context. In translating
many episodes of the *Iliad* Pope can be seen practicing his favorite
pictorial type of composition, working up harmonious groupings of
characters in action, or depicting scenes as fitting backgrounds for
action. When he speaks of "the sounding Shore" in the scene where
Thetis comes to Achilles (p. 57), he is using a phrase based on
Homer's "much-resounding sea," but he introduces it into a passage
where Homer had not used the corresponding phrase in Greek. As
the whole passage in Pope's version makes clear, something quite new
and un-Homeric is being presented: the impression as in Tiepolo's
fresco of a lonely and wild seascape, of a melancholy atmosphere
appropriate to Achilles' "loud lament."

But in judging these Homeric paintings, we must see what Pope—
and contemporary artists—were doing, what they were intentionally
bringing out in Homer. No one, however well indoctrinated in the
technique of oral verse-making, can fail to feel that the *Iliad* is a
poem of vividly heard and seen events, both human and natural. We
hear the roar and slap of waves, the crash of trees cut down in the
forest, the brazen shout of Achilles. We see the wine-dark sea, the
blaze of forest fires and city beacons, the clouds swept from the starry
sky, the old men and Helen on the wall of Troy, Hector bouncing
his son in the air, and Priam putting his hand to the face of Achilles.
In Homer these images are entangled in human actions—of heroes
and men of state, of woodcutters and shepherds, of besieged inhab-
itants of cities. (We have noted in Chapter 2 that Homer "almost never
describes anyone's actual appearance.")

But with Pope we begin to approach the image as art: we are being
asked to contemplate it and enjoy it for the sensuous excitement it
arouses or for the emotion it symbolizes. It is one thing for a Homeric

shepherd to see a stormy mist coming over the sea and to turn away
in terror; another, to enjoy the picturesque melancholy of the scene.
The visual and aural excitement is often there in Homer; but Pope
and seventeenth-century painters of the heroic world were responding to it overenthusiastically and overpictorially. In the battle scene
quoted earlier (p. 60), Homer too tells how a divine light dispels
the "Mist of Darkness," but Pope's "sudden Ray shot beaming o'er
the Plain" and his "scene wide-opening to the Blaze of Light" is by
comparison with the Homeric narrative a baroque *coup de théâtre*.
The illustrations in Pope's text of divine interventions are in much
the same dazzling style (for example, Books V, VIII), but in spite of
some excesses, both Pope and his illustrator strike us as true to our
remembered impressions of sudden shifts of dark and light in many
episodes of the *Iliad*. The "heroic Fires" that Pope adds to the figure of
Nestor in the "Mist of Darkness" scene are again quite Homeric. As
a recent critic has shown, images of fire have a metaphorical value
throughout the *Iliad*, particularly in association with Achilles. In his
Preface "fire" is Pope's prime metaphor for Homer's genius, and in
the translation he may have unconsciously been trying to underline
this quality by lavish use of words like "glittering," "refulgent," "radiant," and "blaze."

In his bravura version of Achilles at the trench—a real epiphany—
Pope gives us all the brilliance and terror of heroic glory and destruc-
tiveness. A brief comparison with the Greek original will show that
the Homeric singer is not always simple and economical. In twenty-
two lines, he heaps up in addition to many images of sound all sorts
of details suggesting "murky fire and brightness:"

. . . with a cloud his head was wreathed by the glorious goddess;
—a golden cloud it was—and from it she kindled a flame far-shining,
as when smoke rising from a burning city strikes the upper air . . .
    and with the sun's setting,
torches flame out in masses, and high above, the radiance
darts up for neighbors round about to see . . .
    so from Achilles' head the flame strikes the upper air . . .
    when they saw the invincible fire
—frightful, above the head of great-hearted Peleus' son—
blazing up, set aflame by the goddess, grey-eyed Athena . . .

In place of Homer's enrichment by adding one narrative detail after
another, Pope gives us brilliant visual effects arranged in the dynamic
oppositions of the couplet. But different as his style is from Homer's,
he has kept Homer's emphasis on the splendor and terror of fire,
both of the burning city and of Achilles.

The original of this passage shows that Homer too has his rhetoric and devices of sound that enhance rhetorical emphasis. Note here the "as when . . ." and "so . . ." of the simile and the matching repetitions of formulas, types of symmetry that are brought out further by alliteration and assonance (especially of endings) and by striking enjambements. We have for example in the last two lines translated: *Deinon/Daiomenon/Daie.* Pope has the same or equivalent resources in English, plus rhyme: "Rays/ Beacons blaze/ Reflecting Blaze on Blaze." Homer also offered Pope the model for the climactic punch of "*Thrice* from the Trench . . . *Thrice*": *Tris men hyper Taphou/ Tris de . . .*

The Roman-English rhetoric of Pope's version of Agamemnon's appeal to his men (p. 59) is certainly coarser and more pompous than Homer's austere and quiet eloquence. But

"Ye Greeks be Men! and Your-selves revere!"

could hardly be bettered, and in Homer's repetition of the *aidos* root there is a cue for Pope's

"Let glorious Acts more glorious Acts inspire" . . .

Again Pope has an advantage over later translators in having a style of eloquence, and a known historic style derived from the Roman. Pope's hero is much more self-conscious than Homer's in proclaiming his valor, and he is more given to expressing himself in maxims of the Roman sententious type. But Homer too has his grave moral sentences, as in the concluding line of Agamemnon's appeal:

When men fall back, there's neither glory, nor any battle-might.

The beautiful couplet in which the death of Patroclus is fore-shadowed (p. 60) also has a solemn Roman tone:

There ends thy Glory! there the Fates untwine
The last, black Remnant of so bright a Line.

But in the original, the formulaic "end of life," *biotoio teleuté,* also has fairly solemn associations, since it is related in form and meaning to the tremendous word used elsewhere by Zeus: "What I speak *shall stand*" ("shall be brought to its appointed end"), *tetelesmenon.* In the somewhat obscure and very human theology of the *Iliad,* the question is at times raised as to whether the will of Zeus may not alter fate, but the event always shows that what must be, must be, that even Zeus must accept what Moira has allotted. In Pope's translation, as Gibbon and others have observed, the use of Hebraic and Miltonic terms often brings his Jove fairly close to the supreme deity of the Old Testament. In the passage quoted earlier (p. 59) Jove is called an "Almighty Pow'r" and "the Sov'reign of the Skies," and in many other contexts Pope, like Milton and the translators of the King James version, invests his Jove-Jehovah with the attributes of modern majesty. But—and here we may again cite the plain translators of the *New Oxford Bible*—Pope's Jove is indisputably a god, tremendous and awful as was Zeus to the gods and heroes of the *Iliad*. Like the heroes, he is more consistently grand in Pope than in Homer, although the translation brings out very well the toughness and social sophistication of Zeus and his "Senate of the Skies."

But the Homeric blend of grandeur, domestic comedy, and personal tragedy in the scene where Zeus foresees the death of his son Sarpedon—one of the great scenes in Homer and a favorite of Pope's —is beyond Pope, and indeed beyond translation. Pope can convey in his Roman-biblical style the majesty of Jove's speech and gestures, and he can describe with elegiac charm how Apollo

> from the War the breathless Hero bore,
> Veil'd in a Cloud, to silver Simois' Shore:
> There bath'd his honourable Wounds, and drest
> His manly Members in th' immortal Vest;
> And with Perfumes of sweet Ambrosial Dews,
> Restores his Freshness, and his Form renews.
> Then Sleep and Death, two Twins of winged Race,
> Of matchless Swiftness, but of silent Pace,
> Receiv'd Sarpedon, at the God's Command,
> And in a Moment reach'd the Lycian Land;
> The Corpse amidst his weeping Friends they laid,
> Where endless Honours wait the sacred Shade.
>
> XVI.825–836

In his version of the scene Pope is high heroic *and* pathetic, but not quite tragic. What we miss is the note of human bewilderment that we cannot fail to recognize in Antigone and Othello, and in Hector and Achilles. In high tragedy the hero discovers that heroic resolve is not enough; and he comes to question the very value that he has asserted more completely than most other men. "Who can control his fate?" Othello asks at the end of the play. To face and express doubt of this kind requires the moral courage and humility that we see in Hector when he is tempted to avoid Achilles and hide in the city, and in Achilles when with Priam before him he has a vision of the inevitability both of heroic action and suffering. Pope's notes on Hector's terror show that he had some understanding of the tragic quality of the scene, though like contemporary critics of the epic he felt bound to justify terror in a perfect hero.

Only the greatest dramatic poets, working easily in their native language, have been able to make their heroes speak so simply and humanly as to convince us that fatal courage is "fortitude to highest victory." For a translator of Homer, the difficulty of striking the right tone in such crucial moments is almost overwhelming. A twentieth-century translator can often command the simple and the human, but the heroic of the unquestioning yet noble kind is alien to him and his world. To put it too plainly: he and his contemporaries no longer quite believe in the heroic ideal, just as they no longer believe in the older unquestioning patriotism. Pope was just able to—because the idea of the patriot-hero was still alive in eighteenth-century England, very nearly the last period when "decent" patriotic verse could be written by an English poet. In Pope's version, Hector becomes a hero of this eighteenth-century patriot-type. Pope's later poetry, where he rarely uses the Roman patriotic style without irony, shows how rapidly the corrosion of the ideal was progressing in his own lifetime. (The same change was also taking place in painting and sculpture.)

We must therefore praise Pope's *Iliad* for what he could do in a style that so easily invited parody. He could and triumphantly did express the noblesse and splendor of the eighteenth-century aristocratic ideal, the closest equivalent he knew for Homer's heroic code. His poem, like Lord Granville's famous gesture, exhibits "the English aristocracy at its very height of culture, lofty spirit, and greatness . . ." Nor is this expression of the aristocratic code a mere distortion of Homer; it represents one level of meaning in the total Homeric vision, one very important aspect of Homer's style. Pope was also fortunate in finding some equivalents for other, if not for all the qualities of Greek epic style. In poems written in the Renaissance heroic tradition, he had at hand an idiom rich in associations going back to Virgil and ultimately to Homer. Thanks to the continuity of this tradition, Pope could use certain kinds of language for convenience and ornament in a way not wholly alien to the ancient Homeric mode of composition. In the heroic couplet he had a strict rhythmical convention that like the hexameter favored the use of fixed phrases and frequently recurring rhetorical patterns. Most important of all, Pope and his contemporaries had a confident belief in a high, *formed*, poetic style, a belief typical of the classic, Mediterranean literary mind. To read Pope's *Iliad* is to have some experience in English of the nature and resources of this mind and of the kinds of expression it has fostered in Greece, Rome, and France. It is a mind and an art that is anti-Gothic, anti-Romantic.

But Pope was decidedly an English poet, and less correct, less classic than he sometimes liked to suppose. The Renaissance tradition in poetry and in art, within which he was writing, was also not quite classic. Since Spenser, "Hobgoblin had always been running away with the garland from Apollo." Nowhere does Pope show the modern and northern temper more clearly than in translating Homer's accurate action reporting into exciting pictorial effects. The reader whose taste is sufficiently impure to enjoy seventeenth- and eighteenth-century mythological and historical painting can also enjoy Pope's *Iliad*. While he reads, as when he is looking at Rubens or Tiepolo, he will not be able to question; he will surely know that he is experiencing one of the compelling visions of the Greek world of gods and of men like gods.

5

FROM THE *ILIAD* TO THE NOVEL,
VIA THE *RAPE OF THE LOCK*

Let me start this fabulous voyage with a scene from Pope's *Iliad* (XIV.179–218), a part of the so-called "Deception of Zeus," which may remind the reader of a scene in the *Rape of the Lock*. A brief recall of the context in the Homeric original may be helpful. Hera, seeing that Poseidon is now fighting for the Greeks, is delighted and plans to deceive Zeus; she seduces him and puts him to sleep, while the Grecians win a great victory over the Trojans. When Zeus awakes and discovers what is going on, he sets in motion new and successful attacks on the Trojan side, in which Patroclus will die, and after which Achilles in revenge returns to battle. So "the will of Zeus is fulfilled."

In Homer, the episode of Zeus's seduction is a piece of high comedy —the contrast between great, powerful divinities and their susceptibility to being deceived and seduced by sleep and love. The implied ironies go deep in the texture of the episode and the whole poem: the weakness of the gods, Homer is saying, is a part of the nature of the gods, and through the frivolous comedy of deception the poet is making one more criticism of his divine society. "The gods," Cedric Whitman says, "are barred by their deathlessness from the dignity of

This essay began in a talk for a humanities class at Yale University, in which I was asked to "carry the students from the *Rape of the Lock* to the novel" (!). In the form printed here, it has been—in Jane Austen's words— "stretched out here and there" with a certain amount of "sense," or "if not, of solemn specious nonsense."

tragedy, or the greatness of self-mastery." But the greatness of the gods is never entirely lost even in moments of ironic inconsistency. When in this scene Zeus tells Hera of all his loves, we feel that he must be a very great god indeed to have begotten so many gods and heroes: Perseus, Minos, Rhadamanthos, Dionysos, Heracles . . .

Here is Pope's version of the scene:[1]

> Meantime *Saturnia* from *Olympus'* Brow,
> High-thron'd in Gold, beheld the Fields below;　　　180
> With Joy the glorious Conflict she survey'd,
> Where her great Brother gave the *Grecians* Aid.
> But plac'd aloft, on *Ida's* shady Height
> She sees her *Jove,* and trembles at the Sight.
> *Jove* to deceive, what Methods shall she try,　　　185
> What Arts, to blind his all-beholding Eye?
> At length she trusts her Pow'r; resolv'd to prove
> "The old, yet still successful, Cheat of Love";
> Against his Wisdom to oppose her Charms,
> And lull the Lord of Thunders in her Arms.　　　190
> 　Swift to her bright Apartment she repairs,
> Sacred to Dress, and Beauty's pleasing Cares.
> With Skill divine had *Vulcan* form'd the Bow'r,
> Safe from Access of each intruding Pow'r.
> Touch'd with her secret Key, the Doors unfold;　　　195
> Self-clos'd behind her shut the Valves of Gold.
> Here first she bathes; and round her Body pours
> Soft oils of Fragrance, and ambrosial Show'rs:
> The Winds perfum'd, the balmy Gale convey
> Thro' Heav'n, thro' Earth, and all th' aerial Way;　　　200
> Spirit divine! whose exhalation greets
> The Sense of Gods with more than mortal Sweets.
> Thus while she breath'd of Heav'n, with decent Pride
> Her artful Hands the radiant Tresses ty'd;
> Part on her Head in shining Ringlets roll'd,　　　205
> Part o'er her Shoulders wav'd like melted Gold.
> Around her next a heav'nly Mantle flow'd,
> That rich with *Pallas'* labour'd Colours glow'd;
> Large Clasps of Gold the Foldings gather'd round,
> A golden Zone her swelling Bosom bound.　　　210
> Far-beaming Pendants tremble in her Ear,

1. The text of this and other quotations from Pope's original poems and from his *Homer* is that of *The Twickenham Edition of the Poems of Alexander Pope*, general ed. John Butt, Vols. I–X (New Haven, 1939–67). Hereafter referred to as *TE*.

From the Iliad to the Novel

Each Gemm illumin'd with a triple Star.
Then o'er her Head she casts a Veil more white
Than new fal'n Snow, and dazling as the Light.
Last her fair Feet celestial Sandals grace.   215
Thus issuing radiant, with majestic Pace,
Forth from the Dome th' Imperial Goddess moves,
And calls the Mother of the *Smiles* and *Loves.*

Pope's gods are great too, though not in quite the same way that Homer's were. Homer's deities were more elementary powers—Zeus is still "the cloud-gatherer" even in this charming narrative—and their desires were more elementary too. In the Greek, Zeus very humanly, directly *wants* Hera:

when he saw her, desire was a mist about his close heart
as much as on that time they first went to bed together
and lay in love, and their dear parents knew nothing of it.
Iliad, XIV.294–296
[Lattimore]

Like two great children at play the son and daughter cheated their parents, Kronos and Rheia. (We get a glimpse in passing of the coarse and happy gods of pre-Olympian times.) By comparison, Pope's gods are Romanized, Hebraicized, and much more solemn. Juno is "Saturnia"; Neptune is her "great Brother"; Jove is "the Lord of Thunders," who, like the Old Testament deity, is manifest in "thunders and lightnings"; and Juno is "th' Imperial Goddess," who moves "with majestic Pace." This last reminds us of Virgil's *vera incessu,* "the genuine pace of a goddess."

In Pope's version greatness and glamour are as often expressed in language reminiscent of *Paradise Lost.* In Juno's chamber

the Doors unfold;
Self-clos'd behind her shut the Valves of Gold.
195–196

In the palace of the fallen angels, Milton tells of

the doors
Opening their brazen folds . . .

and how "a fabric huge" of Pandemonium "Rose like an exhalation." In Pope an "exhalation greets/ The Sense of Gods" from Juno's perfumes. The goddess' beauty is described in language that recalls another woman who was like a goddess,

Shee as a vail down to the slender waste,
Her unadorned gold'n tresses wore
Dissheveld, but in wanton ringlets wav'd . . .

Paradise Lost, IV.304–306

And we hear a little later in Milton of Eve's "modest pride." Compare:

Thus while she breath'd of Heav'n, with decent Pride
Her artful Hands the radiant Tresses ty'd;
Part on her Head in shining Ringlets roll'd,
Part o'er her Shoulders wav'd like melted Gold.

203–206

But it is one thing to compare a woman to a goddess, another to compare a goddess to a woman. Pope's Juno, with her "Charms," "her swelling Bosom," seems more and more a woman of the world,

resolv'd to prove
"The old, yet still successful, Cheat of Love" . . .

187–188

This line, as William Frost tells us,[2] was taken from Tooke (not a play on words, but a reference to the poet Charles Tooke, whose translation of the scene came out in a 1701 *Miscellany* including many of the best-known writers of the Restoration). The line fairly reeks of that society and its jaded loves: we hear in anticipation the tone of Lady Bellaston setting out to seduce Tom Jones. Sexual desires and motives so expressed have been through a considerable social education; though Homer's Hera has her social quality, her mores belong to a high heroic world, more vigorous, less polite. In Pope's translation of the whole episode we find many traces of the idiom, partly Ovidian in origin, of "am'rous" escapades in eighteenth-century verse: "pleasing [and "softer"] Cares," "the Pleasing Fire," "melts . . . in fierce Desires," "Fond Love," "gay [and "soft"] Desire," "Love's entrancing Joys," "Mix'd with her Soul" [not body], "Transport." There is visual splendor in Homer's dressing scene, but much more in Pope's, where the glamour though equally convincing is far more worldly:

Large Clasps of Gold the Foldings gather'd round,
A golden Zone her swelling Bosom bound.
Far-beaming Pendants tremble in her Ear,
Each Gemm illumin'd with a triple Star.

209–212

2. *TE,* VII, cxlv–viii.

80

From the Iliad to the Novel

Pope's comedy, then, arises from a contrast "parallel to Homer's, but not the same," the contrast between solemn Roman deities and all this social gallantry and *luxe*. There is greatness and beauty and comedy, as in Homer, but the definition of the elements that compose these qualities has been altered considerably. This blend, and the character of the translation, can be better understood after a look at the corresponding scene in the *Rape of the Lock:*

> And now, unveil'd, the *Toilet* stands display'd,
> Each Silver Vase in mystic Order laid.
> First, rob'd in White, the Nymph intent adores
> With Head uncover'd, the *Cosmetic* Pow'rs.
> A heave'nly Image in the Glass appears,   125
> To that she bends, to that her Eyes she rears;
> Th' inferior Priestess, at her Altar's side,
> Trembling, begins the sacred Rites of Pride.
> Unnumber'd Treasures ope at once, and here
> The various Off'rings of the World appear;   130
> From each she nicely culls with curious Toil,
> And decks the Goddess with the glitt'ring Spoil.
> This Casket *India's* glowing Gems unlocks,
> And all *Arabia* breathes from yonder Box.
> The Tortoise here and Elephant unite,   135
> Transform'd to *Combs*, the speckled and the white.
> Here Files of Pins extend their shining Rows,
> Puffs, Powders, Patches, Bibles, Billet-doux.
> Now awful Beauty puts on all its Arms;
> The Fair each moment rises in her Charms,   140
> Repairs her Smiles, awakens ev'ry Grace,
> And calls forth all the Wonders of her Face;
> Sees by Degress a purer Blush arise,
> And keener Lightnings quicken in her Eyes.
> The busy *Sylphs* surround their darling Care;   145
> These set the Head, and those divide the Hair,
> Some fold the Sleeve, whilst others plait the Gown;
> And *Betty's* prais'd for Labours not her own.
>   I.121–148

> Not with more Glories, in th' Etherial Plain,
> The Sun first rises o'er the purpled Main,
> Than issuing forth, the Rival of his Beams
> Lanch'd on the Bosom of the Silver *Thames*.
>   II.1–4

As more than one critic has pointed out, it is almost impossible
to tell whether Pope in the *Rape of the Lock* is parodying his *Iliad,* or
whether in his *Iliad* he is imitating the *Rape of the Lock.* (Uncertainty as to dates of composition make this in fact difficult to deter-
mine.) Whatever the explanation, parallels to our passage (and to
many others in Pope's *Iliad*) are not hard to find: "Cosmetic Pow'rs"
and the "Pow'rs" of Olympus; the "heav'nly Image" in the *Rape* and
the "celestial Sandals" in the translation; the "Pride" of the woman
and the "decent Pride" of the goddess; the "Charms" of both, and
the marvelous fragrance—"all *Arabia* breathes" and "she [Juno]
breath'd of Heav'n"; in the *Rape* the "glowing Gems" and in the *Iliad*
the "Colours" that "glow'd" and

> Each Gemm illumin'd with a triple Star.

In the first line of Canto II, "th' Etherial Plain" (a favorite adjective
of Pope's *Iliad*), parallels "th' aerial Way" of the translation.

Finally, the woman, Belinda, emerges as a "goddess" indeed, like
"The Sun" . . .

> issuing forth, the Rival of his Beams

recalling Juno:

> Thus issuing radiant, with majestic Pace,
> Forth from the Dome th' Imperial Goddess moves . . .

We can see that up to a point what Pope was doing in the translation and in the *Rape of the Lock* are very nearly the same—the
creation of divine glamour and beauty; and the impression is achieved
in part in the same way, by the use of Miltonic and Virgilian echoes.

But the effects in the context of the *Rape of the Lock* are hardly
identical. There is a further impression, as in the *Iliad,* of a mysterious and beautiful rite, and of an epiphany, the metamorphosis of a
woman and the birth of a goddess; but the "marvellous" in the *Rape*
is infused with the fine absurdity of the cult of beauty, "beauty" in
the "cosmetic" or "beautician's" sense and in the sense of sexual
attraction. The dressing-table scene is highly aphrodisiac. The most
obvious contrast with the *Iliad* rises from the wit, the kind that
focuses in a phrase like "the sacred Rites of Pride," which is both
climactic and anticlimactic. But this is an easier sort of wit compared with the quiet irony that is felt throughout the scene—all this
preparation for the social game of love, for an afternoon cards-and-
coffee party, all this to flatter a woman's ego.

But Pope, like many ironists, loves the folly he mocks. Inseparable from his wit, often the condition of its surprise, is the wonderful richness of sensuous and literary texture. Let us consider in order a few characteristic expressions, remembering Homer, Milton, and Pope's translation.

Line 122: "Mystic Order" suggests a secret cult known only to the initiate, and also the formulas of cosmetics; "Order" also suggests the harmony of the process. This is a "ceremony of innocence," of the "Fair and Innocent" who should be protected by the Sylphs.

Line 124: In "the *Cosmetic* Pow'rs" and "the glitt'ring Spoil" (132), note the generalizing, eternalizing effect of the article and epithet, as in many epic formulas of Pope's translation. "Glitt'ring" (almost standard in Pope's *Iliad* for heroic splendor) here evokes the beauty to the eye of gems and gold, while suggesting that the glitter is transitory—perhaps fake.

Line 135: The union of the Tortoise and the Elephant is grotesque and prodigious (the elephant, we know, is slow to mate)—perhaps a disturbance of the Law of Nature, perhaps an echo of a far-off primitive world of myth where such things "really" happen.

Line 136: With "Transform'd," the word that sets the note for the rest of the description, we feel the presence of the *Metamorphoses*. A court belle becomes Juno or Venus or an Augustan Queen, "Great *Anna!* whom three Realms obey," the presiding divinity of this not-so-heroic society.

Line 139: "Now awful Beauty puts on all its Arms . . ." is absurd, but taken with "Wonders" and "Lightnings" (like the "thunders and lightnings" on Sinai) the line puts us in mind of the other "awful" deity, the "majestic" goddess of Pope's *Iliad*.

Line 148: The end of the scene is not mere anticlimax, and more than an Ovidian dig at make-up. Betty's "Labours" are "*not* her own." We are witnessing the comically marvelous miracle of a woman's getting herself up for an occasion—the perfect prelude for the beginning of Canto II, where Belinda appears as a sun goddess.

By echoes of heroic-mythical and religious worlds, by immediate appeals of sight, scent, and touch, and by the ordered progress of his verse, Pope has invested the scene and woman's role in social, "am'rous" relations, with wonder, while evaluating the role by the anticipated contrast with the trifling game of love to be played at Hampton Court. And where are we in relation to the translation? Pope has created another parallel to the comedy of contrast in the passage from his *Iliad* and in Homer's original. But with a difference: in Pope's *Iliad* great Roman deities are seen as glamorous belles; here, belles are seen as Roman deities, as heroines in an epic scene. The direction of our amusement has changed, but the techniques of the poetry—the allusions to Milton, Virgil, and other poets—are surprisingly alike.

The direction of our amusement in the *Rape of the Lock*, toward laughter at contemporary foibles and love-making, was not altogether absent from the expected reading of the scene in Pope's *Iliad*. Parody of the heroic was in the air, if not explicit, as in the *Rape of the Lock*. Though Pope's prefatory remarks and most of his performance show him translating resolutely in the high Roman fashion of Dryden and other seventeenth-century predecessors, mocking intonations break in—and where more appropriately than in Book XIV, a scene of Homeric comedy? Though Pope rejected the hearty burlesque of Dryden's version of the quarreling Juno and Jove in Book I, there is at least one couplet to prove that he nearly succumbed to burlesque in rendering Book XIV:

> At length with Love and Sleep's soft Pow'r opprest,
> The panting Thund'rer nods, and sinks to Rest.
>
> 405–406

If we recall the lines on Jove's awful nod in Homer, Virgil, or Dryden, the parodic, if not burlesque, overtone is inescapable. (There is—by the way—nothing in the original like the second line.)

That Pope—and his audience—had other than properly heroic feelings about the episode in Homer, and about the style it suggested, is clear from his Observations, which offer plenty of evidence that Pope kept up the heroic decorum of his version not easily,[3] and that the direction of his personal response to the "Deceit of Jove" was more like that of the poet who had recently been revising the *Rape of the Lock*. His first note on the scene opens like this: "I don't know a bolder Fiction in all Antiquity, than this of *Jupiter's* being deceiv'd and laid asleep, or that has a greater Air of Impiety and Absurdity" (1. 179). Though a Homeric singer might have cheerfully assented to the last phrase, it is unlikely that he would have been troubled, as Pope was, by the lack of truth and morality in the "Fiction." "I must needs, upon the whole, as far as I can judge, give up the Morality of this Fable . . ." "The present Passage will appear with more Dignity," he adds, "if the observation of Diodorus is accepted,

---

3. "The notes of others are read to clear difficulties, those of Pope to vary entertainment. It has, however, been objected with sufficient reason that there is in the commentary too much of unseasonable levity and affected gaiety; that too many appeals are made to the ladies, and the ease which is so carefully preserved is sometimes the ease of a trifler." Samuel Johnson, *Lives of the English Poets,* ed. G. Birkbeck Hill (Oxford, 1905), III, 240.

that the narrative is a symbolic "Representation of a religious Solemnity."

The tone in which Pope introduces his next learned comment is worth hearing: "In the next Place, if we have recourse to Allegory, (which softens and reconciles every thing) it may be imagin'd that by the Congress of *Jupiter* and *Juno,* is meant the mingling of the *Aether* and the *Air* . . ." Citing as an example the lines on Spring from the *Georgics,* he continues, "[Virgil] calls *Jupiter* expressly *Aether,* and represents him operating upon his Spouse for the Production of all things." This pedantic if not salacious fantasy is airily dismissed with

> But, be all this as it will, it is certain, that whatever may be thought of this Fable in a theological or philosophical View, it is one of the most beautiful Pieces that ever was produc'd by Poetry. Neither does it want its Moral; an ingenious modern Writer [*Tatler,* 147] . . . has given it in these Words: "This Passage of *Homer* may suggest abundance of Instruction to a Woman who has a mind to preserve or recall the Affection of her Husband."

More "instruction" in the same vein follows from Pope himself, in "the Spectator tone" that Sherburn detected in the *Rape of the Lock.* The next note (l. 191) descends to the tone of Rymer on *Othello:* "some nice Criticks are shock'd in this Place of *Homer* to find that the Goddess washes herself, which presents some Idea as if she were dirty. Those who have Delicacy will profit by this Remark." The scene of Juno's perfuming herself (ll. 198–203) is commented on in chatty tones containing praise for Greek "Simplicity" in dress, Scriblerian pedantry, and kittenish advice to "the Ladies":

> The good *Eustathius* is ravish'd to find that there are no Washes for the Face . . . the Dress of *Juno* (which is the same they see in *Statues*) has manifestly the Advantage of the present, in displaying whatever is most beautiful: That the Charms of the *Neck* and *Breast* are not less laid open, than by the Modern Stays . . .

Of Venus' "wonder-working Girdle," Pope notes (l. 218) that "The Allegory of the *Cestus* lies very open, tho' the Impertinences of *Eustathius* on this Head are unspeakable." The twentieth-century reader (and Pope, we may assume) may view with skepticism William Frost's comment on the "panting Thund'rer" couplet—that it is "consistent both with his [Pope's] version of the episode as a whole and with his conception of the Juno and Jupiter story in Book XIV as perhaps deriving ultimately from the fertility observances of the eastern Mediterranean."[4] The protective "perhaps" must cover the ironic and sexy tones of Pope's commentary, which are hardly represented by "deriving ultimately from the fertility observances of the eastern Mediterranean." (O Fertility—what crimes are committed in thy name by "anthropological" literary critics!) The "conception" of the gods implied in the language of the translation ("as a whole") is nearer to that of Homer's divine comedy and the worldly comedy of the *Rape of the Lock*. Douglas Knight notes the mixed effect that sometimes results from using the Augustan "high style" in certain contexts,[5] as for example when Paris appeals to Helen to "snatch the hasty Joy":

> Thus having spoke, th' enamour'd *Phrygian* Boy
> Rush'd to the Bed, Impatient for the Joy.
>
> III.557–558

The last line anticipates Byron and in fact echoes Dryden on the illicit love of noble Sigismonda and clownish Guiscard.

We may return to the *Rape of the Lock* for an example of this "effect" in the blended wonder and ridicule of Pope's treatment of the "busy Sylphs." The mixed style in which Pope presents these creatures makes them seem most ambiguous spiritual powers:

> What tho' no Credit doubting Wits may give?
> The Fair and Innocent shall still believe.
> Know then, unnumber'd Spirits round thee fly,
> The light *Militia* of the lower Sky . . .
>
> I.39–42

But the Sylphs *are* the defenders of beauty and innocence—"*Militia* of the Sky." At first this sounds like Milton's guardian corps of angels, but "light" gives them an elfin charm, making them seem diminished compared with angelic powers. "Light" also implies that they may be unsubstantial and unreliable: Pope's style gives an impression of grandeur and of a nobler spiritual world, while imparting charm and ridiculous ineffectiveness to his deities. We are given the lightest assurance that innocence has strength and resources in an evil society.

4. *TE*, VII, cliv.
5. *TE*, VII, clxxxi–iii.

From the Iliad *to the Novel*

But however frail charming Innocence seems, it is preferable to Prudery:

> Soft yielding Minds to Water glide away,
> And sip with *Nymphs*, their elemental Tea.
> The graver Prude sinks downward to a *Gnome*,
> In search of Mischief still on Earth to roam.
> The light Coquettes in *Sylphs* aloft repair,
> And sport and flutter in the Fields of Air.
>
> I.61–66

Pope comes out strongly, here and elsewhere, on the side of generosity and love:

> Some Nymphs there are, too conscious of their Face,
> For Life predestin'd to the *Gnomes'* Embrace.
>
> I.79–80

"Coquettes" may be "light," their realm the less serious one of "air"—of feminine wiles—*but* they sport in *"the Fields of Air."* Again there is a touch of heroic quality, of epic generality, as in "the fields of battle," or in Chapman's "the fields of fight." Just enough weight is given these defenders of innocence to make us regard them with some respect.

Their special skill lies in "guiding" women in "mystick Mazes" of gallantry,

> Oft when the World imagines Women stray,
> The *Sylphs* thro' mystick Mazes guide their Way . . .
>
> I.91–92

They are skillful navigators in the "elemental Tea" of social life. But the power of Ariel is not all-sufficient. At the moment the lock is cut, "resign'd to Fate," he retires. If a woman is to escape Prudery, Innocence must fall, if only in a symbolic game.

The Baron is helped by Clarissa, who

> drew with tempting Grace
> A two-edg'd Weapon from her shining Case . . .
>
> III.127–128

This is the same Clarissa who later appears as the voice of Good Sense. Throughout the fuss that follows the rape of the lock, we see

87

the triumph of the Gnomes and Spleen, of prudishness and ill-nature. The speech of Clarissa in Canto V, which makes its moral point *through* parody, not in spite of it, also makes clear that the only way to rise above prudery and attain inner beauty of soul is to

> keep good Humour still whate'er we lose . . .
>
> V.30

Both Belinda's ravings and the crude boasting of the Baron—the excess of virginity and the excess of triumphant sex—are put in their place. As in a more serious epic, there can be a loss that is not a loss, but glory. Belinda's too is a "fortunate fall."

> Then cease, bright Nymph! to mourn thy ravish'd Hair
> Which adds new Glory to the Shining Sphere!
>
> V.141–142

Beauty and innocence, guided by Good Sense, may find a way. The woman who achieves this balance comes close to being a goddess of love:

> This, the blest Lover shall for *Venus* take . . .
>
> V.135

And what—the reader may well ask—does all this have to do with the novel, with English fiction? Let me suggest a few ways and give an example from a novel related to this kind of poetry. First, we can say that the situation with which Pope deals is very novelistic, a woman and man sparring in a game of love. Second, the situation is novelistic in another sense: the game is in part a social game, and it is played within all the complexities of modern social life. Finally Pope is picturing a particular, historic society, not only an ideal world of heroism and comic fantasy, but the actuality of Queen Anne's London. The setting is local, and the action can be dated, as in most novels. Part of the fun comes from seeing this society in the light of an unchanging heroic one, the "elite" of Homer's imagination.

Two main strands in the developing English novel of the eighteenth century might be noted here: the journalistic, in Defoe, and the parodic, in Fielding.[6] Pope's heroic-comical poem embraces both

---

6. See Ian Watt on Defoe's power of "convincing us completely that his narrative is occurring at a particular place and at a particular time" and on his similarity to Richardson in this respect. *The Rise of the Novel,* 1957 (Berkeley, 1965), p. 24.

modes and anticipates their union in the full-blown prose epic of *Tom Jones*. Let us look now at a scene from a novelist who began with parody, who left parody in the strict sense behind but who owed much to the traditions of satire in which the *Rape of the Lock* was written. It is worth noting that in the latter part of the *Rape*, the to-do over Belinda's loss, dialogue becomes more frequent, and though the heroic style is not sacrificed entirely, the effect comes closer to drama, to comedy of manners. Fielding—to recall something "everyone knows or ought to know"—began as a writer of plays; and many scenes in his novels could be easily transferred to the stage.

Jane Austen had the advantage of Fielding's example before her. (A word of protest should be entered in passing against the current critical fashion of setting up Jane Austen against Fielding.)[7] Jane Austen is also in her way a poet: her control of sentence rhythm, of ironic play on words, is often almost as precise as Pope's. Consider for example the brief dialogue from early in *Pride and Prejudice*, in which the seemingly proud and conceited Mr. Darcy surprises the very penetrating, very self-assured Elizabeth Bennet, by asking her to dance with him:

> After playing some Italian songs, Miss Bingley varied the charm by a lively Scotch air; and soon afterwards Mr. Darcy, drawing near Elizabeth, said to her—
>
> "Do not you feel a great inclination, Miss Bennet, to seize such an opportunity of dancing a reel?"
>
> She smiled, but made no answer. He repeated the question, with some surprise at her silence.
>
> "Oh!" said she, "I heard you before; but I could not immediately determine what to say in reply. You wanted me, I know, to say 'Yes,' that you might have the pleasure of despising my taste; but I always delight in overthrowing those kind of schemes, and cheating a person of their premeditated contempt. I have therefore made up my mind to tell you, that I do not want to dance a reel at all—and now despise me if you dare."
>
> "Indeed I do not dare."
>
> Elizabeth, having rather expected to affront him, was amazed

7. For a balanced view of Jane Austen's relation to Fielding and to Richardson, and to "late eighteenth-century fashions in fiction," see A. Walton Litz: *Jane Austen* (New York, 1965), pp. 3–18. On Fielding and Jane Austen as writers of "anti-romance," in the line of Cervantes, see Harry Levin, "The Example of Cervantes," *Society and Self in the Novel, English Institute Essays, 1955* (New York, 1956), p. 24. The whole essay is of importance for demonstrating how the novelist passes "from the imitation of art through parody to the imitation of nature." (The description also applies to Pope's development as a satirist.)

at his gallantry; but there was a mixture of sweetness and archness in her manner which made it difficult for her to affront
anybody; and Darcy had never been so bewitched by any woman
as he was by her. He really believed, that were it not for the
inferiority of her connections, he should be in some danger.

This dialogue is almost as full of ironic ambiguities as any of the
wittiest passages in the *Rape of the Lock*.[8] Mr. Darcy's question about
"dancing a reel" can be taken as Elizabeth takes it, as expressing
"premeditated contempt" of herself, or as well bred distaste for the
vulgar heartiness of country dancing. When Darcy repeats the question—"with some surprise"—it may be interpreted quite differently,
as another sign of his egotism—that any girl should not jump at the
chance, or as a sign of some interest in Elizabeth, a decided warming
up of this formidable man who dances with no one. After his "Indeed
I do *not* dare," his repeated question can be interpreted as a timid
gesture of love: he was, we discover, "bewitched." If we look at
Elizabeth's remarks, we find that they are equally alive with double
possibilities. Her very knowing rejection—"despise me if you dare"—
is based on *her* suppostion that she has interpreted Darcy's motives
correctly. She "was amazed at his gallantry" implies (though she does
not know it yet) the first sign of an attraction on her part to Mr.
Darcy. Her "mixture of sweetness and archness" bewitches, when she
intended the opposite effect, to cut Darcy down to size. Note also
that her "archness" defends her "sweetness" from any over-easy giving
in. (We may recall Belinda and her defenders.)

But there are no sylphs here—or rather, they have undergone a
new transformation, having become a part of the inner consciousness
and life of the heroine. Their skillful navigation now takes the form
of Elizabeth's artful way of turning off Darcy's attempts to win her
interest. A new diplomacy of the heart has taken the place of Pope's
epic machinery. As in the *Rape of the Lock*, the strategy that attempts to defend innocence also attracts the attacker. The sylphs
were not altogether reliable defenders: they made Belinda more
"bewitching" than ever.

There is a deeper likeness to Pope that can be seen by relating this
and similar dialogues to the whole of *Pride and Prejudice*. Elizabeth,
like Pope's heroine, is being educated (though she doesn't suspect it)
in Good Sense; just as Darcy is being educated in love and openness
of mind. Through the irony of the dialogue we are being gently re-

8. A more detailed analysis of "Popian" irony in this and other passages
is given in R. A. Brower, *The Fields of Light* (New York, 1951), pp. 167–
170.

minded that the egotistical pride of Darcy and the self-assurance of Elizabeth are not adequate attitudes for a mature man and woman. Both—without knowing it—are very "gnomish." The small hints of possible illumination, of generous response, point to another way, a way between frigidity or pride and mere helpless subjection to another personality. Jane Austen would call it the way of "rational happiness"—the reward of Pope's "Good Sense."

To all this let me add a brief epilogue by way of suggesting that our voyage has been a little more than fabulous. There is no case, or at best a slight one, for proving direct influence of Pope or of the *Rape of the Lock* on Jane Austen. It can be said, however, that her literary temper, the temper expressed through the ironic dialogue and comment of her drawing- and morning-room comedies, had its natural alliances with that of the earlier eighteenth century and with the Augustans, rather than with her immediate ancestors, the sentimental, domestic, and gothic novelists. Certain traits of mind, views of character and social life, with their accompanying modes of irony and moral evaluation, which become salient in Jane Austen, had been anticipated in eighteenth-century satire. The line of connection and development is suggested by Rachel Trickett in her admirable study of eighteenth-century poetry, *The Honest Muse:*

> The movement from fable to fact in subject-matter, and from myth to history as a mode of understanding and reflecting experience, is as vividly reflected in the poetry of the Honest Muse as in the development of the new literary form of the novel to which these changes gave rise.

The Augustan poets, particularly the satirists, "shared the common assumption of the time that men and manners, matter of fact rather than fiction, were the true substance of an art which, at its highest, must come home to the business and the bosom of every man."[9]

By family relationship, Jane Austen had at least one link with the great world of Pope and his contemporaries: she was "great-grand-niece of the magnificent first Duke of Chandos," and it is likely that both her sister's and her mother's first name came from the Duke's second wife, the Duchess Cassandra.[10] Though Chandos was almost certainly not Pope's Timon, his house, Canons, was grand enough to make the identification a natural one.

9. Rachel Trickett, *The Honest Muse* (Oxford, 1967), p. 15.
10. D. J. Greene: "Jane Austen and the Peerage," *PMLA,* 68 (1953), 1019.

Jane Austen's easy familiarity with eighteenth-century writers is well known, especially with "dear Dr. Johnson." She did not often model her style closely on her hero, though she made one unfortunate attempt to imitate him in verse. She loved Cowper and Crabbe, and quoted one of Cowper's most Augustan poems. She had a replay of Pope *On the Art of Sinking* in her brother James's periodical, *The Loiterer*: the ironic "Rules for *Prose Composition*" (in No. 5)[11] is a "compendium of those affectations in style and manner which were ridiculed in the Austen household," and which Jane often made fun of in her *Juvenilia*. Even Johnson and Pope are parodied, Pope in a letter from a young lady crossed—many times!—in love. A friend now widowed tries to brighten her up by introducing the subject of riding:

> Then repeating the following line which was an extempore and equally adapted to recommend both Riding and Candour— "Ride where you may, Be Candid where you can," she added, "I rode once, but it is many years ago"—She spoke this in so low and tremulous a Voice, that I was silent—.
>
> *A Collection of Letters*, Letter the Second

The context in the original must have been congenial to the novelist:

> Eye Nature's walks, shoot folly as it flies,
> And catch the Manners living as they rise;
> Laugh where we must, be candid where we can . . .

(These lines are a better introduction to Jane Austen's novels than to the "specious" and "solemn" argument of the *Essay on Man*.) Walton Litz says that Jane Austen's "works must be seen against the background of an eighteenth-century dialectic involving Reason and Feeling, Judgment and Fancy . . . By education and temperament, Jane Austen was uniquely suited to dramatize in her art the classic debates of the century that lay behind her."[12] "Sense and Sensibility" might serve as a subtitle for the *Rape of the Lock*, as "Benevolence and Prudence" might for *Tom Jones*. Both novelists—Fielding quite consciously—belong to the "line of Pope."

Richard Simpson, one of the earlier critics to point out Jane Austen's links with the Augustans, echoes Lewes' and Macaulay's view of her as close to Shakespeare in "her power of composing

---

11. Litz, p. 46. On *The Loiterer* and its possible effect on Jane Austen's "comic techniques," see pp. 15–17.
12. *Ibid.*, p. 8; compare p. 135.

characters. She does not give any of them a hobby-horse, like
Sterne, nor a ruling passion, like Pope, nor a humour, like Ben
Jonson, nor a trick, like Mr. Dickens."[13] We may want to qualify this
if we think of the fixed characters or "fools" in Jane Austen, and we
can accept the remark about the "ruling passion" only if we add—not
"like Pope" at his best. The lines just quoted from the *Essay on Man*
suggest that the doctrine of the "Ruling Passion" was not likely to
offer an adequate rationale for Pope's mature satirical portraits. The
great passage on Man,

> Chaos of Thought and Passion, all confused . . .

expresses better than his theory Pope's sense of the paradoxical
complexity of human nature. In the *Epistle to Cobham*, the satire in
which he tried hardest to impose the doctrine on particular cases,
the portraits keep exceeding their assigned Passion. In the first half
of the poem Pope sets forth a quite different account of "human
kind," expressing over and over his skepticism about easy explana-
tions.

> Our depths who fathoms, or our shallows finds,
> Quick whirls, and shifting eddies, of our minds? . . .
> On human actions reason tho' you can,
> It may be Reason, but it is not Man:
> His Principle of action once explore,
> That instant 'tis his Principle no more.
> Like following life thro' creatures you dissect,
> You lose it in the moment you detect.
> > 29–30; 35–40

The dazzling contradictions of Wharton's character hardly illustrate
his Ruling Passion, "the lust of Praise."

> A constant Bounty, which no friend has made;
> An angel Tongue, which no man can persuade;

13. Richard Simpson, "Jane Austen," *The North British Review*, 52
(1870), 136, quoted in *Jane Austen, The Critical Heritage*, ed. B. C.
Southam (London, 1968), p. 249. For Lewes' and Macaulay's views, see
Southam, items 26, 30, 36. "It is clear that she began, as Shakespeare
began, with being an ironical censurer of her contemporaries. After form-
ing her prentice hand by writing nonsense, she began her artistic self-
education by writing burlesques . . . her parodies were designed not so
much to flout at the style as at the unnaturalness, unreality, and fictitious
morality, of the romances she imitated." Simpson, "Jane Austen," p. 130.

> A Fool, with more of Wit than half mankind,
> Too quick for Thought, for Action too refined.
>
> 198–201

Though we may trace the lines of a moral dialectic in many of Pope's satirical portraits, the greatest ones—like the central characters of Jane Austen's novels—cannot be reduced to a single pair of warring vices and virtues. Though Jane Austen and Pope were equally clear about the meaning of the large moral abstractions on which their judgments rested, in their great cases they expressed a common love of "intricacy" in character. Belinda surprises us by being more than a featherhead, and Darcy by being more than an allegorical embodiment of Prejudice. Elizabeth Bennet may speak for both the novelist and the satirist: "intricate characters are the *most* amusing." When Pope tells Swift that "Your lady friend Martha Blount—is *Semper Eadem*, and I have written an Epistle to her on that qualification in a female character . . ." he is not giving an adequate account of the tenderly mocking picture with which he concludes the *Epistle to a Lady,*

> And yet, believe me, good as well as ill,
> Woman's at best a Contradiction still . . .
>
> 269–270

"Heav'n . . . Blends," he continues,

> Reserve with Frankness, Art with Truth allied,
> Courage with Softness, Modesty with Pride;
> Fixed Principles, with Fancy ever new;
> Shakes all together, and produces—You.
>
> 277–280

Pope did not always write like this, but he did more than once, in poems to Martha Blount, and in the *Rape of the Lock:*

> Her lively looks a sprightly mind disclose,
> Quick as her Eyes, and as unfix'd as those:
> Favours to none, to all she Smiles extends:
> Oft she rejects, but never once offends.
> Bright as the sun, her Eyes the Gazers strike,
> And, like the Sun, they shine on all alike.
> Yet graceful Ease, and Sweetness void of Pride,
> Might hide her Faults, if *Belles* had Faults to hide:
> If to her share some female errors fall,
> Look on her face, and you'll forget 'em all.
>
> II.10–18

94

From the Iliad to the Novel

"The tone is ironical," as Cleanth Brooks reminds us, "but the irony
is not that of a narrow and acerb satire; rather it is an irony which
accords with a wise recognition of the total situation."[14]

In this "Shakespearean" treatment of the heroine and in other
features, the *Rape* differs markedly from its more obviously mock-
epic predecessors. After reviewing Pope's indebtedness to Tassoni,
Boileau, and Garth, Joseph Warton concludes "that the *Rape of the
Lock* . . . contains the truest and liveliest picture of modern life; and
that the subject is of a more elegant nature, as well as more artfully
conducted than that of any other heroi-comic poem."[15] The important
difference lies in the subject: "While Boileau and Garth describe the
quarrels of lazy priests and grubby physicians, Pope is concerned with
a quarrel in the *beau monde*."[16] Pope's world is "beautiful" in every
sense, and his poem presents a credible society of families and lovers
in "a palpably credible plot."[17] This world of parodied crises and of
deeper and more permanent moral and emotional concerns lightly
implied in an ironic surface approaches closely to the fictional crea-
tions of Jane Austen. Fielding had led the way in his dramatic scenes
from the life of a hero who was both warm-hearted and imprudent;
and Crabbe, another sturdy Augustan, may have offered models
nearer to Jane Austen's chosen milieux in tales like "The Frank
Courtship," "Arabella," and "The Lover's Journey," with their scenes
of village middle-class wooing and romantic deceptions coolly un-
masked. But the outright irony of Crabbe was not adequate to the
more complex vision of Jane Austen. To bring the multiple per-
spectives of irony *and* tenderness to bear simultaneously on the social
case, whether of Elizabeth Bennet or Marianne Dashwood, or Emma
Woodhouse, demanded another model for revising the prose sentence
to serve its new function. And where could the last of the Augustans
and the first of the nineteenth-century novelists find a more apt
teacher than in the master of "intricacy" and politeness, the creator
of an idealized yet imperfect Martha Blount and Arabella Fermoor?
If we shudder at the notion of conscious or unconscious "influence,"
we may change our metaphor and suggest that in Jane Austen the
mind and art of Pope found its reincarnation, as the heroic-comical
poem found *its* reincarnation in novels of "Love and Friendship."

14. *The Well Wrought Urn* (New York, 1947), p. 94.
15. *Essay on the Genius and Writings of Pope* (London, 1782), I, 254–
255.
16. Ian Jack, *Augustan Satire* (Oxford, 1952), p. 85.
17. The phrase, and the point, is G. S. Rousseau's: *Twentieth Century
Interpretations of "The Rape of the Lock"* (Englewood Cliffs, N.J., 1969),
Intro., p. 3.

95

6

A POET'S *ODYSSEY*

The reader of Robert Fitzgerald's translation of the *Odyssey* will be certain of one thing—that the *Odyssey* is a *poem*. What seems obvious to anyone familiar with the original needs stressing because for the past seventy years or more the *Odyssey* has often been handed over to the prose writers, while the *Iliad* has usually been claimed by the poets. Whatever the reasons for this division of labor—and to explore them would carry us into the history of literary taste—the results as measured by popularity have seemed to justify the feeling that the *Odyssey* did not need verse, whereas the *Iliad* did. For a literary public bred on fiction, for whom the long poem was unreadable or dead, a "good story" of married life and romantic adventure seemed to go naturally in prose, and for everyone who has read the versions of William Morris or William Cullen Bryant, there must have been thousands who have read and enjoyed the prose translations of George Herbert Palmer, Samuel Butler, T. E. Shaw, and E. V. Rieu. Palmer, whose version is still the best in prose, wrote in his preface that he aimed "to employ persistently the veracious language of prose, rather than the dream language, the language of poetry"—a remark that tells us much about poetic style in 1891, and something about Palmer's reading of the *Odyssey*. Although Palmer acknowledges the importance of rhythm in a prose version, he clearly implies that any "systematic arrangement" of sounds would be a distraction from veracity, not, as we might think, the necessary condition for achieving

Reprinted from a review of *Homer: The Odyssey*, trans. Robert Fitzgerald, *Poetry*, 98 (1961).

poetic truth. Butler's plainness (less evident than he supposed) led the way to Lawrence's novel with its archaic and poetic perversities, and his example apparently justified the journalism of Rieu's paperback. The downhill reformation of translation style that began with the revolt against Murray was thus complete.

But while it is easy enough to be plain, it is very much harder to be plain and make a poem. Fitzgerald has succeeded magnificently in this difficult task and has given us a translation that far surpasses the prose versions in faithfulness to the dramatic and poetic life of the *Odyssey*. He has succeeded first in the most difficult feat of all, in finding a rhythm and a level of diction that make us feel, as we should, that the *Odyssey* is the most continuously beautiful of all epics in the Western tradition. The line he uses is based on blank verse, but the rhythm has been affected by the poet's aiming at another line, the Homeric hexameter, with its laying down of successive phrases and masses of sound. It is easy to find a good example:

No words were lost on Hermês the Wayfinder,
who bent to tie his beautiful sandals on,
ambrosial, golden, that carry him over water
or over endless land in a swish of the wind,
and took the wand with which he charms asleep—
or when he wills, awake—the eyes of men.
So wand in hand he paced into the air,
shot from Pieria down, down to sea level,
and veered to skim the swell. A gull patrolling
between the wave crests of the desolate sea
will dip to catch a fish, and douse his wings;
no higher above the whitecaps Hermês flew
until the distant island lay ahead,
then rising shoreward from the violet ocean
he stepped up to the cave. Divine Kalypso,
the mistress of the isle, was now at home.
Upon her hearthstone a great fire blazing
scented the farthest shores with cedar smoke
and smoke of thyme, and singing high and low
in her sweet voice, before her loom a-weaving,
she passed her golden shuttle to and fro.
A deep wood grew outside, with summer leaves
of alder and black poplar, pungent cypress.
Ornate birds here rested their stretched wings—
horned owls, falcons, cormorants—long-tongued
beachcombing birds, and followers of the sea.
Around the smoothwalled cave a crooking vine

held purple clusters under ply of green;
and four springs bubbling up near one another
shallow and clear, took channels here and there
through beds of violets and tender parsley.
Even a god who found this place
would gaze, and feel his heart beat with delight:
so Hermês did; but when he had gazed his fill
he entered the wide cave. Now face to face
the magical Kalypso recognized him,
as all immortal gods know one another
on sight—though seeming strangers, far from home.
But he saw nothing of the great Odysseus,
who sat apart, as a thousand times before,
and racked his own heart groaning, with eyes wet
scanning the bare horizon of the sea.

V.43–83 (in Greek)

The first thing to note is that the movement of these lines is always going forward, narrative expectation and sound being so well paired that it is hard to end the quotation. It is this hidden rhythm inaccessible to analysis that is most Odyssean and most rare in translation. If we look at the Greek we shall see innumerable local effects that suggest the pattern of Homeric verse. For example, the ending of the first line with its weighty epithet, and the way in which clauses and adjectives follow in the familiar additive style:

> . . . Hermês the Wayfinder,
> who bent to tie his beautiful sandals on,
> ambrosial, golden, that carry him over water
> or over endless land . . .

The slight awkwardness of grammar in the next three lines beautifully reproduces the tension and climax of the Greek. Homer too makes us wait for "awake," and he slips in "when he wills" at exactly the same point in the line. (There are moments when we feel that the bard is doing awfully well in rendering Fitzgerald!)

But the finding of a rhythm necessarily implies the creation of a style. Fitzgerald's modeling of diction is masterly, particularly in striking the right level for the English reader while skillfully alluding to the traditional oral style. The passage shows very well how Fitzgerald handles two features of this style that are most troublesome for the translator—the fixed epithet and the simile. "Hermês the Wayfinder," for example, translates only one of two epithets used here, but it gives active and accurate meaning to a noun (*diaktoros*) usually translated tiresomely as "conductor" or "messenger." The second expression, *argeiphontes*, is again omitted when it recurs only six lines later. "The desolate sea" and "the violet ocean" renew phrases that have become unhappily fixed in classroom translations ("barren," "violet-colored"). "Divine Kalypso" is added, though the equivalent is frequent elsewhere in Homer. In general, Fitzgerald exercises a nice balance between freedom and accuracy, apparently feeling with Pope that English taste will not stand Homeric frequency of repetition. His tact in handling similes is shown by the fine example describing Hermês' gull-like flight. Instead of the standard "As" and "So," we are brought in direct touch with Homer's image:

[Hermês] veered to skim the swell. A gull patrolling . . .

Fitzgerald's freedom stands in sharp contrast to the austere precision with which Lattimore has rendered epithet and simile in his *Iliad*. Though I have been assured by an expert that the *Odyssey* is not measurably less formulaic in style than the *Iliad*, I suspect that many readers will share my impression that the *Odyssey* is less heroic and less ceremonial in style. Similes are in fact less frequent and certainly unobtrusive. Fitzgerald's omissions and shortenings have a further advantage in increasing speed of narration and in keeping the length of the poem close to that of the original. He also possesses a fine ear for Homer's rhythmic paragraphing, as can be seen in the economical rounding off of the first section of this passage:

Divine Kalypso,
the mistress of the isle, was now at home.

Elsewhere, Fitzgerald uses breaks in the page very effectively (if occasionally too often for my taste) to give us the illusion of hearing the recitation of the singer and his actors.

But a poet-translator of the *Odyssey* cannot simply rely on a standard rhythm or idiom which he applies through thick and thin. The *Odyssey* includes a much greater variety of poetry than the *Iliad*, and the translator must be able to shift as easily and as often as the Homeric singer. In the passage we have quoted the poetry moves from sea-voyaging to luxurious domesticity to marvelous gardening to divinity, and finally to poetry of simple longing for home. Fitzgerald manages all of these familiar Odyssean modes while maintaining the good neutral style that is never ostentatiously "poetic" or "modern." At the same time he has the happy gift of surprise. We keep coming on words that strike us as new, only to find that they were "there" in the Greek, that is, they were there for a translator who sees into the life of words. So "in a swish of wind" catches the breathiness of Homer's *pnoié,* and the hunting gull of the simile *is* "patrolling" the waves: if the verb is modern, it is also accurate. The pungent details of the description are almost all Homer's, and if "purple" and "green" are not named, they are present by sensuous implication and quite typical of other scenes in the poem.

Perhaps the most difficult kind of poetry for the translator of the *Odyssey* to recapture is the poetry of hard-boiled fun and resourceful cunning. Fitzgerald is remarkably adept at catching the tone of Odysseus' jokes, as in his wily dialogue with the Cyclops:

> "you ask my honorable name? Remember
> the gift you promised me, and I shall tell you.
> My name is Nohbdy: mother, father, and friends,
> everyone calls me Nohbdy."
>
> And he said:
> "Nohbdy's my meat, then, after I eat his friends.
> Others come first. There's a noble gift, now."
>
> IX.364–370

Another tough pun comes out exactly right in the translation of the episode where Odysseus takes on the fat beggar, Iros:

> So now Odysseus made his shirt a belt
> and roped his rags around his loins, baring
> his hurdler's thighs and boxer's breadth of shoulder,
> the dense rib-sheath and upper arms. Athena   .
> stood nearby to give him bulk and power,
> while the young suitors watched with narrowed eyes—
> and comments went around:
>
> "By god, old Iros now retiros."
>
> "Aye,
> he asked for it, he'll get it—bloody, too."
> "The build this fellow had, under his rags!"
>
> XVIII.66–74

Here as in Homer is the rugged warrior of Troy, heroic Odysseus. Any fear that Fitzgerald's accent might be too gentle vanishes when we see this fighter and when we hear him speak out loud and bold in another interchange with the Cyclops:

> "We are from Troy, Akhaians, blown off course
> by shifting gales on the Great South Sea;

A Poet's Odyssey

homeward bound, but taking routes and ways
uncommon; so the will of Zeus would have it."
                                        IX.259–262

In the creation of dramatic life through speech Fitzgerald meets the
final test for the translator of Homer, and here he has been well prepared by his experience in translating Greek tragedy. Homer's
speeches, as critics have often pointed out, are composed within the
formulaic style, and in a sense everyone, from nurses to monsters to
gods, speaks alike. (If Fitzgerald occasionally nods, Homer has been
there before him.) At his best Fitzgerald has caught the true dramatic
trick of striking through the Homeric idiom to the implied voice. He
is less "Homeric," inevitably—for Homer's secret is contained in his
language—but he keeps us in touch with the men and women behind
the Greek by finding equivalent tones in English. We hear with surprising distinctness young Nausicaa and her queen mother, the old
nurse Eurycleia, the noble-crafty Penelope, and dozens of others. Fitzgerald also has a trick of his own, a kind of shorthand indirect discourse that goes straight to the heart of the matter, singling out the
salient dramatic fact from Homer's Greek. Here is a beautiful example
from the scene in which Eurycleia recognizes her master:

> Then he kept still, while the old nurse filled up
> her basin glittering in firelight; she poured
> cold water in, then hot.
>   But lord Odysseus
> whirled suddenly from the fire to face the dark.
> The scar: he had forgotten that. She must not
> handle his scarred thigh, or the game was up.
> But when she bared her lord's leg, bending near,
> she knew the groove at once.
>   XIX.386–393

"The scar"—that is purely English inner dramatic style—but it is
marvelously like what happens as we read Homer's more stylized,
more leisurely idiom, with its apt placing of the key word (*oulen*) at
the head of the verse.

It should be clear by now that the art of making a poem in translating the *Odyssey* is also the art of making a story and a drama.
Fitzgerald's command of the plain style and his mastery of rhythm
in the line and paragraph account in large measure for our sense of
swiftness and direction in the narrative line, qualities in which he
very nearly equals Homer. His economy in the handling of epithet
and simile also contribute to the rapidity and clarity of narration in

101

parts and in the whole. Our very palpable grasp of the voice and the role of each actor is matched by the sensuous sharpness of detail in descriptions of natural settings or of splendid palaces or of simpler scenes such as the cave of the Cyclops or the cabin of Eumaeus. The fun and the violence, the homeliness and the elegance are present in the particulars of narration and speech, as well as in the large gestures and actions of the characters. As we read the closing episodes of the slaughter in the hall and the reunion of Penelope and Odysseus, we are confident that the emphases and the blend of elements are and have been right throughout. The English reader without Greek cannot have all of Homer's poem in this version, but he can discover something of that surprising combination that is the *Odyssey*—a poem of marriage and family, of husband and wife, father and son, that is also a poem of heroic adventure and romantic temptation, a poem of all that denies and revolts against "home." Fitzgerald shows that the translator may through poetry point toward the richness of life which the original poem celebrates.

7

DRYDEN'S EPIC MANNER AND VIRGIL

"A heroic poem, truly such, is undoubtedly the greatest work which the soul of man is capable to perform."[1] While the solemnity of this pronouncement is certainly more characteristic of Rapin than of Dryden, the reverence for epic poetry is quite typical of the author of *An Essay of Heroic Plays*. As every reader of Dryden knows, the influence of Renaissance epic theory is all but omnipresent in his critical essays and prefaces. It is equally well known that the epic manner Dryden often adopted in his verse owes much in a general way to the idea of the heroic poem. But fewer readers, I believe, realize the extent to which Dryden's epic style is directly indebted to his "master," Virgil.

When Dryden tried most consciously to follow the theories of heroic poetry, almost invariably he heightened his style by means of echoes and imitations of the "best poet." In such passages we find the heroic convention revived and reinforced by an uncommon familiarity with Virgil and the Virgilian style. But the connection between Virgil and the Renaissance idea of the epic was not made by Dryden; in fact, from early in the sixteenth century Virgil played only too prominent a part in the voluminous speculations on the "truly heroic poem."[2] Naturally we must not hope to draw too fine a

Reprinted, with revisions, from *PMLA*, 55 (1940), 119–138.

1. *Dedication of the Aeneis* in *Essays of John Dryden*, ed. W. P. Ker (Oxford, 1926), II, 154.

2. See J. E. Spingarn, *A History of Literary Criticism in the Renaissance* (New York, 1908); B. J. Pendlebury, *Dryden's Heroic Plays: A Study of*

line between the influence of Virgil and that of Homer in shaping
these tenuous theories, since with very few exceptions the critics
cite precedents in both poets. Besides, there are some writers, such as
Hobbes and Madame Dacier, who give Homer, and not Virgil, the first
place in their observations. But in spite of references to Homer and
Aristotle the theorists commonly betray an over-fondness for Virgil
and "the pure idea of a Virgilian poem."[3] The Maronolatry of sixteenth-century Italian critics such as Vida and Scaliger needs no emphasizing, while among French critics of both the sixteenth and
seventeenth centuries the bias in favor of the Virgilian epic is more
than evident. Le Bossu, the most famous of the French writers on the
epic, does not praise Virgil at the expense of Homer; but the theories
he sets forth find much more support in the *Aeneid* than in the *Iliad*
or the *Odyssey*. In general, the Renaissance critics and poets alike
were in their approach to the epic much nearer to Virgil than Homer.
They could with reason cite Virgil's example in justifying some of
their most important doctrines, such as the insistence on a conscious
moral or patriotic purpose in the epic, the demand that the hero be
an exemplar of virtue, and the emphasis on the allegorical interpretation of the action.

If we wish to see quite clearly the influence of the Virgilian tradition in such theorizing, we need only turn to Dryden himself. As
will be remembered, Dryden long cherished the notion of writing a
poem according to the heroic formula. In his remarks on this project
he showed that he was as loyal to Virgil as many of the Continental
theorists:

> I could not have wished a nobler occasion to do honour . . .
> to my king, my country, and my friends; most of our ancient
> nobility being concerned in the action . . .[4] after Virgil and
> Spenser, I would have taken occasion to represent my living
> friends and patrons of the noblest families, and also shadowed
> the events of future ages, in the succession of our imperial line.[5]

The project shows clearly the influence of Virgil in the consciousness
of purpose with which the poem is planned and more particularly in
the patriotic nature of the purpose. For a seventeenth-century poet,

---

the Origins (London, 1923); George Saintsbury, *A History of Criticism and
Literary Taste in Europe*, II, *From the Renaissance to the Decline of
Eighteenth Century Orthodoxy* (Edinburgh and London, 1902); F. Vial, L.
Denise, *Idées et doctrines littéraires du XVIIᵉ siècle* (Paris, 1928).

3. Ker, *Essays of Dryden*, I, xvii.

4. *The Works of John Dryden*, ed. Sir Walter Scott, revised and corrected by George Saintsbury (Edinburgh, 1882–93), V, 196.

5. Ker, *Essays of Dryden*, II, 38.

as for Virgil, the heroic fable was not an end in itself, but a vehicle employed for a given object. Dryden further showed his kinship with Virgil in preferring the Augustan age to the era of the Homeric bards: "The times of Virgil please me better, because he had an Augustus for his patron; and, to draw the allegory nearer you [the Earl of Mulgrave], I am sure I shall not want a Maecenas with him."[6] Despite the obvious effort to turn a compliment, Dryden was expressing an instinctive choice: he was well adapted to an age of patronage, and like Virgil was not averse to suggestions from above.

Dryden never wrote his Virgilian epic, but he was much influenced by the ideal and found other channels that offered him at least a partial fulfillment of it. At the beginning of his career, he found an outlet in the rhymed heroic plays with which he achieved such great success between 1664 and 1676. Like all of Dryden's works in which he adopted the epic tone, these plays were indebted in a general way to the Renaissance heroic tradition. But they owed their epic quality more directly to a dramatic theory that had been gradually formed through the combined efforts of critics and playwrights. The importance of this application of epic theory to the drama is well summarized by B. J. Pendlebury:

> Since then the most striking characteristics of the heroic play, the epic construction, the unity of tone, and the predominance of the hero, cannot be regarded as being inherited from Beaumont and Fletcher, it is obvious that their origin must be sought in that critical theory of heroic poetry which, though it had long been connected with dramatic theory in Italy and France, and had been adopted to some extent by Davenant, Dryden may be said to have been the first Englishman to apply consciously and thoroughly in the actual composition of plays.[7]

It was Davenant who introduced Dryden to the epic theories of Tasso; it was Davenant, too, who suggested to Dryden the notion of a genre that should combine both epic and drama. In the *Preface to Gondibert* Davenant had declared that he had constructed his poem on the outlines of a play;[8] while Hobbes, in his *Answer*, went so far as to declare that "the heroique poem narrative is called an epique poem. The heroic poem dramatique is tragedy." That Dryden's conception of the

6. *Works*, Scott, Saintsbury, V, 196.
7. Pendlebury, *Dryden's Heroic Plays*, p. 8.
8. Sir William D'Avenant, *Gondibert, an Heroick Poem* (London, 1651), "The author's Preface *To his much honour'd friend*, Mr. HOBS (*sic*)," pp. 1–70; "The Answer of Mr Hobbes to Sr Will. D'Avenant's Preface Before Gondibert," pp. 71–88.

heroic play was derived largely from Davenant and Hobbes is only too evident from the *Essay of Heroic Plays*. "For heroic Plays," he wrote, ". . . the first light we had of them, on the English theatre, was from the late Sir William D'Avenant." Observing further that "what was wanting to the perfection" of Davenant's *Siege of Rhodes* ". . . was design, and variety of characters," he went on after Hobbes to add that ". . . an heroic play ought to be an imitation, in little, of an heroic poem." Proceeding on this principle, he criticized Davenant for failing to attain the grandeur of style and spaciousness of design proper to the epic: "In the scanting of his images and design, he complied not enough with the greatness and majesty of an heroic poem."

Such criticisms may imply a theory of drama and dramatic style that strikes us as absurd; but even a bad theory can be very influential, as the heroic plays go to prove. Seeking to give these dramas "the majesty of an heroic poem," Dryden borrowed heavily from the one epic style with which he was most familiar. The more epic the scene, the more certain he was to adopt a phrase from the *Aeneid* or to imitate some Virgilian expression. As he gradually became convinced that his purpose was to dramatize heroic poetry, he made an increasing effort to approximate the epic tone. We meet with many more reminiscences of Virgil in the two later heroic plays, *The Conquest of Granada* and *Aureng-Zebe*, than in the two earlier ones, *The Indian Emperor* and *Tyrannic Love*. Dryden also used his Virgilian echoes for a more definite end in the later plays, notably in *The Conquest of Granada*, with which he published his theory of epic-drama, *An Essay of Heroic Plays*.

Most of the Virgilian echoes in *The Indian Emperor* are of the decorative type so common throughout Dryden's poetry. Two fairly characteristic examples are the reference to the race of Nisus and Euryalus,[9] and the echo of Virgil's *sequiturque sequentem*. The first occurs in a passage of courtly love; the second, in a song. Two others, "drowned in his sleep" and "when all are buried in their sleep," are reminiscences of a Virgilian metaphor that was a favorite of Dryden's. But in three other passages the imitations play a rôle that is more than purely decorative:

> Behind the covert, where this temple stands
> Thick as the shades, there issue swarming bands
> Of ambushed men . . .

9. Complete references to this and all other texts quoted from Dryden and Virgil are given in *PMLA*, 55 (1940), 119–138.

As when, upon the sands, the traveller
Sees the high sea come rolling from afar . . .

As callow birds—
Whose mother's killed in seeking of the prey,
Cry in their nest, and think her long away;
And at each leaf that stirs, each blast of wind,
Gape for the food, which they must never find:
So cry the people in their misery.

While none of these examples have exact parallels in Virgil, all three suggest his manner; and the third, amusingly enough, Dryden has marked by a hemistich, which at this period he considered eminently Virgilian. All three appear in situations of martial excitement: the approach of Cortez's troops, the pursuit of the defeated Montezuma, and the panic in the besieged city. In each case the simile is "turned on" to give the passage something like epic grandeur. This is good epic practice. In the battle narratives of the fourth, fifth, and twelfth books of the *Iliad*, similes appear in much greater numbers than elsewhere. Virgil also makes freer use of figures (often imitated from Homer) in the martial scenes of the ninth and eleventh books of the *Aeneid*.

Dryden, being a dramatist, suffered from a limitation which affected neither of the ancient poets: he could not give such descriptions in his own person. The second of the three examples, an elaborate sea simile, is spoken by Montezuma, who is fleeing from the enemy and who has heretofore shown no knowledge of marine matters. As Dryden later noted, "the image had not been amiss from another man, at another time." But the impulse that led Dryden to employ it—the desire to elevate his style in a passage of great excitement—was not altogether wrong. The other two similes are more plausibly introduced. The first is put in the lips of a mere messenger, in a speech that describes action off scene. The third is similarly used, in lines which depict the sufferings in the city. In all three passages we have indications of a stylistic device that was to be more purposefully employed in *The Conquest of Granada* and in *Aureng-Zebe*.

In the second of Dryden's heroic plays, *Tyrannic Love*, there is no marked increase in the number of Virgilian echoes; but most of the examples occur in passages of approximately epic character. A legitimate and necessary part of the epic, it will be remembered, was the "machine"—almost any supernatural device used to adorn the tale or to account for what would be incredible if attributed to chance or to a merely human agent. In dramatizing the martyrdom of St. Catherine of Alexandria Dryden found ample justification for venturing into "those enthusiastic parts of poetry." As before, Virgil comes to his aid; and of the three reminiscences occurring in the "machines" of the play, two contain literal translations from the *Aeneid.* The first is found in lines describing the prophetic hocuspocus of the state magician:

> When first a hollow wind began to blow,
> The sky grew black, and bellied down more low;
> Around the fields did nimble lightning play,
> Which offered us by fits, and snatched the day.[10]

The lines recall a famous description from the *Aeneid,* rather baldly suggested by the tell-tale Latinisms "offered us by fits" and "snatched the day." The second of these echoes occurs also in a scene of supernatural character, in lines picturing the life of evil spirits: "We wander in the fields of air below," which is partly a literal translation of *vagantur/aëris in campis (Aeneid* VI.886–887). The last of the triad is a long and rather beautiful reworking of Virgil's descriptions of Venus, particularly that in the first book of the *Aeneid.* In this passage, which describes the translation of St. Catherine, we have again a narration of wondrous off-stage action.

Another narrative from the same play announces the death of a hero, Charinus, the son of the Emperor Maximin. In lines (as Dr. Johnson would say) "of glorious depravity" Charinus' fall is described. He stood,

> like Capaneus defying Jove;
> With his broad sword the boldest beating down.[11]

Bombastic as the narrative is, it has a partially Virgilian origin: the noble scene from the *Aeneid* when Pallas' body is brought back to Evander. In the play, as the procession draws near, Maximin hears "the hoarse murmurs of a trumpet's sound." The phrase is one of several in which Dryden tried to convey the effect of Virgil's *clangor tubarum.* These allusions and imitations from *Tyrannic Love,* like those from *The Indian Emperor,* again suggest that in scenes of epic

10. Cf. *Aeneid* I.85–90, especially 88, *eripiunt subito nubes caelumque diemque.*
11. Cf. *Aegaeon qualis . . .*
> *Iovis cum fulmina contra . . .*
> *Aeneid* X.565–567.

character, whether of martial or supernatural tone, Dryden tried to heighten his style in an appropriate manner. And when he did so, echoes from Virgil came.

This suggestion will be reënforced by a study of the next heroic play, *The Conquest of Granada.* In the opening scene of the play the audience learns of Almanzor's feats in a great bullfight that has just taken place. This scene, as even a brief glance will show, is nothing more than a long narrative mechanically split up into speeches. Using his vigorous declamatory vein, Dryden obviously has tried to imitate the Games of the *Aeneid,* an episode that he especially admired. Within fewer than a hundred lines, he introduced seven or eight reminiscences of Virgil and five "Virgilian" hemistichs. The whole movement of the verse is improved over that of the preceding plays. It is more sonorous and more stately; the rhythmical groups are more varied, a single group extending over five or six lines, as in Virgil. Near the beginning of the passage the epic style is suggested by a somewhat awkward Latinism, "the darted cane." The bulls are described in language that recalls the *Georgics:* "with high nostril snuffing up the wind," echoing

> bucula caelum
> suspiciens patulis captavit naribus auras.
> *Georgics* I.375–376

A longer description shows the blending in memory of various Virgilian elements:

> One bull, with curled black head, beyond the rest,
> And dew-laps hanging from his brawny chest,
> With nodding front a while did daring stand,
> And with his jetty hoof spurned back the sand;
> Then, leaping forth, he bellowed out aloud:
> The amazed assistants back each other crowd,
> While monarch-like he ranged the listed field;
> Some tossed, some gored, some trampling down he killed.

In addition to specific imitations,[12] we should note the Latin use of the participle ("listed") and the epanaphora that Virgil used so frequently. The lines in which Dryden sketches Almanzor's steed also owe much to Virgil, as readers of the *Georgics* will recall.

But we find Virgilian influence of a more poetic character in the speech that closes this narrative:

12. Cf. *Georgics* III.51–55, 233–234.

109

Mirror on Mirror

Not heads of poppies (when they reap the grain)
Fall with more ease before the labouring swain,
Then fell this head:
It fell so quick, it did even death prevent,
And made imperfect bellowings as it went.
Then all the trumpets victory did sound,
And yet their clangours in our shouts were drown'd.

With this compare:

> purpureus veluti cum flos succisus aratro
> languescit moriens, lassove papavera collo
> demisere caput pluvia cum forte gravantur.
> *Aeneid* IX.435–437

In this passage Dryden is not merely blending two parts of a Virgilian simile into one, or recalling, with no little success, the sonorous trumpets of the *Aeneid;* he is writing in a style that in great part owes its variety of movement and mastery of sound to a thorough appreciation of Virgil's artistry. Hence the easy sweep of the lines with their characteristically Virgilian parentheses and the effective use of the caesura after "head" (whatever is the true explanation of the hemistichs); hence too the suggestive use of rime and assonance in "sound . . . shouts . . . drown'd." The whole of this epic prelude to the play shows that the full-blown epical manner and the imitation of Virgil were connected in Dryden's practice. But since he now realized the absurdity of characters who fought with mouthfuls of classical similes, he tended to restrict this manner to appropriate scenes. (The satirist will soon exploit the latent absurdity of expressions like "imperfect *bellowings.*")

Dryden continued to imitate Virgil in less heroic scenes. There are scattered about in *The Conquest of Granada* some remarkably close imitations of passages from the *Aeneid:* the dream simile (Book XII), the picture of Venus (Book I), and the curse of Turnus. That Virgil was much in Dryden's mind while writing the heroic plays is suggested by his later defense of a passage from *The Conquest of Granada:*

> Spite of myself I'll stay, fight, love, despair;
> And I can do all this, because I dare.

"This passage," G. R. Noyes notes,[13] "is parodied in *The Rehearsal.* Dryden, in the second and third quartos, defends it by citing in the

13. *Selected Dramas of John Dryden* (Chicago, 1910), note to p. 92, l. 105, at p. 440.

110

margin Virgil's phrase 'possunt quia posse videntur' (*Aeneid* V.231)."

Aureng-Zebe, the last of the purely heroic plays, is no less remarkable for the number and significance of its recollections of Virgil. The exposition, like that of *The Conquest of Granada,* is an epic narrative in dialogue, a description of the war that has broken out among the sons of the Emperor. The opening lines, august and portentous in tone, rise to a climax in a simile drawn from Virgil:

> As at a signal, straight the sons prepare
> For open force, and rush to sudden war;
> Meeting, like winds broke loose upon the main,
> To prove, by arms, whose fate it was to reign.

Within a few lines another simile of much the same type is used to describe the machinations of the ministers, "Whispering, like winds, ere hurricanes arise." Abbas, one of the lords, comes in to tell of the approach of even greater forces: "The vale an iron harvest seems to yield," a line including a literal translation of the *ferrea telorum seges* of Virgil. Once more a narrative in heroic style sets the tone of the play. A glance over the other echoes from *Aureng-Zebe* will reveal a number that are pedantically faithful: "argued me of fear," "birds obscene," "conscious virtue." The general character of the night-battle in the city is reminiscent of the fall of Troy, and the last important echo comes in a narrative speech, Abbas' report of another battle off-stage. His description of the union of the rival forces culminates in lines recalling the famous Laocoön passage:

> In either's flag the golden serpents bear
> Erected crests alike, like volumes rear,
> And mingle friendly hissings in the air.

As we have seen, in narrative passages describing a martial exploit or an act of divine intervention, Dryden often used Virgilian allusions to suggest the heroic tone. With the increase in the epic scope of the plays, he tended to restrict this style to the exposition, probably feeling that in an opening scene he might adopt a more expansive and leisurely manner than in the heat of the action. In chorus-like narratives, where the individuality of the characters was less important, he felt free to indulge in elaborate similes and detailed descriptions closely patterned after Virgil.

But in their larger features the heroic plays owe relatively little to Dryden's "master." Their epic scope, their unity of tone, and the superhuman stature of their protagonists were due in large part to Renaissance epic theory, although Virgil's example probably reenforced the influence of the theory at many points now unobservable to us. Occasionally, as in the emphasis on "piety" in the character of Aureng-Zebe, Dryden was following Virgil's example quite directly. But this play, like the others, was only one of the substitutes for the epic that Dryden always planned, and never wrote. "Some little hope, I have yet remaining," he wrote in the *Dedication to Aureng-Zebe,* "and those too, considering my abilities, may be vain, that I may make the world some part of amends, for many ill plays, by an heroic poem."

Although Dryden never tried again to transfer epic to the stage, he could not simply give up a dramatic style that he had used for more than a decade. The best plays he ever wrote, *All for Love* (1677) and *Don Sebastian* (1689), are essentially dramas of "love and honor"; while plays or operas of less literary value, such as *King Arthur*[14] and *Cleomenes* (1692), include characters and passages in the old heroic vein; and Virgilian allusions are still being worked in to suggest the epic tone. In *All for Love,* the defeat of the Egyptian navy is announced in words that recall the *Aeneid* (and *Paradise Lost*):

> O horror, horror!
> Egypt has been; our latest hour is come:
> The queen of nations, from her ancient seat,
> Is sunk for ever in the dark abyss.
>
> venit summa dies et ineluctabile tempus
> Dardaniae. fuimus Troes, fuit Ilium et ingens
> gloria Teucrorum.
>
> II.324–326

In *The Spanish Friar* (1680? 1681?), in two speeches describing martial uprisings, there are two similes based on Virgil's account of the war of the bees. About four years later, in the opera *Albion and Albanius* (1685), Dryden again took Virgil as his guide in describing the intervention of the gods and in picturing the world below. The opera had one scene of martial character dealing with the disturbances previous to the exile of the Duke of York ("Albanius" in the opera, later James II). Dryden here made a direct allusion to the passage of the *Aeneid* in which Allecto is summoned to arouse Queen Amata's wrath:

> Alecto, thou to fair Augusta go,
> And all thy snakes into her bosom throw.

14. This opera was nearly finished before the death of Charles II (1685).

Dryden's Epic Manner and Virgil

In the next play, *Don Sebastian* (1689?), Dryden used a bee simile of the same type as those in *The Spanish Friar*. The passage is another description of an uprising:

> All crowd in heaps, as, at a night alarm,
> The bees drive out upon each other's backs,
> To emboss their hives in clusters . . .

Dryden perhaps owed a deeper debt to Virgil in *Don Sebastian* than in any of the later plays. "In the drawing of his character," he wrote, "I forgot not piety, which anyone may observe to be one principal ingredient of it, even so far as to be a habit in him." Sebastian is depicted as a second Aeneas:

> he was a man,
> Above man's height, even towering to divinity:
> Brave, pious, generous, great, and liberal;
> Just as the scales of heaven, that weigh the seasons.
> He loved his people; him they idolized.

In the year after *Don Sebastian*, *King Arthur* was produced. Whether Dryden felt any irony in using for an opera-masque the grand conception that he was to have carried out in a perfect epic, we cannot know. He certainly tried to inject heroic quality into the opera, writing a libretto of some dignity (and some "frantic sallies"). Echoes from Virgil appear in two of the more exalted passages; the first, a description of supernatural manifestations, would have pleased the Elizabethan "Senecans":

> But straight a rumbling sound, like bellowing winds,
> Rose and grew loud; confused with howls of wolves,
> And grunts of bears, and dreadful hiss of snakes;
> Shrieks more than human; globes of hail poured down
> An armed winter, and inverted day.

In the *Aeneid* the Sybil's approach is announced by similar wonders:

> sub pedibus mugire solum et iuga coepta moveri
> silvarum, visaeque canes ululare per umbram
> adventante dea . . .[15]

15. *Aeneid* VI.256–258. Compare also the storm from the fourth book of the *Aeneid* especially,
> Interea magno misceri murmure caelum
> incipit, insequitur commixta grandine nimbus . . .
> *Aeneid* IV.160–161.

The second passage indebted to Virgil is a speech in which Arthur
offers to end the war by single combat:

> As once Aeneas, my famed ancestor,
> Betwixt the Trojan and Rutilian bands,
> Fought for a crown and bright Lavinia's bed,
> So will I meet thee . . .

But in spite of epic touches, the opera remains a fairy story, a sorry
substitute for a "true heroic poem."

In his last tragedy, *Cleomenes* (1692), Dryden seems to have re-
verted to his more purely heroic manner, particularly in the charac-
terization of the hero, who is as bold, proud, and stoical as Almanzor.
The play opens with a ranting declamation in which Cleomenes describes his downfall:

> Unbounded empire hung upon my sword:
> Greece, like a lovely heifer, stood in view,
> To see the rival bulls each other gore,
> But wished the conquest mine.
> I fled; and yet I languish not in exile;
> But here in Egypt whet my blunted horns,
> And meditate new fights, and chew my loss.

This tasteless—not to say comic—simile, which recalls the opening
scene of *The Conquest of Granada*, is based on a famous passage
from the *Georgics:*

> pascitur in magna Sila formosa iuvenca:
> illi alternantes multa vi proelia miscent
> vulneribus crebris, lavit ater corpora sangius,
> versaque in obnixos urgentur cornua vasto
> cum gemitu, reboant silvaeque et longus Olympus.
> nec mos bellantis una stabulare, sed alter
> victus abit longeque ignotis exsulat oris . . .
>
> et temptat sese atque irasci in cornua discit
> arboris obnixus trunco . . .
> III.219–225; 232–233

Virgil also had used a simile of the same type in describing Turnus:

> utque leo, specula cum vidit ab alta
> stare procul campis meditantem in proelia taurum . . .
> *Aeneid* X.454–455

Dryden's "meditate new fights" suggests that he had a partial memory of these particular lines.

We may now turn back to the early years of his career and observe traces of his epic style in his non-dramatic poetry. At the time when Dryden was writing the heroic plays, he made his one and only attempt to write a long narrative poem of a partially epic character— the *Annus Mirabilis* (1667). We can agree with Dryden that however heroic the material may have been, the poem itself is *"historical,* not *epic."* But the *Annus Mirabilis* possesses a clinical interest for anyone who wishes to see Dryden's heroic style in the making. "Virgil," he declared in the *Preface,*

> has been my master in this poem. I have followed him everywhere, I know not with what success, but I am sure with diligence enough; my images are many of them copied from him, and the rest are imitations of him. My expressions also are as near as the idioms of the two languages would admit of in translation.

One of many typical instances will indicate the quality of images so diligently composed:

> Behind, the gen'ral mends his weary pace
> And sullenly to his revenge he sails;
> (p) So glides some trodden serpent on the grass,
> And long behind his wounded volume trails.[16]

(p) *So glides,* &c. From Virgil: *Quum medii nexus, extremaeque agmina caudae Solvuntur; tardosque trahit sinus ultimus orbes,* &c.

Here as elsewhere, the poem offers depressing evidence of the superficial and imitative qualities of Dryden's early style. Although he adopted many devices used by Virgil—elaborate similes, declamatory speeches, and supernatural signs—he introduced them so deliberately that the effort appears more heroic than the result.

But it was in satire that Dryden made the most apt use of his epic manner. Here he developed a style that was a compound of the heroic and the satirical much in the manner of Boileau, for whose work he expressed great admiration. In describing Boileau's method in *Le Lutrin,* Dryden gave a fair account of his own satirical style:

> He writes it [*Le Lutrin*] in the French heroic verse, and calls it an heroic poem; his subject is trivial, but his verse is noble.

16. Ll. 489–492. All references to Dryden's verse, except in the plays, are to *The Poetical Works of John Dryden,* ed. G. R. Noyes (Cambridge, Mass., 1909).

I doubt not but he had Virgil in his eye, for we find many admirable imitations of him, and some parodies . . . And, as Virgil in his fourth Georgic, of the Bees, perpetually raises the lowness of his subject, by the loftiness of his words, and ennobles it by comparisons drawn from empires, and from monarchs . . . we see Boileau pursuing him in the same flights, and scarcely yielding to his master. This, I think, my Lord, to be the most beautiful and noble kind of satire. Here is the majesty of the heroic, finely mixed with the venom of the other; and raising the delight which otherwise would be flat and vulgar, by the sublimity of expression.

In a similar manner, Dryden employed in his satires the vein of his better heroic plays, heightening his style by epic devices and by imitations and parodies of Virgil. Dryden's satires have a grandeur that Pope rarely ever attained, except in the fourth book of the *Dunciad*.

Absalom and Achitophel (1681), as many readers have noted, exhibits in general structure a number of features common to epic poetry. The satire opens in a leisurely fashion with a narrative explaining the situation and preparing the way for the declamations of Achitophel. In the central part of the poem we have a kind of epic catalogue transformed into a series of magnificent satirical portraits. And the conclusion comes with a Jovian warning from the King, whose words are ratified by a sign from on high:

> He said. Th'Almighty, nodding, gave consent;
> And peals of thunder shook the firmament.
> Henceforth a series of new time began,
> The mighty years in long procession ran:
> Once more the godlike David was restor'd,
> And willing nations knew their lawful lord.

While this description may have been suggested by either Homer or Virgil, the chances are in favor of a Virgilian origin, especially since Dryden alludes to the famous line in the fourth *Eclogue: magnus ab integro saeclorum nascitur ordo.* There are further signs of Virgilian influence in less significant passages. For example, when Dryden addressed the muse with the words, "Indulge one labor more, my weary muse," he was following quite literally the first line of the tenth *Eclogue: Extremum hunc, Arethusa, mihi concede laborem.* In another passage, for the sake of rhythmical variation he introduced a pseudo-Virgilian hemistich, "And theirs the native right . . ."

A later passage offers the best illustration of how Dryden used Virgilian allusions to give his satire the tone of serious epic poetry.

Turning in the second section of the poem from his catalogue of the King's enemies, he gives a brief account of the loyal nobles, with Barzillai (the Duke of Ormond) heading the list. Dryden digresses slightly at this point to honor Ormond's son, Thomas, who had recently died:

> His eldest hope, with every grace adorn'd,
> By me (so Heav'n will have it) always mourn'd,
> And always honor'd, snatch'd in manhood's prime
> B'unequal fates, and Providence's crime;
> Yet not before the goal of honor won,
> All parts fulfill'd of subject and of son:
> Swift was the race, but short the time to run.
> O narrow circle, but of pow'r divine,
> Scanted in space, but perfect in thy line!
> By sea, by land, thy matchless worth was known,
> Arms thy delight, and war was all thy own:
> Thy force, infus'd, the fainting Tyrians propp'd;
> And haughty Pharaoh found his fortune stopp'd.
> O ancient honor! O unconquer'd hand,
> Whom foes unpunish'd never could withstand!
> But Israel was unworthy of thy name;
> Short is the date of all immoderate fame.
> It looks as Heav'n our ruin had design'd,
> And durst not trust thy fortune and thy mind.
> Now, free from earth, thy disencumber'd soul
> Mounts up, and leaves behind the clouds and starry pole.

Besides "unequal fates," which translates the *iniqua fata* of the *Aeneid*, we may note three other echoes of Virgil. The first is near the beginning of our passage:

> By me (so Heav'n will have it) always mourn'd,
> And always honor'd, snatch'd in manhood's prime,

a couplet that recalls Aeneas' words on the anniversary of his father's death,

> iamque dies, nisi fallor, adest, quem semper acerbum,
> semper honoratum (sic di voluistis) habebo.
> > V.49–50

In the noble line, "O ancient honor! O unconquer'd hand," we hear Anchises' praise of the young Marcellus and his house,

117

Mirror on Mirror

heu pietas, heu prisca fides invictaque bello
dextera!

VI.878–879

And in the last of these reminiscences,

Now, free from earth, thy disencumber'd soul
Mounts up, and leaves behind the clouds and starry pole;

Dryden offers a version of lines that he imitated in another poem,

Candidus insuetum miratur limen Olympi
sub pedibusque videt nubes et sidera Daphnis.

Eclogues V.56–57

He presumably drew the general notion for the passage from
Virgil's tribute to Marcellus, unconsciously adapting his other allusions to fit this conception, as when he applied to the young Earl of
Ossory Aeneas' words on the death of Anchises. By preserving Virgil's
anaphora and parenthetical phrase in the couplet beginning "By me
(so Heav'n will have it)," Dryden has fashioned lines that recall
remarkably well the movement of the original. Aeneas' tribute to his
father occurs in a speech, the address to his men after landing in
Sicily. The tone of his words is not intimate, but appropriate to public
utterance; sincere, but formal. The most striking qualities of Dryden's lines—measured dignity, aristocratic formality, oratorical ex-
altation, and worshipful tone—are characteristic of the lines on
Anchises and Marcellus in the *Aeneid*.

Blessed with the right occasion, Dryden succeeded in giving to his
own verse some of the qualities of Virgil's oratorical style. By introducing speeches of this type into the context of satire, he produced
a rather remarkable effect, imparting to *Absalom and Achitophel* a
grandeur out of proportion to the characters and events that were
being treated. While the tone is obviously mock-epic, it is mock-epic
with the minimum sacrifice of epic seriousness. If we want a standard
of comparison, we have only to glance at Garth's *Dispensary* or the
1729 *Dunciad* to find examples of a style that has reduced the epic
to a much lower level. The impressiveness of Dryden's satire as compared with that of conventional mock-epic is traceable to Dryden's
talent for suggesting the tone of serious heroic poetry, a talent which
was materially sustained by his exceptional familiarity with the style
of the *Aeneid*.

The Medal (1682) is less heroic than *Absalom and Achitophel*,
perhaps because of its occasion. Dryden did not make any notable use

of Virgil in this poem, or in *The Second Part of Absalom and Achitophel* (1682). We may note in the later poem a Virgilian allusion in the very first line of the part generally attributed to Dryden.

It was in *Mac Flecknoe* (1682?) that Dryden made his finest satirical use of the heroic manner, truly combining the "venom" of the one style with the "majesty" of the other, notably in the famous lines,

> At his right hand our young Ascanius sate,
> Rome's other hope, and pillar of the State.
> His brows thick fogs, instead of glories, grace,
> And lambent dulness play'd around his face.

By comparing the original passages from Virgil we can appreciate Dryden's transformation:

> hinc pater Aeneas, Romanae stirpis origo,
> sidereo flagrans clipeo et caelestibus armis
> et iuxta Ascanius, magnae spes altera Romae . . .
> > *Aeneid* XII.166–168

> ecce levis summo de vertice visus Iuli
> fundere lumen apex, tactuque innoxia mollis
> lambere flamma comas et circum tempora pasci.
> > *Aeneid* II.682–684

The "method," as Eliot said, "is something very near to parody": Dryden has managed to suggest Virgil's style while producing an entirely different effect. He displayed a similar power of imaginative synthesis in another passage where he was again reshaping Virgilian elements to suit his special end:

> The sire then shook the honors of his head,
> And from his brows damps of oblivion shed
> Full on the filial dulness: long he stood,
> Repelling from his breast the raging god:
> At length burst out in this prophetic mood.

Here Dryden combined the Homeric (and Virgilian) picture of Zeus with Virgil's description of the inspired Sibyl:

> At Phoebi nondum patiens immanis in antro
> bacchatur vates, magnum si pectore possit
> excussisse deum . . .
> > *Aeneid* VI.77–79

While in these two passages Dryden made his best satirical use of Virgilian allusion, he maintained throughout the poem the exalted tone proper to epic narrative and in at least one other instance echoed Virgil directly:

> Now Empress Fame had publish'd the renown
> Of Sh————'s coronation thro' the town.

Dryden used a familiar tag (not necessarily Virgilian) to give a final heroic touch to his poem:

> He said: but his last words were scarcely heard;
> For Bruce and Longvil had a trap prepar'd,
> And down they sent the yet declaiming bard.

In *Religio Laici* (1682), which Dryden described as an example of "the legislative style," he found little place for the epic manner. His aim, as he pointed out in the preface, was to imitate the epistolary style of Horace. But in the preface to his next "ratiocinative" poem, *The Hind and the Panther* (1687), Dryden declared that, in the First Part, he had "endeavor'd to raise, and give it the majestic turn of heroic poesy," but in the actual writing he did not confine the epic touches to The First Part. The whole of the closing scene of The Second Part was modeled on the seventh book of the *Aeneid*. It is true that the style of the opening section is more august, showing traces of the formal diction that Dryden later used in his *Virgil*. We note such familiar phrases as "vocal blood," "confess'd in sight," and "vital air." There are also, in The First Part, two further reminiscences of Virgilian lines: "Cov'ring adult'ry with a specious name." and

> The surly Wolf with secret envy burst,
> Yet could not howl; the Hind had seen him first.[17]

We may note in The Third Part a long Virgilian simile, and a fable strongly influenced by the *Georgics*.

In the verse published between *The Hind and the Panther* (1687) and the *Virgil* (1697), Dryden had little opportunity outside the drama to make use of his heroic style. But the translation of the *Aeneid* at last gave him a real opportunity to write in a purely epic vein. Dryden now felt that he might indulge in all the Virgilianisms that he had long been cultivating. Elsewhere[18] I have described the

17. Cf. *Eclogues* IX.53–54.
18. "Dryden's Poetic Diction and Virgil," *Philological Quarterly,* 18 (1939), 211–217.

qualities of the style that he created, in particular its circumlocutions and Latinized vocabulary.

But although the language of the *Fables* is fairly heroic, the writing is on the whole more straightforward and simple, a change due in part to Dryden's improved taste and, more especially, to the example of Chaucer. It is also partly attributable to the nature of the material that Dryden was translating. The stories from Chaucer were hardly epic, in spite of Dryden's insistence on the heroic qualities of *Palamon and Arcite;* while Ovid's fanciful tales and Boccaccio's melodramatic narratives lent themselves to a less exalted manner than that of Virgilian epic. Though moderating the high-heroic style of the *Aeneid,* Dryden still retained many of his epic expressions, and still sought to elevate the tone by the use of Virgilian allusions. Even in his Chaucerian renderings he found opportunities to introduce reminiscences of a definitely epic character. As Christie has noted, when Dryden described the funeral rites for Arcite, he had "in his mind Virgil's account of the burial-rites after the battle in *Aeneid* XI."[19] A comparison of the three passages shows that Dryden completely transformed Chaucer's lines by his use of a balanced antithetical style that owes much to Virgil.

In other poems of this collection there are frequent Virgilian allusions introduced to give the epic tone. In describing the suicide of Sigismonda, Dryden borrows a detail from Dido's death scene in the fourth book of the *Aeneid:* "This done, she mounts the genial bed." So Dido ordered her sister to place on the pyre *exuviasque omnis lectumque iugalem* (IV.496). When she was ready to die, like Sigismonda, she lay down upon her wedding-bed:

> hic, postquam Iliacas vestis notumque cubile
> conspexit, paulum lacrimis et mente morata
> incubuitque toro . . .
>
> IV.648–650

In *Theodora and Honoria,* when describing a scene of supernatural horror, Dryden again had recourse to Virgil: "Air blacken'd, roll'd the thunder, groan'd the the ground," recalling, *sub pedibus mugire solum* (*Aeneid* VI.256). In *The Flower and the Leaf,* as in *Palamon and Arcite,* a whole passage, the description of the jousting knights, has been remodeled under the influence of a similar passage in the *Aeneid.* In general conception, movement,[20] and in explicit details,

19. *Poetical Works of John Dryden,* ed. W. D. Christie (London, 1925), p. 560, note.
20. "In the passage on the jousting knights Dryden has remembered the metrical pattern which he used some years before to describe the Trojan boys [in his *Aeneis*]." Mark Van Doren, *The Poetry of John Dryden* (New York, 1920), p. 285.

Dryden has drawn upon Virgil; and interestingly enough, he has added an allusion taken from a completely different context.

The connection between Virgil and typically heroic motifs was almost mechanically regular throughout Dryden's poetic and dramatic works. When Dryden's immediate theme was a martial exploit, a prince's death, a supernatural manifestation, "games" of warriors, or even a scene of heroic courtesy, when, in other words, his subject was obviously suitable for epic narrative, he almost invariably turned to Virgil (consciously or unconsciously) for help in expression. In many cases the epic tone of a passage was in great measure conveyed by some Virgilian allusion or by the incorporation of a Virgilian phrase. But it is apparent from the examples we have quoted that the epic touches so introduced were often adventitious in character and superficial in effect. As Dryden knew, he could not make the *Annus Mirabilis* into a true "Heroic Poem" by scattering allusions over the surface. Nor could he by similar methods turn *The Conquest of Granada* into a dramatized *Aeneid*. But in certain passages and in certain poems of less grandiose pretensions, when the avowed purpose was to convey the impression of epic rather than the reality, Dryden found in the use of Virgilian allusions the surest means of giving to his verse "the majestic turn of heroic poesy."

8

THE HERESY OF PLOT

It does not take a historian to see that the spirit of the mid-twentieth century is reactionary—whatever meaning, favorable or unfavorable, we attach to that adjective. The tendencies in the great world are obvious; a minor sign in the minor world of literary criticism is that Aristotle is again in fashion, which is in turn a sign of a desire to move away from the critical principles and techniques characteristic of the past twenty-five or thirty years. The temper of the time is "either-or"; and the critic, like the liberal in politics, is asked to be either for or against Aristotle or Arnold or the nineteenth century or somebody or something. A strayed explicator who comes into a conference on the *Poetics* and modern criticism is puzzled, especially if he has read Aristotle and found on reflection that he must be both a New Critic and an Aristotelian. Without assuming the role of a Jeremiah, he feels he should hold up a warning hand—a kid-gloved hand, of course—to fellow readers who are about to take Aristotle as their guide. Before embracing critical principles of the fourth century B.C. or of the nineteenth century, it is well to consider what we are embracing. In our eagerness to correct excesses of recent criticism, we may sacrifice important gains in awareness and method, and forget, as John Crowe Ransom suggests, that a "linguistic revolution" separates the twentieth century from the nineteenth and earlier centuries. Shakespearean criticism offers a good example of the

Reprinted from *English Institute Essays, 1951*, ed. A. S. Downer (New York, Columbia University Press, 1952).

difficulties of the new reaction: we may read Bradley with a more tolerant eye than we did twenty years ago, but are we therefore to unlearn what we have learned from Stoll and Knights and Empson?[1]

On the present occasion it would be easy to produce a caricature of an Aristotelian critic and draw the appropriate moral. But to be just to Aristotle, to face the obscurities of his text, to acknowledge his points of weakness and strength is another matter. If we want to learn from him, we must translate his concepts to our purposes, eliminating if possible the liabilities. Radical translation is needed not only because the *Poetics* is written in Greek but also because Aristotle is talking much of the time from the writer's point of view, a fact that has often proved troublesome to critics, more especially since the Renaissance. As modern literature gained its distinctive character, and as readers were compelled to adjust their sights to both Sophocles and Shakespeare, the problem of "turning Aristotle's statements around" and making them relevant was staggering. Mild critical schizophrenia resulted; the Aristotelian Dryden of the Preface to *Troilus and Cressida* is hardly recognizable in the genial appreciator of Shakespeare and Chaucer.

With the passage of time, the difficulties have increased. A contemporary reader who asks himself whether the *Poetics* has any relevance to his interpretation of a poem or play or novel will sympathize with Dryden. The Great Amphibium who can breathe the lucid air of the *Poetics* and swim in the deceptive currents of the *Seven Types of Ambiguity* has yet to be born. While waiting—we can try to translate Aristotle and indicate the kind of practice that might bridge the two worlds of critical activity.

But why concern ourselves with Aristotle? Because he is the clearest and most influential exemplar of a position. He stands for the familiar principle that literature offers a representation of human life and that the basic order of a work is the arrangement of successive "actions." Aristotle will not let us forget that literature, if literature at all, is dramatic.

But what is our own position? In reading Aristotle nothing is easier to forget than where we are. The standard translators and commentators on the *Poetics* are firmly planted in the nineteenth century, a world in which plots were certainly plots; and less conservative interpreters, the ritualists, though they wrote in the earlier decades of this century, show more than a trace of nineteenth-century

1. In *The Structure of Complex Words* (Norfolk, Conn., 1951) Empson is much concerned with the problem of combining "pattern" and "character" approaches to Shakespearean drama. The interesting chapter "Honest in *Othello*" represents a move toward Bradley, a protest against the view that "coherence of character is not needed in poetic drama, only coherence of metaphor and so on."

nostalgia for primitive and simply unified societies in a happy, happy past. The romanticism of Murray's translations and his interest in ritual are not unconnected. But I am thinking of a critical reader aware that he is functioning here and now, a reader who has undergone the critical revolution initiated by Eliot and Richards in the twenties and early thirties. This revolution, particularly in the analysis of the text that it popularized, might be described as a reaction of "Cambridge" against the Oxford of Bradley and Pater.

The mark of the reader-critic bred in the "Cantabrigian" climate is a consciousness that he is a reader, that the experience of literature is a complicated event in response to words on a page—hence his realization that he can describe the event only by quotation and continual reference to the language of the work being interpreted. But the kind of analysis accompanying quotation is important and more characteristic. The principle, or the intellectual bias, that determines the analysis is a renewed awareness of the multiple meanings of words and of the abstract character of all language, in particular the language of literary criticism. Our critical reader is sensitive to the fact that when he speaks of a work as "tragic," or when he refers to a "character," he has gone through a process of selecting and relating one sort of item from the great range of items of experience symbolized and generated by a writer's words.

Although he employs many old and new critical abstractions, his effort is directed toward discovering the felt order of a particular literary event. He knows that he cannot communicate the order directly or render it adequately by descriptive gestures, though of course he uses every expressive resource at his command. He aims rather to delineate the verbal arrangements that control and shape the total ordered response.

That it is difficult for such a reader to assimilate Aristotle is comically obvious. But the ghost of Aristotle, or of something very like Aristotle, keeps haunting him. How, without sacrificing valuable principles of linguistic and esthetic analysis, is he to deal with dramatic structure in anything like Aristotle's sense of the term? How can a mind that is positivist in bent have any commerce with even a reformed Platonist? To focus on a point where the *Poetics* seems at once most compelling and most alien to our critical reader, how can he think of action in an Aristotelian sense without falling into the "heresy of plot"? He is haunted by another fear which may seem paradoxical, that he may slip via this heresy into the "religion of ritual." But discussion of that error belongs to another essay.

What do we mean by the melodramatic phrase "heresy of plot"? Nothing very sensational; it is the notion that in a poem or a play or a novel there is an order of events that may be thought of in complete isolation from other structures and that "somehow" exists independent of the language of the work. So described, the idea is revolting; no self-respecting contemporary critic is guilty of this. Crude hypostatizing of plot and separation of plot from expression is a nineteenth-century error, left behind with character sketches and the well-made play. But is this quite true? It is difficult to catch a modern literary critic in the act of "talking plot"; but we can still find ample evidence of the heresy in numerous contemporary handbooks on interpreting drama. There are generalized discussions of rising and falling action, of plot as logical sequence of incidents; the point of view of the writer-builder is often confused with the reader's, and so forth. More significant is the silence that eddies about these discussions and the eager loquaciousness when the subject of verse drama appears. As Eliot has observed: "It is unfortunate when they [people] are repelled by verse, but can also be deplorable when they are attracted by it—if that means they are prepared to enjoy the play and the language of the play as two separate things." Though the student is warned that they must not be separated, the warning comes late after pages of talk in which they have been separated in practice.

It is not my business to decide whether Aristotle is guilty of this gross heresy, but to use the questions it raises in order to define his position on dramatic structure and its relation to *lexis*, or expression. Can we translate Aristotle's statements in terms meaningful to a present-day reader and make them relevant to interpretation? We begin with the baffling term *praxis*, "action" in the most general sense, as in "tragedy is a representation not of human beings, but of action and life" (1450a 16, 17).[2] The last two terms are probably synonymous; *praxis*, as Cornford notes, is sometimes the Greek word for "experience." Readers of the *Ethics* will agree that for Aristotle "life" must be activity, human behavior, and must include inner conscious, as well as overt bodily, action.

When Aristotle talks of *praxis* in a particular sense, definition becomes harder. As examples of "one action," that is, a single, unified action (1451a 16–36; 1459a 17–1459b 7), he cites the *Iliad* and the *Odyssey*, poems that have the narrative variety of novels. But Aristotle does not say what this "one action" is. He notes that unlike the *Cypria* the Homeric epics offer matter for only one, or at the most two, trage-

2. The line references are to *The Poetics of Aristotle*, ed. S. H. Butcher, 4th ed. (London, 1907). Except where otherwise noted, quotations in English from the *Poetics* are taken from Butcher's translation. In a few instances small changes, usually no more than a word or two, have been made. The other editions most frequently consulted were: *Aristotle on the Art of Poetry*, ed. Ingram Bywater (Oxford, 1909); *Aristoteles Poetik*, ed. Alfred Gudeman (Berlin, 1934); Lane Cooper, *Aristotle on the Art of Poetry*, rev. ed. (Ithaca, N.Y., 1947).

dies, which leaves us where we were. If we say that the action of the *Iliad* is the "wrath of Achilles," that of the *Odyssey*, "Odysseus' trying to get home," what is the meaning of "action" common to these two very different abstractions?

We turn with relief to *mythos*, or plot, a term that has pleasantly concrete attributes: here is something we can get our teeth into "literally," as undergraduates say. There is the solid body of the biologist and the equally solid "body" of the work of art, whether painting or poem. The plot of a tragedy is a "putting together, a composition of parts"; and the parts are "incidents," or *pragmata* (1450a 15; 1450b 22–35). As long as "dramatic incident" is used for bodily movements on the stage, the illusion of the objective concrete plot is easily maintained. But with *pragmata* in the sense of the "other kinds of dramatic action," the mind of the playwright enters; and the comparisons with enormously large and extremely small organisms suggest a kind of intellectual "seeing" of the whole by both poet and spectator.

What is seen, the incidents so easily assumed, is not defined. If Aristotle uses *logos* as equal to *mythos*, we have examples of plots and incidents in the generalized "stories" (*logoi*) of the *Iphigenia at Tauris* and the *Odyssey*. But these two scenarios do not help us much in defining an incident. We say, "something that one of the agents does or suffers." But if we look at Aristotle's examples—and they are of the sort we all give—we find extraordinarily different kinds of statement: "A young girl is sacrificed; sometime later her brother arrives"; or, "A man is away from his own country for many years; he is jealously watched over by Poseidon and yet alone, quite on his own." An element of the plot may be the simplest sort of physical event: "Someone arrives." Or it may be a complicated set of relationships between agents, implying distinct attitudes; or it may be a total impression of a situation. If we refer either outline to the works, we become even less sure of exact definitions of plot or incident. More than half of Aristotle's Iphigenia story consists of statements of events that Euripides recounts in the prologue; they are included in the plot, in spite of the fact that they seem to be "outside the drama." The remarks about Odysseus' isolation and his relations to Poseidon hardly correspond to discrete segments of narrative or even to happenings; they represent complicated abstractions based on grouping and comparison of narrative facts and on inferences as to their meaning.

In addition to plot as an arrangement of incidents, there is also in the *Poetics* quite a different definition of plot, as Francis Fergusson has pointed out. But it, too, depends on the organic analogy and is even more purely "Aristotelian," the plot being compared to the *arche*, or soul, of a tragedy (1450a 37, 38). The analogy is almost overpoweringly suggestive;[3] the soul in relation to the body is much more than the formal cause; it is also the efficient and the final cause. By comparison, the plot is "the origin of movement" in a play, and also "what determines its essential nature." "Essential nature" must mean intelligible order or form, but the exact philosophical meaning of Aristotle's terms cannot be pressed here or elsewhere in the *Poetics*. The point of the metaphor lies in its exaggeration, in the insistence on "plot" as the most important ordering principle in a work of literature. This broad sense of the word is clearer from the curious analogy that follows: "Character holds second place. A similar fact is seen in painting. The most beautiful colours, laid on without order, will not give as much pleasure as the chalk outline of a human figure." The stress of the comparison is on "without order" and "outline of a figure." "Plot" must be an ordered sequence of expressions (the chalk lines) that build up in the reader's consciousness a recognizable pattern of human behavior. Here, as we shall see, is a conception of plot that may be useful to a modern reader.[4]

But in the ease with which Aristotle elsewhere separates the pleasures of recognizing likeness from the medium that projects it, there is a glimpse of the heresy with which we began. In most of the *Poetics* the body-structure analogy is very much in evidence; and by a paradoxical law of critical economy, as the plot and incidents become more material, the words, the cells that compose them, oddly disappear. But the too, too solid flesh rarely melts. It may be said that Aristotle was too Greek, too aware of poetry as a craft of words, to think of literary structure apart from the words that "make" it. He was certainly free from any taint of the nineteenth-century heresy of spirit, of poetry as a nonliterary essence. It is also clear from his initial discussion of media that he is mainly concerned with mimesis through language (*mimesis en logois*). But from the order of importance in which Aristotle lists media, it appears that *lexis* (diction, style, or expression) is to him of minor importance.

We ask whether Aristotle in fact talks of the plot as existing and producing its effect independently of language, or if not, how he does describe the relationship between the two. We must not get into the solemn position of accusing Aristotle of using abstractions; but one sign of critical health is the degree of discomfort shown by a critic while using his machinery. And it must be admitted that Aristotle is

3. See S. H. Butcher, *Aristotle's Theory of Poetry and Fine Art*, 3rd el. (London, 1902), pp. 345, 346.
4. Aristotle does not here or in his remarks on the pleasures of recognition reduce the pleasure of art to recognition of likeness. He is defining the pleasure that comes from viewing likenesses; the other pleasures have other sources, in execution, coloring, and so forth (1448b 15–19).

extremely comfortable in classifying plots, their elements, and types. His units of analysis, we should note, are not verbal, but dramatic, that is, stage actions or reported actions; and he cites examples. But by citing the *Oedipus* too often, abstract model and example tend to become identical. In reading the *Poetics*, who comes very close to the felt particular moments of the *Oedipus* or the *Iphigenia?* Who could, in the seminar shorthand of this curious Greek, which no translator would dare to imitate? Only in discussing recognitions does Aristotle refer more exactly to speeches. But he does not quote from most of the texts, not from the *Odyssey*, or the *Iphigenia*, or the *Oedipus*, or the *Choephori.* In citing the last of these, it is the syllogism that interests him, not dramatic speech.

Perhaps the silence about language is only a matter of attention; but there are two points at which Aristotle seems to go out of his way to eliminate the medium. The first comes in a discussion of "spectacle" (1453b 3–8):

> For the plot ought to be constructed in such a way that anyone, by merely hearing an account of the incidents and without seeing them, will be filled with horror and pity at what occurs. That is how anyone hearing the story of Oedipus would be affected. To rely on spectacular means is less artistic.[5]

Though "hearing" implies words of some sort, Aristotle shows little or no concern about them.[6] Any telling will do that keeps the order of incidents (whatever we mean by an incident). The mere chain of events, if heard, will produce tragic pity and fear. If we translate "anyone hearing the story of *The Oedipus*" (Sophocles's play), then Aristotle shows an even greater indifference to the telling. The test of his statement is to compare the *Oedipus* of Seneca: the generalized story of the *Oedipus Rex* is there, but it does not work. Although several Sophoclean scenes are followed closely, the swiftness and anger and dread so constantly underlined in the speeches of the Greek play have disappeared. Though there are, as Robert Frost says, "re-tellable stories," retelling is something more than "arranging incidents."

The other passage (1456b 2–8) is more obscure; Butcher's version preserves some of its ambiguities.

5. Translation from *Aristotle* by Philip Wheelwright (New York, 1951), p. 307.
6. Bywater confidently explains (*ad loc.*) that "As the poet is an imitative artist in language, a *mimetes en logo* . . . it follows that the poetic effect has to be produced by language, and not by means other than language."

Now, it is evident that the dramatic incidents must be treated from the same points of view as the dramatic speeches, when the object is to evoke the sense of pity, fear, importance, or probability. The only difference is, that the incidents should speak for themselves without verbal exposition; while the effects aimed at in speech should be produced by the speaker, and as a result of the speech. For what were the business of a speaker, if the thought were revealed quite apart from what he says?

With that triumphant question in our ears, we can hardly suppose that Aristotle could for long think of a plot as working its effect apart from special handling of words. But the ambiguity is the familiar one: what are "the incidents" that "speak for themselves without verbal exposition," or explanation? If they are overt stage movements[7] of the actors, the meaning is perhaps clear enough. But as soon as we think of writing a play—which is what Aristotle is talking about— the haziness of his account is evident: he has nothing[8] to say about how actions get into the play and how they are made to produce the effects he insists on as necessary.

In discussing the plot Aristotle is on the whole indifferent to the verbal medium; at his best he implies that it exists; at his worst he lapses into talk about the direct effect of incident. But these may be local defects of Aristotle's method of dividing and conquering the field he is studying. Perhaps we shall find what we want in his treatment of *lexis*, a term as hard to define as *praxis*. It means in the most general sense "expression through language" (1450b 14, 15),[9] probably as Bywater says, "expression of whatever is in the mind" of the characters. The so-called inner life of a character being made up of the "ethical element" and the "intellectual and affective elements," *lexis* is mainly a medium for expressing them. As usual, plot is lost sight of; there is some reference to character and thought, none to action. In the more detailed account of *lexis* the term is limited to the choice of words conventionally appropriate to tragedy, epic, and

7. In the fifth century, when the author was director or working with the director, he could work out a completely nonverbal "rhetoric of action," as Bywater calls it. But Bywater's phrase and Aristotle's term are ambiguous and include all the countless kinds of action that may be expressed.

8. This is all the more strange since he has just been insisting that "speech" produces all the various kinds of "thought," or we might say "psychic life," of the agents: "proof and refutation; the excitation of feelings, such as pity, fear, anger, and the like; the suggestion of importance or its opposite" (1456a 36–1456b 2). He then moves on, in our passage, to say that the "dramatic incidents" must be made to produce similar effects. The same types of thought must be conveyed through the poet's handling of incidents. Aristotle is no less dark than Butcher; the passage has been translated in various ways.

9. In 1460b 11 *lexis* is expression of the poet's whole mimetic act.

iambic poetry. In this culinary account of style as combining foreign and ornamental and current and metaphorical words, and so forth, there are only two or three points where Aristotle refers to the connection between words and what is being expressed or indicates that a change in a word changes the experience of the listener.

In the *Rhetoric* we find a more refined account of the relation between words and the structures of thought, emotion, character, and narrative. Discussion of diction is as limited as in the *Poetics*, the object being to show speakers how to satisfy current Attic standards; but Aristotle has another and more generous standard of propriety, essentially a dramatic one (*Rhetoric* III.7). A speaker must use language in a way to project the role he has assumed. He must use words appropriate to what he feels or wants his hearers to feel; he must select idioms that will delineate a certain "disposition" (*hexis*) and so convey the impression, let us say, of a farmer or of an educated man. Such advice could serve as a basis for critical interpretation of dramatic speech.

In both treatises it is what Aristotle does not say that is disturbing. His omissions in discussing metaphor and rhythm and sound are well known; they result in part from overemphasis on the logical and dramatic structure of a speech or a poem. The golden sentences about metaphor seem to open extensive vistas: "The greatest thing by far is to have a command of metaphor. This alone cannot be imparted by another; it is the mark of genius, for to make good metaphors implies an eye for resemblances" (1459a 5–9). But what follows? We are told that metaphors are best suited to iambic verse, that is, to the dialogue of tragedy. In the *Rhetoric* Aristotle stresses the value of metaphor in producing a sense of actuality (*energeia*), of having things "before your eyes" (*Rhetoric* III.10). But the figure is regarded in general as a local expressive device, a way of surprising and pleasing an audience. There is no thought of any larger unifying function of metaphor. Similarly, rhythm and musical sound (*harmonia*) are only incidental embellishments; there is no suggestion that the order of argument or plot may be subtly modified by sound pattern. In general, the scant treatment of metaphor and sound is reflected in the slight attention given to the chorus in Greek tragedy. The *Poetics* does not offer much support for replacing analysis in terms of plot by analysis in terms of ritual sequence.[10] The attitude expressed in the *Rhetoric* toward the finer arts of language offers equally cold com-

---

10. But Jane Harrison, the *magna mater* of the ritualists, has said that if we want to grasp the relation between dramatic art and ritual "it is essential we should understand . . . the chorus, strangest and most beautiful of all" the surviving ritual forms in Greek drama. J. E. Harrison, *Ancient Art and Ritual* (New York, 1913), p. 122.

fort to explicators: "All such arts are fanciful and meant to charm the hearer. Nobody uses fine language when teaching geometry." (*Rhetoric* III.1.) The suspicion arises that this excellent geometrician did not know what poetry was; in other words, his "art of poetry," *mimesis en logois,* excludes much that we feel essential.

It may now seem more than generous to return to our original questions: What can a contemporary critical reader "do" with the Aristotelian account of dramatic structure? And how can he translate it to his advantage?

He begins by accepting the Greek prejudice that literature is "of"[11] human action and life. With plot as a composition of incidents, our critic will not have much to do, though he grants that the notion has a limited usefulness for a playwright. Ibsen's often quoted account of how he composed *The Wild Duck* seems to be a good example: "I have just completed a play in five acts—that is to say, the rough draft of it; now comes the elaboration, the more energetic individualisation of the persons and their mode of expression." But this statement hardly represents what Ibsen did when he wrote the play, as Archer's comparison of the draft and the final text shows. The sentence emerging in the mind and arriving on the page must have borne a total freight of incident and speaking tone and symbolic implication, all of them, in James's phrase, "intimately associated parts of one general effort of expression." Although an abstract structure of incidents may be present to the writer planning his play or novel, only plot "written" concerns the literary critic.

In plot as *arche,* as "origin of movement" and "intelligible order," he can find an idea adaptable to his purposes. For the writer it is what Elizabeth Bowen means by plot as "the knowing of destination." Aristotle makes the shift to the reader's point of view with his analogy of "the chalk outline," the perceived order that we take as standing for a human figure. In terms of reading experience, plot is one of the orders that we apprehend in our response to a writer's words, the order of meanings that we take as "of" a man living. It is a sequence of ordered meanings going toward a destination; plot includes movement. For this definition "dramatic sequence" is a more appropriate term.

How do we translate "dramatic sequence" in relation to our reading of a poem, play, or novel? We start from Aristotle's reminder that personality in literature is expressed by a selection of words and idioms, and we remember that our term is analytical, a way of directing attention to one abstracted aspect of literary experience. In re-

---

11. For definition of this "of" (*mimesis*) see Philip Wheelwright, "Mimesis and Katharsis: an Archetypal Consideration," *English Institute Essays, 1951,* pp. 3–30.

ferring to dramatic structure, we think first of meanings and uses of language that compose a distinct speaking voice; we hear someone speaking in a role, if only the role of "poet." We hear the voice as speaking to "someone" and infer various relationships between the fictional speaker and the auditor. We describe the total of their relationships as a "situation." The slightest shift in tone brings a shift in relation, and drama begins with this movement.

> Had we but world enough and time,
> This coyness, lady, were no crime.

The intimate companionship of lover and mistress in "we" is finely altered by "lady," with its note of detached, ironic decorum. The situation in the second line is not the same as in the first—an example of a small-scale dramatic sequence. By "dramatic structure" (or design) we mean one of these inferred sequences of changing human relationships. "Human," because the relations and changes belong to the distinct impersonation evoked by the words.

This definition may be "blown up" and made sufficiently complex to fit a play by Shakespeare or a novel by James, though the interrelations become innumerable and the changes correspondingly large in scale. In longer works we usually come on points of major change, often with a "recognition" in a derived Aristotelian sense. We have Elizabeth in *Pride and Prejudice* saying, "Until this moment, I never knew myself," or Oedipus, "All comes true now!" or Antony, "I am so lated in the world that I / Have lost my way forever." We accept the implication of Aristotle's remark that tragedy is not possible without plot; no rendering of life will affect us much that does not give us a sense of movement and of reaching points of radical readjustment in relationships. But we wear the peripatetic robe with a difference; the contrast between our definitions and Aristotle's appears in the analysis indicated, in what we "do" with them. At this point someone is saying with an earlier dramatic critic, "Bless thee, Aristotle! Thou art translated!"

We may follow Quince a step further: "To show our simple skill / That is the true beginning of our end." We began with the aim of indicating a kind of translation and practice that might bridge the gap between the Aristotelian position and that of contemporary critical readers. While adopting a disinfected definition of plot, we are still thinking of the reader as exposed to the totality of the language of a poem or play and as responding to the "total connotations" of words. We see in this whole structures as potent and as "real" as the dramatic: designs in image, metaphor, and irony. We remember also that the different sorts of connotation are the connotations of the same words. In the glow of imaginative experience, there is no immediately felt distinction between a "plot" meaning and a metaphorical one; to the cool eye of analysis a single key word may be seen as the focus for several distinguishable designs—metaphorical, ironic, and rhythmic. When we return to our reading, we may feel at the edge of consciousness a double action of drama and metaphor or of drama and irony, or of drama and rhythm.

We experience this double or even triple action most keenly at an "Aristotelian" moment when the dramatic sequence reaches a point of decisive change. Let me try to interpret one of these moments, keeping in mind the language that shapes and projects it: the point in Act V of *The Tempest*,[12] when Prospero describes the behavior of the king and his courtiers as they return from madness to sanity. Shakespeare has been preparing for this readjustment by a movement both dramatic and metaphorical. The play has been moving from a scene of tempest toward a promise of "calm seas, auspicious gales," through a series of punishments or trials toward a series of reconciliations and restorations. Although as Dr. Johnson would say there is a "concatenation of events" running through Prospero's "project" and though the play has a curiously exact time schedule, there is often little connection in time or logic between dialogues or bits of action. To be sure, Shakespeare has the Elizabethan conventions "on his side," but the freedom of his dramatic composition in *The Tempest* never seems merely conventional or capricious, because the connection through analogy is so energetic and pervasive. Recurrent analogies—of sea and tempest, noise and music, sleep and dream, of earth and air, freedom and slavery, usurpation and sovereignty—are linked through the key metaphor of "sea-change" into a single metaphorical design expressive of metamorphosis, or magical transformation. Shakespeare is continually "prodding" us—often in ways of which we are barely conscious—to relate the passing dialogue to other dialogues by a "super-design" of metaphor.

If we now read Prospero's words announcing the great changes that are taking place, we shall see many references back to the metaphorical preparation for this moment. We shall also realize that various dramatic lines and various lines of analogy converge almost simultaneously.

> A solemn air and the best comforter
> To an unsettled fancy, cure thy brains,
> Now useless, boil'd within thy skull! There stand,
> For you are spell-stopp'd.

12. The following analysis is adapted from my essay, "The Tempest," in *The Fields of Light* (New York, 1951).

Holy Gonzalo, honourable man,
Mine eyes, even sociable to the show of thine,
Fall fellowly drops. The charm dissolves apace;
And as the morning steals upon the night,
Melting the darkness, so their rising senses
Begin to chase the ignorant fumes that mantle
Their clearer reason.—O good Gonzalo!
My true preserver, and a loyal sir
To him thou follow'st, I will pay thy graces
Home, both in word and deed.—Most cruelly
Didst thou, Alonso, use me and my daughter:
Thy brother was a furtherer in the act;—
Thou'rt pinch'd for 't now, Sebastian.—Flesh and blood,
You, brother mine, that entertain'd ambition,
Expell'd remorse and nature; who, with Sebastian,—
Whose inward pinches therefore are most strong,—
Would here have kill'd your king; I do forgive thee,
Unnatural though thou art!—Their understanding
Begins to swell, and the approaching tide
Will shortly fill the reasonable shores
That now lie foul and muddy. Not one of them
That yet looks on me, or would know me,—Ariel,
Fetch me the hat and rapier in my cell:—[*Exit Ariel.*]
I will discase me, and myself present,
As I was sometime Milan.—Quickly, spirit;
Thou shalt ere long be free.

If this is a climactic moment, what is happening dramatically?
The "men of sin," like Ferdinand, have come to the end of trials which
began with the storm and continued through various "distractions."
Now, as Prospero explains, they are undergoing a moral, as well as a
mental, regeneration; they are "pinch'd" with remorse and are being
forgiven. In a few moments, "Th' affliction of Alonso's mind amends,"
he resigns Prospero's dukedom, and "entreats" him to pardon his
"wrongs."

But these are the prose facts, the bare bones of the changes in
dramatic relationships. We cannot feel the peculiar quality of what
is taking place or grasp its meaning apart from the metaphorical language through which it is being expressed. And the expressions ac-
quire their force and precision from the metaphorical preparation
glanced at earlier. The courtiers' senses are restored by "an airy
charm," by magic similar to that worked by Ariel and his spirits. The
allusions to "heavenly music" and "solemn air," in contrast to the
"rough magic" that Prospero has abjured, remind us that these

changes will be musically harmonious, like the songs of Ariel, not noisy and confused like the storm sent to punish these men and reveal their "monstrous" guilt. Toward the end of the speech, the imagery recalls the tempest metaphor, but it is altered so as to express the mental and moral changes that are taking place. The return of understanding is like an "approaching tide" that covers the evidence of a storm (both "foul" and "muddy" have storm associations from earlier occurrences).

The metaphor that best expresses this "clearing" is the one for which the preparation has been most complete.

> The charm dissolves apace;
> And as the morning steals upon the night,
> Melting the darkness, so their rising senses
> Begin to chase the ignorant fumes that mantle
> Their clearer reason.

"Dissolving" and "melting" and "fumes" take us back at once to the grand transformations of the masque and "the cloud-capp'd towers" speech, to earlier cloud-changes both serious and comic; and they take us back further to the association of clouds with magical tempests, inner storms, and clearing weather. We read of the moral and psychological changes with a present sense of these analogies. They are qualified for us as a dream-like dissolution of tempest clouds, as events in the "insubstantial" region where reality and unreality merge.

It is through such links that Shakespeare concentrates at this dramatic moment the fullest meaning of his key metaphor. There is, of course, no separation in the reader's experience between dramatic fact and metaphorical qualification. The images that recur take us back to felt qualities, but to felt qualities embedded in particular dramatic contexts. "Melting," for example, carries us to the supernatural dissolution of "spirits . . . melted into air, into thin air"; but it also reminds us of the masque pageantry and of Prospero's calming of Ferdinand's fears. We hear Prospero's soothing and mysterious voice in both the earlier and the later uses of the word. The dramatic links and the analogical links are experienced at once; metaphorical design and dramatic design are perfectly integrated.

"Metamorphosis" is the key metaphor to the drama, but not the key metaphor to a detachable design of decorative analogies. Through the echoes in Prospero's speech of various lines of analogy, Shakespeare makes us feel each shift in dramatic relationships as a magical transformation, whether it is the courtiers' return to sanity, or Prospero's restoration to his dukedom, or Ariel's flight into perpetual summer. While all the "slaves" and "prisoners" are being freed and all the "sovereigns" are being restored, the sense of magical change is never lost. The union of drama and metaphor is nowhere more complete than in *The Tempest*.

That is to say, the composition of *The Tempest* is "poetic" in a sense that revives the central Aristotelian meaning of *poietike*, and that extends and adjusts its implications to fit contemporary views of the reading experience and of the relation between structure and language. The poetic art of literature, *mimesis en logois*, is for Aristotle primarily a rendering of human behavior in terms of dramatic sequence, the medium of language being assumed, but often overlooked. A typical contemporary definition of poetic art might run: "an exploitation of the resources of words," or "creation through words of orders of meaning and sound." The aim of this paper has been to take a step toward harmonizing these two sorts of definition, both of them useful, both inadequate. The kind of definition and practice we want may be illustrated from the single word "dissolves" in Prospero's speech. We note first that the word bears the weight of certain limited dramatic relationships: the voice heard in the faintly Latinate, elevated "dissolves" has the objectivity and remoteness characteristic of Prospero. He observes with detachment and without anger. "Dissolves" reminds us that his vengeance is coming to an end; that the courtiers are moving out of their trance and recognizing their guilt. (The word also gives us a cue as to the actors' movements and facial expression.) It is heard in an even iambic rhythm, "The charm dissolves apace," and in the balanced rhetorical pattern of a classical simile, "as . . . so." Prospero's stance in relation to himself and the others is further modified by the steadiness and intellectual "command" of this speech and verse movement. And the analogies with earlier dissolvings and clouds are bringing in all their qualifications, sensuous and philosophic. The Aristotelian sense of "poetic" directs us to the salient dramatic relations and to their place in the movement of the play, and to the total human experience rendered by *The Tempest*. The modern sense of "poetic" directs us to a fuller perception of the variety of meaning and design and to the close interaction of meanings, the fine qualification of one kind of design by another. All structural links, large and small, from an obvious change in narrative fact to a phrasal echo, are perceived in the resonances of particular words.

The Aristotelian emphasis seems, perhaps, the right one now; twenty-five years ago the emphasis on the word seemed equally right. Both are right enough for literature and for criticism in the long run. But an adequate theory cannot be summoned on demand. We may doubt whether the growth of critical intelligence comes by direct steps from theory to practice; it comes rather from feeling our way and fitting our theories to what we must say at our moment in history if we are not to become tools of our machines. The redefinition of plot as dramatic sequence perceived in the progress of meanings is a sample of the kind of adjustment wanted—an account of literature that will do justice to its dramatic character without falling into an Aristotelian separation of plot and character from diction. An adjustment by theory or practice that does not face the liabilities and the obscurities of Aristotle's position (or of any similar position) will not be worth much, even for a short run. That is my excuse for spending so much time in translating and evaluating Aristotle's statements: it is hard to say exactly what we are trying to adjust to. If the result has been sufficiently grim, my success may have been greater than I am inclined to suppose.

9

POETIC AND DRAMATIC DESIGN IN VERSIONS
AND TRANSLATIONS OF SHAKESPEARE

The typical "heresy" among critics of poetic drama two generations back was to analyze the experience in terms of dramatic "form"— plot,[1] character, rising and falling action. The typical heresy of the present generation has been to reduce the well-made play to the well-wrought urn. *King Lear* is no longer a bad play, but a supreme lyric poem on order and disorder in nature. Both extremes of interpretation betray the same defect, the assumption that the play as poem and the play as drama are separable entities. Although every critic "knows better," acting better is another matter. Whether we are formalists in the old sense or the new, what we lack is not principles, but control of critical discourse, mastery of a critical style for describing the experience of drama, a style that will continually acknowledge the claims of the poetic and the dramatic. This essay attempts to move in the direction of creating such a style by exploring in a new setting the connection between poetic and dramatic structures. The "new setting" offered is comparison of versions and translations of Shakespeare's plays.

The aim of this study was first suggested by T. S. Eliot's admirable remark in his essay on *Poetry and Drama:* "When Shakespeare, in one of his mature plays, introduces what might seem a purely poetic line or passage, it never interrupts the action, or is out of character, but

Reprinted from *Poetics* (Warsaw, 1961).
1. See Chapter 8, "The Heresy of Plot."

on the contrary, in some mysterious way supports both action and character."[2] Another point of departure was Roman Jakobson's paper, *Linguistics and Poetics.* In his analysis of Antony's funeral oration from *Julius Caesar,* Jakobson showed that by starting from the simplest uses of language, one could see that "The main dramatic force of Antony's exordium . . . is achieved by Shakespeare's playing on grammatical categories and constructions."[3] It should be noted that my approach to the problem of the poetic and the dramatic is not that of an expert in linguistics, but of a literary critic,—not with the aim of making "censorious verdicts," but rather with the Arnoldian purpose of preparing for "the judgment which almost insensibly forms itself in a fair and clear mind, along with fresh knowledge." Like many English and American critics since the Richardsian revolution, I am concerned with interpreting works of imaginative literature, "imaginative" in the sense of offering experiences of a high degree of interconnectedness. (Readers may dine at journey's end with Coleridge and with Arnold.) Such works may be described as both "poetic" and "mimetic." (Compare above, pp. 128, 137.) In drama, obviously enough, all verbal resources, nonpoetic as well as poetic, are subdued to the mimetic function.

Translations offer most useful examples for exploring the connection between the two kinds of design because of the two necessary yet conflicting purposes of the translator. (1) He attempts to give the reader the same dramatic experience as that offered by the original (e.g., the experience of the voice, the role, the attitudes that equal "Hamlet"). (2) He attempts to produce this identity of effect through a different verbal medium, in another language. What happens when he undertakes this impossible task? What can we learn from his attempt about the interconnection of the poetic and the dramatic?

Although we know that the poetic and the dramatic are inseparable in our response to the words in a play of Shakespeare, we can nevertheless attend even to a single word in two very different ways, as a sign within a system of poetic parallels, or as a sign within a system of mimetic enactments. A tiny example will serve to remind us of both kinds of attention and their union in a complete response. Consider Hamlet's dying words, "the rest is silence."[4] We can attend to these words as drama: Hamlet dies, Hamlet cannot mend his wounded name, or even completely express his wish that Horatio will do it for

---

2. T. S. Eliot, *On Poetry and Poets* (New York, 1957), pp. 88–89.
3. *Style in Language,* ed. Thomas Sebeok (New York, 1960), p. 375.
4. The text quoted in this paper is *Hamlet,* ed. G. L. Kittredge (Boston, 1939), with the exception of J. D. Wilson's reading of "sullied" for "solid" in "this too, too sullied flesh."

him. The incompleteness of the gesture is very Hamletian, as he has
not been quite able to act out the heroic role, though

> he was likely, had he been put on,
> To have prov'd most royally . . .

"The rest" extends into

> The undiscover'd country, from whose bourn
> No traveller returns . . .

But it is unlikely that "rest" and "silence" would open up so richly in
dramatic implication if we did not hear them in a particular aural
context:

> He has my dying voice.
> So tell him, with th' occurents, more and less,
> Which have solicited—the rest is silence.
>
> [Fortinbras]

There are no fewer than nine sibilants and as many aspirates in the
two lines ending with "silence." The rhythmic swing shifts with "more
and less" into extreme regularity which contrasts oddly with the break
in syntax after "solicited." A length of utterance and a weight of emphasis is given to both *rest* and *si-* that they would not have in ordinary speech, and the relatively unexpected feminine ending completes
the dying fall of the line. The line has barely ended when we hear its
reprise in

> angels sing thee to thy rest!

The alert auditor will recall the other most potently simple line of the
play,

> Rest, rest perturbed spirit!

Hamlet's prayer has been answered, the arc of his desire has been
completed. We began a minute ago with consonants and metrical
stress, we are now talking about the *dramatic* line and its course in
the play. But we reached this further range through the beautiful
circuit and subterfuge of the heard verbal pattern. The extension of
"the rest" into that "undiscover'd country" grew out of the lengthened
utterance and the syllabic and metrical pauses. To extend the sound

141

was to increase the area of reference. We may refrain from demonstrating the effect of re-ordering the lines or changing their diction.

Restoration improvers of Shakespeare had a heartier taste, and their versions—made in part with the laudable purpose of modernizing Shakespeare's grammar—illustrate nicely the inseparability of grammar from poetry. They also offer instructive examples of what happens to dramatic values when the poetic medium is altered. They also show that the *disiecta membra* of Shakespeare's poetic pattern will not reassemble and work in a new dramatic context. Nahum Tate's "happy ending" of *King Lear*—a version that satisfied Dr. Johnson's demand for "justice"—is surprisingly enough filled with echoes of the imagery and thematic motifs of the play: "The wheel of fortune now has made her circle" . . . "The winds be hush'd" . . . "All nature pauses" . . . "storm of fortune" . . . One can imagine a caricature of the standard analysis of Shakespearean imagery in which it was solemnly shown that indeed the closing scene beautifully recapitulates the design of the play, that the drama comes full circle in its metaphorical course. And it would all be true—if we disregard the fact that we lose utterly the sense of different voices, that every character begins to sound like Prospero in his most priestlike moments. Everyone is also speaking in a form of blank verse barely distinguishable from heroic couplets except for the lack of rhyme. While a dramatic and moral case can be made for a happy ending, it may be doubted whether Shakespeare himself could have created a speech rhythm capable of convincing us that Shakespeare's Lear would "talk" such an ending.

Dryden's *Troilus and Cressida* is a more respectable example of Restoration "improvement" than Tate's *Lear,* and his transformations are also much more instructive. The blank verse is not despicable, and there is evidence that Dryden had a clear understanding of much that Shakespeare was doing. He is equally clear about the necessity of "correcting" Shakespeare's style, a necessity imposed by the state of the language, which he contrasts with that of Greek in the age of Aeschylus, when "the Greek tongue was arriv'd to its full perfection."[5] Consider the application of this doctrine in the reworking of Ulysses' great speech on "degree":

> *Ulysses. Troy* had been down ere this, and *Hectors* Sword
> Wanted a Master but for our disorders:
> The observance due to rule has been neglected;
> Observe how many *Grecians* Tents stand void

---

5. *Dryden: The Dramatic Works,* ed. Montagu Summers (London, 1932), V, 11. The text of Dryden's *Troilus and Cressida* quoted in this chapter is from this edition.

Upon this plain; so many hollow factions:
For when the General is not like the Hive
To whom the Foragers should all repair,
What Hony can our empty Combs expect?
O when Supremacy of Kings is shaken,
What can succeed: How cou'd Communities
Or peacefull traffick from divided shores,
Prerogative of Age, Crowns, Scepters, Lawrells,
But by degree stand on their solid base!
Then every thing resolves to brutal force
And headlong force is led by hoodwink'd will,
For wild Ambition, like a ravenous Woolf,
Spurd on by will and seconded by power,
Must make an universal prey of all,
And last devour it self.

The essential points in the Shakespearean argument are preserved, and key lines are kept or intelligently paraphrased. The case is clinched by the striking metaphor of the "ravenous Woolf"; but somehow the final line seems tame: we hardly feel that this beast will bite, let alone "devour itself." Comparison with Shakespeare's text[6] shows why the metaphorical climax works so much better there than here. The whole speech has built up a highly particularized definition of "degree" as illustrated in different orders of society and in the cosmos, the disturbance of degree being expressed in violent metaphors of storm and disease (with related imagery of feeding). The final paradox has behind it a peculiar structure:

Strength should be lord of imbecility,
And the rude son should strike his father dead;
Force should be right; or rather, right and wrong,
Between whose endless jar justice resides,
Should lose their names, and so should justice too.
Then everything includes itself in power,
Power into will, will into appetite;
And appetite, an universal wolf,
So doubly seconded with will and power,
Must make perforce an universal prey,
And last eat up himself.

I.iii.114–124.

6. The text of Shakespeare's *Troilus and Cressida* quoted in this chapter is from the edition of Alice Walker, general ed. J. D. Wilson (Cambridge, 1957).

Not only is "eat up himself" a cruder idiom; it is the summing up of a metaphorical and grammatical pattern. In substituting "ambition" for "appetite" Dryden shows that he had not felt the way in which this image of self-cannibalism is prepared for. We have a whole series of grammatical "ingorgings" in which we hear one verbal mass, one name, being eaten up, included, within another: right in force; "right and wrong" in an "endless jar"; right, wrong, and justice "lose their names," absorbed in "everything"; "everything includes itself in power"; "power into will"; "will into appetite" (and perhaps also will and power become seconds, substitutes for appetite). Finally we hear the universal eater consumed by the universal eaten (since appetite by eating everything has become everything eaten). Appetite has been verbally self-consumed a half-dozen or more times before the final paradox is released. Dryden's version is a perfect example of poetic excitement diminished by the loss of a peculiar grammatical figure. But the dramatic loss is equally great. In the Shakespearean original we get a special sense of a mind thinking and feeling its way through the process of moral and social decay that is only named by the argument from degree. The fine intelligence projected by the poetic progression, by the complexity of its grammatical unfolding, largely disappears in the lines by Dryden. His Ulysses is a pronouncer of clear and distinct platitudes, much nearer to the public speakers of *Julius Caesar* than to the tortured thinkers of this most metaphysical play. "Character" in this speech of Shakespeare is as much grammar as metaphor.

The reduction in style in this crucial passage of *Troilus and Cressida* —one that presents the key metaphor of "degree" in imagery that recurs throughout the play—has its effect much later in the main dramatic crisis, Troilus' discovery of Cressida's falsity:

[*Troilus.*] Was Cressid here?
Ulysses.   I cannot conjure, Trojan.
Troilus. She was not, sure.
Ulysses.   Most sure she was.
Troilus. Why, my negation hath no taste of madness.
Ulysses. Nor mine, my lord; Cressid was here but now.
Troilus. Let it not be believed for womanhood!
Think we had mothers. Do not give advantage
To stubborn critics, apt without a theme
For depravation, to square the general sex
By Cressid's rule; rather think this not Cressid.
Ulysses. What hath she done, prince, that can soil our mothers?
Troilus. Nothing at all, unless that this were she.
Thersites. Will 'a swagger himself out on's own eyes?

Troilus. This she? No; this is Diomed's Cressida.
If beauty have a soul, this is not she;
If souls guide vows, if vows be sanctimonies,
If sanctimony be the gods' delight,
If there be rule in unity itself,
This is not she. O madness of discourse,
That cause sets up with and against itself!
Bifold authority! where reason can revolt
Without perdition, and loss assume all reason
Without revolt. This is, and is not, Cressid!
Within my soul there doth conduce a fight
Of this strange nature, that a thing inseparate
Divides more wider than the sky and earth;
And yet the spacious breadth of this division
Admits no orifex for a point as subtle
As Ariachne's broken woof to enter.
Instance, O instance! strong as Pluto's gates:
Cressid is mine, tied with the bonds of heaven.
Instance, O instance! strong as heaven itself:
The bonds of heaven are slipped, dissolved and loosed,
And with another knot, five-finger-tied,
The fractions of her faith, orts of her love,
The fragments, scraps, the bits and greasy relics
Of her o'ereaten faith are given to Diomed.

V.ii.125–160.

The "revolt" of reason is expressed here not by sensuous imagery, but by mad "discourse" in which the same logical and grammatical routines repeat and repeat that "is" and "is not" are equal. Dryden's reduction shows that as in ritual, belief in nonsense depends largely on suggestive repetition:

> *Troilus.* Was *Cressida* here?
> *Ulysses.* I cannot conjure Trojan.
> *Troilus.* She was not sure! she was not.
> Let it not be believ'd for womanhood:
> Think we had Mothers, do not give advantage
> To biting Satyr, apt without a theme,
> For defamation, to square all the sex
> By *Cressids* rule, rather think this not *Cressida.*
> *Thersites.* Will he swagger himself out on's own eyes!
> *Troilus.* This she! no this was *Diomedes Cressida.*
> If beauty have a Soul, this is not she:
> I cannot speak for rage, that Ring was mine,

145

By Heaven I gave it, in that point of time,
When both our joys were fullest!—if he keeps it,
Let dogs eat *Troilus.*

But the elimination of logical and grammatical hypnosis has a further effect. The great culminating metaphor,

The bonds of heaven are slipped, dissolved and loosed,

cannot be reached, the cosmic overtones disappear, and the connection of Troilus' personal chaos with the social and moral chaos described in Ulysses' speech and dramatized in the war scenes, utterly disappears. (It is not surprising that the accompanying imagery of foul feeding is also lost.) The bonds of metaphor are loosed, and with them the Shakespearean vision of the link between war and lechery is also broken. Not only do we lose a thematic design, but the large philosophic meaning of Troilus' act is lost, and it becomes a much smaller thing. The disturbance in the mind of Shakespeare's hero opens up into a vision of irrationality not only in the history of his love, but in the human mind and the cosmos. Again we find ourselves talking about losses in dramatic as well as philosophic meaning. Dryden's Troilus is less disturbed by the revolt of reason than by seeing his ring on Diomede's hand. Shakespeare's hero has been transformed from a Proustian dialectician with a heroic accent into an angry young man. In correcting grammar Dryden "corrected" a great deal else. Although we sometimes talk of plot and character as surviving in translation while poetry is lost, we must observe that if poetry is completely lost, plot and character tend to become unrecognizable.

In a translation of *Hamlet,* a play in which the relations between word and act are so subtly portrayed, we should expect to find that changes in poetic form produce equally subtle dramatic disturbances. Gide's French version[7] reminds us at once that the limits imposed by a particular language are also limits of imaginative power. Consider this exchange from *Hamlet,* in which the Queen reminds her son that the death of his father is a "common" occurrence:

Queen.   If it be,
Why seems it so particular with thee?
Hamlet. Seems, madam? Nay, it is. I know not "seems."
'Tis not alone my inky cloak, good mother,
Nor customary suits of solemn black,

7. *Hamlet, édition bilingue traduction nouvelle de André Gide,* ed. Jacques Schriffin (New York, 1945).

Nor windy suspiration of forc'd breath,
No, nor the fruitful river in the eye,
Nor the dejected haviour of the visage,
Together with all forms, moods, shapes of grief,
That can denote me truly. These indeed seem,
For they are actions that a man might play;
But I have that within which passeth show—
These but the trappings and the suits of woe.

I.ii.74–86.

These lines give us our first distinct sense of Hamlet's role—his voice, and run of speech—and at the same time they set going a theme and a metaphor of considerable importance in the play. Gide translates:

La Reine. Alors pourquoi si particulière votre apparence?
Hamlet. Apparence? Eh! non! Madame. Réalité. Qu'ai-je affaire avec le "paraître"? Non plus mon manteau couleur d'encre, ni ma coutumière livrée de deuil, ne parvient à me satisfaire—ni les gémissements qu' exhale une poitrine haletante, ni le ruissellement des pleurs, ni l'allongement désolé du visage, ensemble avec les dehors et les symboles du chagrin—ni tout ce qui paraît et dont par jeu, ma bonne mère, n'importe qui peut se vêtir— mais j'ai ceci en moi qui surpasse l'apparence; le reste n'est que faste et parure de la douleur.

The mistranslation of "seems it so particular" leads to a very Gallic reduction, an example of what Yves Bonnefoy calls the "platonic" character of French poetic language ("le français de la poésie est 'platonicien,' l'anglais de Shakespeare une sorte d'aristotélisme passionnel").[8] "Apparence" and "réalité" are undoubtedly among the larger meanings of Hamlet's words: the theme looms large in the play, although never expressed in these terms. (Only in Wittenberg would Hamlet talk like this.) In the original we have instead Hamlet's characteristic iteration—words, words, words. In his three previous lines, his first in the play, there are two puns (telescoped iterations) and an echo of his mother's "common." Next we hear both voices leaning heavily on "ē" sounds, while Hamlet's line plays metrical tricks with his mother's evenly iambic question:

Queen.   If it be,
Why seems it so particular with thee?
Hamlet. Seems, madam? Nay, it is. I know not "seems."

8. "Shakespeare et le poète français," *Preuves* (June 1959), no. 100, p. 47.

"Seems" stands out because of the rude reversal of stress followed by a suppression of the unstressed syllable and by still another reversal. The metrically surprising breaks due to punctuation and the third reversal in "I know not seems" give the final word an odd salience to ear and mind.

> Seems, madam? Nay it is. I know not *"seems."*

The effect is very like another pun, since the second "seems" by a grammatical sleight of words now has also the meaning of "is." ("Your *seems* equals my *is.*") We have been beguiled into taking "it" as referring to "seems," since the reference of "it" has become fairly vague. The line offers a kind of grammatical poetry very like Wallace Stevens': "To seem it is to be"—and, we might add, poetry with a similar effect of logical wit. The important point is that Shakespeare's words by being thrown into new metrical and grammatical positions turn up successively the new meanings that Gide extracts so neatly. Here if anywhere we can see the necessary bonds between elementary grammatical and metrical orderings and particular dramatic significance. Break the relation, as in Gide's version, and the Hamletian voice and playing disappear, and we have the classic *Hamlet* without Hamlet. The opposition of appearance and reality, when abstracted so, is not what Shakespeare "means" here or elsewhere in the play. Furthermore, the playing with words, the fine consciousness of what words can do, leads at once into the central metaphor of Hamlet's role, the hero as actor, player:

> These indeed seem,
> For they are actions that a man might play . . .

Hamlet is here anticipating the language of his "player's" soliloquy (II.ii.575–633). Though Gide's "par jeu" can refer to the theatre, it hardly has the strong and immediate reference of English "play" in the context of *Hamlet*, a word used in various forms some thirty-five times, often with specific reference to the theatre. (French usage forces both Gide and Bonnefoy to use such words as "acteur," "théâtre," "scène," where English uses "player," "play," "playing.") To lose the distinct force of "play" in this speech is to miss the initial disclosure of the metaphor that reminds us most forcibly of Hamlet's ability to "act" in one sense and not in another.

It is in the "player's" soliloquy that we see Hamlet "unpack his heart with words" in a style that leads him from mere play-acting to using a play to "catch the conscience of the king." He proceeds from analysis of the player's art to shocked awareness of what the player would do with *his* cue for passion, to a rehearsal of new roles—the peppery fighter and the bloody avenger: "O, vengeance!" With bitter clarity Hamlet now turns sharply to see that he has himself been play-acting, and with "About, my brain!" he begins to speak in that lively, active tone that will recur whenever he sets to work in earnest (cf. III.ii.1–57; III.iv.199–211; IV.vii.43–49; V.ii.1–70, 203–35). The art of the speech does not lie in the argument, but in the "turnings" of words that serve as notations for the flow of thought and feeling. One small example from Shakespeare and from Gide will again show how a slight shift in poetic means has a far-reaching dramatic effect:

> Am I a coward?
> Who calls me villain? breaks my pate across?
> Plucks off my beard and blows it in my face?
> Tweaks me by th' nose? gives me the lie i' th' throat
> As deep as to the lungs? Who does me this, ha?
> 'Swounds, I should take it! for it cannot be
> But I am pigeon-liver'd and lack gall
> To make oppression bitter, or ere this
> I should have fatted all the region kites
> With this slave's offal. Bloody, bawdy villain!
> Remorseless, treacherous, lecherous, kindless villain!
> O, vengeance!
> Why, what an ass am I! This is most brave . . .
>
> II.ii.598–610

Hamlet. Qui me traitera de lâche? me donnera du poing sur la gueule, m'arrachera le poil et me soufflètera? Qui me tirera par le nez? Qui me renfoncera la protestation dans la gorge jusqu'au fond des tripes?

Allons! Qu'il vienne celui qui fera cela, que, parbleu, je n'aurai pas volé! Car il faut croire que je n'ai qu'un foie de pigeon, incapable, sous l'oppression, de fiel amer; ou sinon j'aurais déjà gorgé tous les vautours du royaume les viscères de ce goujat. Sanglant, obscène, scélérat! Scélérat éhonté, libidineux, perfide! O vengeance!

Quoi! Quel âne je suis! Quel beau courage il a . . .

Note first the blood-and-thunder vocabulary and a style reminiscent of a crude avenging hero, if not of Pistol (cf. *Henry V*, III.vi.26–30; IV.iv.15–16, 41). The alliteration, the homoeoteleuton, the sheer mass of the words when taken together, are too much. But the tricks have a dramatic point, as we see from Gide's version. Consider especially *libidineux, perfide* for "treacherous, lecherous." In the double

149

rhyme we hear not only "lustful" and "faithless," but the flickering light of parody, the mocking echo of the avenger's style. Lose that note and we lose a fine anticipation of the self-mockery that breaks out in "This is most brave!" The continuous psychological turning of the original speech is in Gide broken by a crude shift. The integrity of dramatic life, the illusion of a sentient being, is dependent on the verbal illusion.

The player metaphor in *Hamlet* is closely allied to the two major themes of playing madness and of melancholy, the true melancholy from which Hamlet suffers, and which he sometimes feigns. Each of these themes is introduced early in the play by a metaphorical expression that recurs in many variants. These varying yet related analogies accentuate, qualify, and connect much that is said and done in *Hamlet,* and at times the action, as often in Shakespeare, is little more than a playing out of the metaphors. To sacrifice the character of the initial image is to lose therefore a clue to large dramatic patterns and meanings. The first hint of playing madness comes in

> To put an antic disposition on . . .

"Put on" (which recurs in many forms) is another version of both the player's metaphor and the "appearance-reality" theme. "Antic" carries at once suggestions of the antic (the Elizabethan "fool"), the fantastic (the eccentric), and the madman. Hamlet touches on all these characters in his bewildering, never-to-be-classified moods. The compactness and the range of implication of "put on" and "antic" exemplify very well the "opening up," the *ouverture,* as Bonnefoy calls it, of the English word in contrast to the *fermeture* of the French, as in Gide's *buffoner,* which gives us one kind of fooling only.

The theme of melancholy is set first by an almost equally memorable expression, the Ghost's

> Taint not thy mind . . .

"Taint," in its Shakespearean associations with melancholy and corruption (cf. *Twelfth Night,* III.iv.13) is allied at once with the disease-rottenness theme that has already been underlined in a dozen or more different expressions. Gide's "Garde ton esprit pur" eliminates the connection and gives no hint of what is to come. Bonnefoy's translation,

> Ne souille pas ton âme . . .

150

picks up nicely his

> O souillures, souillures de la chair!
> . . . this too, too sullied flesh . . .

and shows the poetic dramatist at work in the act of translation. (Note again the abstractness of the French idiom.)

But as Jakobson has reminded us, Shakespeare is not always explicitly metaphorical; he has a style, dramatically of great power, that works by other figures. Antony's funeral oration and the scene in which it stands (*Julius Caesar* III.ii.79–265) offer little to the searcher for recurrent images that build up large metaphors in the course of the play. *Julius Caesar* is a highly individual work in the Shakespeare canon, quite special in poetic style and dramatic quality. With the exception of *Coriolanus*—which is however rich in image and metaphor—it is the most purely oratorical of all the plays. Dramatic speech is always public speech, often distinctively persuasive. The most private soliloquies, Brutus' meditations on Caesar's death and on his inner "state of man," are quite public and impersonal in tone when compared with similar speeches in *Hamlet* and *Macbeth*. There is also a marked tendency for characters to use the third person of themselves or of other characters they are addressing; and there is a not unrelated fondness for prosopopoeia, for the use of semi-allegorical abstractions to describe[9] both outer and inner action. In a style that lends itself to rhetorical questions and apostrophes, we are not surprised to find much use of grammatical figures of the sort Jakobson points out in the "Friends, Romans, and countrymen" speech.[10]

Some further peculiarities of poetic form may also be noted. The recurrent "ambitious/ambition" and "honourable man/men" has an almost refrain-like effect since in all but one case the words close end-stopped lines. The one exception is very telling,

> Ambition should be made of sterner stuff . . .

where the first word jumps out in its personified role. The recurrences of "honourable" and "ambitious" fall into a curious pattern that produces something like stanzas: (Numbers in the table refer to numbers of lines *between* each recurrence).

9. That Shakespeare makes use of similar devices elsewhere (especially of the pompous third person in the tragedies and the Roman plays) does not diminish their effect in *Julius Caesar*. See my *Hero and Saint: Shakespeare and the Graeco-Roman Heroic Tradition* (Oxford, 1971), p. 219, n. 2.
10. The text quoted is *Julius Caesar*, ed. G. L. Kittredge (Boston, 1939).

honourable man (men)	ambitious (ambition)
0	7
3	3
6	1
4	0
0	3
	0

Roughly speaking, the two patterns are opposites: the echoes of "honourable man" tend to occur farther apart; while the echoes of "ambitious" tend to come closer together. As we hear "ambitious" more frequently, a surprising interchange of meaning has taken place with "honourable." By gradually reducing all of Brutus' statements about ambition to lies, "honourable man" becomes equivalent finally to liar, slanderer. At the same time examples from Caesar's life, sympathetically described by Antony, are quietly equated with "ambition": "grievous fault" and "grievously answer'd," "faithful and just to me," "ransoms did the general coffers fill," "When that the poor have cried, Caesar wept," "he did thrice refuse [the crown]": "Ambition" made of such "stuff" and applied to Caesar becomes a noble term; "honourable" redefined and applied to Brutus and the conspirators becomes a base one. Shakespeare shows the mob being gradually corrupted by this degradation:

> Caesar has had great wrong . . .
> . . . 'tis certain he [Caesar] was not ambitious.

They complete the equation with

> They were traitors. Honourable men!

The poetic design, like the argument, has a special dramatic value. The movement is not, as in Hamlet's player soliloquy, of the kind usually called "development of character." Rather the movement is toward the goal of persuasion, and we marvel at the exhibition of forensic art. We have little sense of growth in Antony himself. Indeed we have seen enough of this "shrewd contriver" to expect some such performance. We are again reminded of allegory, of allegorical illustration of an essential quality through a fixed character. In general, the noble Romans of *Julius Caesar* are of this dramatic type, public historic images, relatively static compared with the fluctuating tide of Shakespearean life in Hamlet, Lear, and Othello.

Bonnefoy's version[11] of Antony's oration will confirm and support

11. Texts quoted are from *Hamlet, Jules César* (Paris, 1959).

our impression of the special nature of the "poetic" and the "dramatic" in this play.

> *Antoine.* Romains, mes amis, mes concitoyens, écoutez-moi!
> Je viens ensevelir César, non le louer.
> Le mal que les hommes ont fait vit après eux,
> Le bien, souvent, est enterré avec leurs os,
> Qu'il en soit ainsi de César . . . Le noble Brutus
> Vous a dit que César fut ambitieux.
> S'il a dit vrai, certes la faute est grave,
> Et grave aussi en fut le châtiment.
> Ici, avec la permission de Brutus, et des autres,
> (Car Brutus est un homme honorable,
> Ils le sont tous, d'ailleurs, tous honorables)
> Je viens parler sur la dépouille de César.
> Il était mon ami, fidèle et juste,
> Mais Brutus dit qu'il fut ambitieux
> Et Brutus est un homme honorable.
> Il a conduit bien des captifs à Rome
> Dont la rançon remplit nos coffres publics :
> Cela vous semble-t-il d'un ambitieux?
> Quand les pauvres souffraient, César pleurait.
> L'ambition doit être plus rigide.
> Mais Brutus dit qu'il fut ambitieux
> Et Brutus est un homme honorable.
> Et tous vous avez vu qu'aux Lupercales
> Trois fois je lui offris la couronne royale,
> Qu'il refusa trois fois. Fût-ce par ambition?
> Mais Brutus dit qu'il fut ambitieux,
> Et Brutus est, bien sûr, un homme honorable.
> Je ne critique pas ce qu'a dit Brutus,
> Mais je dois dire, ici, ce que je sais.
> Vous l'avez tous aimé. Non sans raison.
> Quelle raison vous retient donc de le pleurer?
> O Jugement! tu ne vis plus que chez les bêtes
> Et les hommes n'ont plus de sens . . . Excusez-moi,
> Mon coeur est là, dans cette bière, avec César,
> Et je ne puis parler, tant qu'il me manque.

Note at once how well the main pattern of lines and "stanzas," is preserved. In one detail it might be argued that the French word order is superior to the English: not "honourable man," but *homme honorable.*" The antiphony of *ambitieux* and *honorable* is heightened as we hear the two words sung out at the end of the lines. The grammatical and rhetorical figures by which Brutus' assertions are reduced to questionable statements, in which his abstracts become "linguistic fictions" (and personifications) are closely paralleled in the French. But the most poetic and most Shakespearean device, the pun on "brutish" disappears with a softening of the metaphor as rendered in *tu ne vis plus*. This toning down takes place with the one expression reminiscent of the more characteristic metaphors of the other tragedies, the one that recalls the single dominant image strain in the play. Beasts, especially brutish ones, are associated with the less noble, less Roman actions and with the portentous "change" of things

> . . . from their ordinance,
> Their natures, and preformed faculties,
> To monstrous quality . . .
>
> I.iii.66–68.

The dramatic force of the metaphor is clear in

> Caesar should be a beast without a heart
> If he should stay at home today for fear.
>
> II.ii.42–43.

Readers of *King Lear* and *Othello* will note the anticipation of one of the great Shakespearean metaphors, the "monstrous" transformation of the human, which is acted out in the blinding of Gloucester and in Othello's torturing of Desdemona.

In an expression such as "brutish beasts," where the poetic and dramatic texture is most finely woven, translation becomes nearly impossible. Nor is there any sure way of matching one of the finest shifts in Antony's speech, the twisting of Brutus' "hear me for my cause" to

> You all did love him once, not without cause.
> What cause witholds you . . .

The echo neatly recalls Brutus' innocence, and the abstraction illustrates Antony's power of ironic attack. But though French easily admits *Écoutez-moi plaider ma cause . . .*, it cannot follow the pattern of the echo,

> Vous l'avez tous aimé. Non sans raison.
> Quelle raison vous retient donc de le pleurer?

The repetition of *raison* is a nice stroke, and the next line is an example of fine remembering (conscious or not) in the Shakespearean manner:

> O Jugement! tu ne vis plus que chez les bêtes
> Et les hommes n'ont plus de sens . . .

Brutus had said:

> Et pour juger le mieux possible, tenez vos sens en éveil.

By and large the translation is most successful (judgment is contagious!), not only in such details, but in the over-all tone and rhythm. To ask why is not to minimize Bonnefoy's feat, but to see more clearly the quality of this Shakespearean poetic-dramatic style. It is peculiar enough in English, less so in French. Bonnefoy has remarked that *Julius Caesar* is the "most French" of Shakespeare's plays; he might have said, the most "Corneillian." In adopting the Roman oratorical tone, in the balance of phrasing ("to bury Caesar, not to praise him"), in the use of abstractions (especially personifications) and of apostrophes and rhetorical questions, Shakespeare like Corneille is writing within a Latin tradition common to many Renaissance poets and orators. It need hardly be said that highly sensuous metaphors and strains of echoing images are less frequent in the plays of Corneille and Racine than in Shakespeare's. There is however in Corneille a kind of petrified imagery of horror combined with personification that is ultimately Senecan:

> *Chimène.* Sire, mon père est mort; mes yeux ont vu son sang
> Couler à gros bouillons de son généreux flanc;
> Ce sang qui tant de fois garantit vos murailles,
> Ce sang qui tant de fois vous gagna des batailles,
> Ce sang qui tout sorti fume encor de courroux . . .
> Son flanc étoit ouvert; et pour mieux m'émouvoir,
> Son sang sur la poussière écrivoit mon devoir;
> Ou plutôt sa valeur en cet état réduite
> Me parloit par sa plaie, et hâtoit ma poursuite . . .
> *Le Cid*, 659–663; 675–678.

Compare Antony's:

> Woe to the hand that shed this costly blood!
> Over thy wounds now I do prophesy
> (Which, like dumb mouths, do ope their ruby lips
> To beg the voice and utterance of my tongue) . . .

mothers shall but smile when they behold
Their infants quartered with the hands of war,
All pity chok'd with custom of fell deeds . . .

III.i.258–261; 267–269.

As a further example of the elevated exclamatory Roman tone (with
an apostrophe and active personifications), consider:

Horace. Quelle injustice aux Dieux d'abandonner aux femmes
Un empire si grand sur les plus belles âmes,
Et de se plaire à voir de si foibles vainqueurs
Régner si puissamment sur les plus nobles coeurs!
A quel point ma vertu devient-elle réduite!
Rien ne la sauroit plus garantir que la fuite.
Adieu: ne me suis point, ou retiens tes soupirs.

Sabine, seule. O colère, ô pitié, sourdes à mes désirs,
Vous négligez mon crime, et ma douleur vous lasse,
Et je n'obtiens de vous ni supplice ni grâce!
Allons-y par nos pleurs faire encore un effort,
Et n'employons après que nous à notre mort.

Horace, 1391–1402.

The *empire* of passion *sur les plus belles âmes* may remind us that
the *ton* here is Louis Quatorze, not Elizabethan.

From this too brief comparison, it is sufficiently clear that there is
a style of poetic drama in *Julius Caesar* that has its counterpart in
French dramatic tradition. It is also fairly obvious that despite the
success of *Julius Caesar* there is no established tradition of this sort
in English. Our translators have never quite known "what to do" with
Corneille and Racine. (Note also that the style of Jonson's Roman
plays has remained alien to English popular taste.) Although Dryden
and the "improvers" of Shakespeare were more or less consciously
trying to create a taste for the French manner, they did not succeed.
If we wish to find an equivalent in English for the French classical
style, we must go to Pope's *Eloisa to Abelard* and to his satires, where
we have a poetry of grammar and rhetoric that is profoundly Latin
in origin and in practice. But Pope too has seemed less "poetic" to
readers who take explicit metaphor and sensuous image as the exclu-
sive marks of true poetry.

It is not without significance that Pope is a master of poetry of
irony, a kind of poetry in which general truths are evaluated by
witty oppositions, in which the drama lies in the play of speech
tones and not in the "development of character," in which "charac-

156

ters" in another sense serve as illustrations of clashing truths, or of the clash between truth and reality. Antony's oration too might slide easily into a satire, even into couplets:

> I speak not to disprove what Brutus spoke,
> But here I am to speak what I do know.

The peculiar quality of character in *Julius Caesar*—its relative fixity and forensic flavor—the high irony of Brutus' naiveté (what a fine stroke that Antony pronounces the eulogy on his career) are thus not unconnected with a special poetic medium.

It need not be said at this point that comparing translations is useful for defining particular styles in Shakespearean drama and for seeing how the dramatic experience is controlled by the finer orderings of language that we call "poetic." The attempts of the imitator or the translator to go against the genius of his language offer concrete illustrations of the styles they are trying to reproduce however ineptly. As we explore their efforts and see more clearly the connections between poetic and dramatic design, we also see that the explicitly metaphorical and the "grammatical-figurative" styles are constantly merging. Under Richards' broad definition of metaphor as "thinking of one thing in terms of another," both are metaphorical, analogical modes. The value of the linguistic approach lies in reminding us of the *palpability* of language in poetry, of the primitive fact that we reserve the term for experiences embodied in words uttered in rhythmic order.

At the beginning of this essay I expressed the hope that explorations of this kind might be of some value for literary criticism, that is for the total critical act, the confronting of a work by nothing less than our whole intelligence. The aim, though never to be realized, is necessary, especially at the present stage in criticism of Shakespeare. The excesses of character analysis have now been matched by excesses in analysis of image and metaphor. As Empson has implied, it is now time for us to read Bradley again: he can do us no harm![12] If we do read Bradley, we may be surprised to discover that much that has been hailed as new has a place in his work, for example, the study of recurrent images and symbolic "atmospheres" and actions.[13] Structural linguistics now beckons to new excesses. The proper response for the critic of Shakespeare is not a return to irresponsible explorations of Hamlet's "soul," but to use analysis of language where

12. See Chapter 8, "The Heresy of Plot," p. 124, note 1.
13. See for example comments on *King Lear* and *Macbeth*, *Shakespearean Tragedy* (New York, 1955), pp. 213–216, 277–278.

and when he can, in order to understand more exactly the words through which Hamlet's "soul" is given a life beyond words:

> Words move, music moves
> Only in time; but that which is only living
> Can only die. Words, after speech, reach
> Into the silence. Only by the form, the pattern,
> Can words or music reach
> The stillness, as a Chinese jar still
> Moves perpetually in its stillness.

10

SEVEN AGAMEMNONS

This study starts from a remark which a great teacher of Greek[1] was fond of repeating to his classes. "A translation," he would say, "is like a stewed strawberry." Everyone familiar with translations *and* stewed strawberries will appreciate the perfect justice of this criticism. Certainly everyone who has read a Greek play and a translation of a Greek play realizes bitterly what a transformation has taken place in the "stewing." There is of course no escaping such transformations; every time we read a foreign or an English text, we remake what we read. Avowed translations are merely the most accessible and disturbing evidence of what happens when we read any text, particularly a text by an earlier author, whether foreign or English. Translations forcibly remind us of the obvious fact that when we read, we read from a particular point in space and time.

When a writer sets out to translate—say, the *Agamemnon*—what happens? Much, naturally, that we can never hope to analyze. But what we can see quite clearly is that he makes the poetry of the past into poetry of his particular present. Translations are the most obvious examples of works which, in Valéry's words, are "as it were created by their public." The average reader of a translation in English is looking for an experience of the type that has been identified with "poetry" in his reading of English literature. The translator who wishes to be read must in some degree satisfy this want.

From *On Translation*, ed. Reuben A. Brower (Cambridge, Mass., 1959).
1. Harry de Forest Smith, teacher of Greek at Amherst College, 1901–1939.

The conditions of translating make this almost inevitable, for the translator in seeking to preserve a kind of anonymity, in seeking to eliminate himself—to let his author speak—often finds that the voice which actually speaks is that of his own contemporaries. This twofold character of anonymity and "contemporaneousness" can be illustrated from famous translations in which several writers have taken part. A reader quite familiar with Dryden will find it impossible to distinguish Dryden's own translations of Juvenal from those of his helpers. What reader of Pope's *Homer* could confidently separate—on internal evidence alone—the passages by Pope from those supplied by Broome and Fenton? A reader unacquainted with the work of Lang, Leaf, and Myers might not believe that three different writers could attain the same degree of unctuous infelicity. If we should define the poetry of Pope or of Dryden from their translations alone, we should find we were omitting most of what distinguishes them from their contemporaries. The prose in which Lang and his associates have immortalized Homer is a mosaic of contemporary poeticisms.

When we say of all these translators that they gave their readers what they expected in poetry, what do we mean by "expect" and "poetry"? We mean that readers assume that they will have the kind of experience which they enjoy in reading poems written originally in their own language. "Kind of experience" is of course an experience through words. The readers of translations look to find words used as other poets use them. They demand, in Johnson's phrase, "those poetical elegancies which distinguish poetry from prose." Though the eighteenth-century audience was more certain what "elegancies" were, the twentieth-century audience has some similar expectations, such as a greater frequency in the use of metaphor than in prose, a predilection for terms which are *not* recognizably the "elegancies" of the Romantics, an approximation to the vocabulary and rhythm of speech, a preference for the act, the immediate sense impression, to the abstraction, and so on.

But we are not to suppose that these expectations are merely rhetorical, that the intelligent reader separates the use from the meaning. Nor are the meanings which satisfy the reader in search of poetry merely "poetic." It is true that there are always stock poetic meanings which become consecrated as "poetic" in each literary era, for instance, the meanings of the "lonely lake" in the nineteenth-century, of the "heroic" in the eighteenth century, or of "melancholy" in the late sixteenth and the seventeenth centuries. And readers have never found it hard to convince themselves that these "poetic" meanings satisfy a special "poetic faculty." But even these meanings are never merely "poetic" or "literary" or whatever word we wish to use to label such set reactions to a set vocabulary. The stock "heroic" meaning of the eighteenth century corresponded to something more than the recurrent attitudes evoked by scores of neoclassical epics; it also equaled a certain misreading of ancient history and a code of aristocratic behavior which was in some degree an actuality of contemporary social life. When an eighteenth-century reader found Pope speaking of the women of Troy as "dames," he found at once many kinds of satisfaction. The word belonged to what he recognized as the language of verse; it suggested to him the "high heroic" vein; and it reminded him agreeably of the society to which he belonged while satisfying that society's standard of decorum. Therefore, as we can see from this brief sketch, when we say that a translator gives his readers the kind of experience they expect in poetry, we are saying a good deal. He offers a series of satisfactions no one of which (with the possible exception of meter) is confined to poetry. But taken together they may be said to form a definition of poetry for a group of contemporary readers.

Translations—exactly because of the peculiar conditions of their manufacture—are of special interest to a critic of poetry; for they show him in the baldest form the assumptions about poetry shared by readers and poets. To paraphrase Collingwood, every poem is an unconscious answer to the question: "What is a poem?" But the question is never the same question, any more than the question "What is a man?" is the same question when asked in 1200 or 1600 or 1900. Recently, while reading some translations of Aeschylus' *Agamemnon*, it struck me that the study of translations, especially from a literature produced by a civilization very different from our own, was one of the simplest ways of showing what is expected at various times in answer to the question of "What is poetry?" In the following essay on six translations from the *Agamemnon*, I want to give an example of a method and suggest its usefulness when applied in studying translations of an ancient author which have been made over a long period of time. For instance, a study of English translations of Homer along with the writings of contemporary literary theorists should show us vividly the continuous evolution among English readers of their definition of poetry and their historical picture of ancient Greece.

To show how the implied definitions of "poetry" vary in this set of translations from Aeschylus, we must begin with our reading of the Greek text. Of the *Agamemnon* as an absolute, a fifth-century absolute, we have no knowledge. We can only read Aeschylus in the context of our knowledge of the fifth century, which is a very different thing. I am going to begin with a recent translation of the two passages to be studied, using the Greek text to correct and amplify this version, in order to make quite clear the readings which will serve as a basis for comparison. Later we shall look at this translation, too, as an exhibit of assumptions about poetry. The first passage to be considered is from the herald's speech to the leader of the chorus in answer to an inquiry about Menelaus. The herald replies, telling of the storm which scattered the ships soon after they left Troy.[2]

> For they swore together, those inveterate enemies,
> Fire and sea, and proved their alliance, destroying
> The unhappy troops of Argos.
> In night arose ill-waved evil,
> Ships on each other the blast from Thrace
> Crashed colliding, which butting with horns in the violence
> Of big wind and rattle of rain were gone
> To nothing, whirled all ways by a wicked shepherd.
> But when there came up the shining light of the sun
> We saw the Aegean sea flowering with corpses
> Of Greek men and their ships' wreckage.
> But for us, our ship was not damaged,
> Whether someone snatched it away or begged it off,
> Some god, not a man, handling the tiller;
> And Saving Fortune was willing to sit upon our ship
> So that neither at anchor we took the tilt of waves
> Nor ran to splinters on the crag-bound coast.
> But then having thus escaped death on the sea,
> In the white day, not trusting our fortune,
> We pastured this new trouble upon our thoughts,
> The fleet being battered, the sailors weary,
> And now if any of *them* still draw breath,
> They are thinking no doubt of us as being lost
> And we are thinking of them as being lost.
> May the best happen. As for Menelaus
> The first guess and most likely is a disaster
> But still—if any ray of sun detects him
> Alive, with living eyes, by the plan of Zeus
> Not yet resolved to annul the race completely,
> There is some hope then that he will return home.

The noisiness of the images and the shocking character of some of the metaphors here are not surprising to a reader of Aeschylus in

---

2. For the Greek text see *Agamemnon*, ll. 650–680, *Aeschyli Tragoediae*, ed. A. Sidgwick (Oxford, 1902). For the Greek text of the next two passages quoted in translation, see ll. 737–743 and 772–781.

162

Greek. By a Sophoclean standard this storm narrative is *démesuré*. The language is at some points remote from—and at others, close to—the norm of conversational prose as we find it in Xenophon and Plato. Over against a "sea flowering with corpses," we can set "proved their alliance"—which in Greek as in English suggests military and political contexts—and the everyday interjection "May the best happen," which is not a solemn prayer but just "Let's hope that it will all turn out for the best." The speaker here is given the language not merely of an impersonal voice from the stage, but of a blunt herald who had answered the chorus' first question flatly with "I tell no lies."

If we look at the Greek, we shall see that this translation needs some explaining and correcting. "Ill-waved," though literal enough, loses the associations of fated disaster which the compounds have in Greek. As Verrall observes, δυσκύμαντα ("ill-waved") is a word which merges meanings of swelling, labor, and storm. "Butting with horns" is an image comparing the crashing ships to a flock, which is continued in "Whirled all ways by a wicked shepherd." The storm is like a bad shepherd (bad at his herding, not morally evil), who drives (spins) the flock in circles. The "flowering sea" image is less surrealist in effect if we see in it, as Verrall does, a last glimpse of the flock metaphor: a faint reference to a field in flower after a rain. "Saving Fortune" is both simply "our good luck which saved us" and a half-deified, half-personified power, nearer to "chance" than to *Fortuna*. The "tilt" ("pitch") is not matched in Aeschylus. Aeschylus speaks quite plainly of the ship's being filled with water from the waves. "White day" has even more of a sudden "blanket-of-light" effect in the Greek, since it comes right after "death on the sea" ("sea-Hades"), with its associations of blackness and night.

"We pastured this new trouble." The bucolic character of this idiom sets a typical problem for the poet-translator. The question is how much of the literal meaning survives in the metaphor. The verb in its more common use in Greek means "to tend cattle." Perhaps, though it seems unlikely, Aeschylus' phrase was no more suggestive to Greek readers of "tending cows" than "brooding" is suggestive to English readers of "setting hens." The present translation seems to me very good, just because the verb was not commonly used in the sense of "tending thoughts," that is, "pondering," "going over them." The only instance cited by Liddell and Scott is from the *Eumenides*. Liddell and Scott do cite examples of the verb in the sense of "cheat," "beguile" (with hopes) and wrongly include the present passage under this meaning. But Aeschylus is not saying here that "trouble is beguiled." "Trouble is looked over," "given range in thought," as appears from the lines which follow. Some of the other surprising metaphors in the passage remind us that we are not to suppress the literal level of the meaning for fear of incongruity.

There is only one place where this translation differs on a point of narrative fact from the others we shall use:

As for Menelaus
The best guess and most likely is a disaster.

The translation is apparently based on two emendations both of which should probably be rejected: μογεῖν for μολεῖν and δ'οὖν for γοῦν. The original readings are best supported by Wilamowitz. Verrall defends μολεῖν (but not γοῦν) for less acceptable reasons.[3] Without the emendations, the translation runs: "Except that Menelaus will come home, if, at least, any ray . . ." For the purposes of our comparison a textual difference of this type matters remarkably little, since the differences in translation we are discussing are due to other causes.

The next passage to be used is from the chorus on Helen:

So I would say there came
To the city of Troy
A notion of windless calm,
Delicate adornment of riches,
Soft shooting of the eyes and flower
Of desire that stings the fancy.

It would be hard to improve on this translation. "Notion" gives suggestions of an impersonal abstraction which are very near to those of the Greek term. The only clearly inadequate term is "the fancy." The Greek word rendered by "fancy" is θυμός, the part of man affected by strong emotion. We no longer think of emotions as having a single, definite location in an organ (as implied in the Greek term); but we must here revert to that archaic view and translate "desire that stings the heart." "The fancy," which is a nineteenth-century "faculty," is not archaic enough.

Helen is one of Aeschylus' symbols for the pride which brings ruin. Later in the same chorus he contrasts this *hybris* with *dike* ("rightness," "justice") in lines which show the Aeschylean blend of personalized image and generalization:

But Honest Dealing is clear
Shining in smoky homes,

3. For another reading see G. Murray, ed., *Aeschyli Tragoediae* (Oxford, 1938), *ad loc.*

Honours the god-fearing life.
Mansions gilded by filth of hands she leaves,
Turns her eyes elsewhere, visits the innocent house,
Not respecting the power
Of wealth mis-stamped with approval,
But guides all to the goal.

Dike is rendered "Honest Dealing," a translation which may shock
readers who put Justice invariably for *dike*, cheerfully assuming that
dike is always *dike*. This translation attempts to give the meaning
defined by Aeschylus' context. Aeschylus has been saying that not
mere wealth, but wrongdoing brings ruin to a house. In the quoted
strophe he defines *dike* by its opposite: gaining great wealth by
wrong methods ("filth of hands") and hence enjoying wealth which
does not deserve to be honored. The metaphor means that such
wealth is like counterfeit coins, stamped with a value they do not
possess. We should note that Aeschylus does not say that Honest
Dealing is found among the poor because they are poor. Honest Dealing honors the man who acts as he ought to, making his money
by fair means. Honest Dealing does not turn away from rich men,
but from men who get their wealth dishonestly.

In comparing this basic text with various versions and in comparing the versions with each other, it is necessary to keep in mind what
we are doing. We are trying to see what the comparison tells us
about the translator's definition of "poetry." This definition will be
one shared by his contemporaries. But we do not expect to form-
ulate a complete definition of poetry for each of the historical periods from which the translations come. We are trying to demonstrate
a method of using translations, not to reach general formulas, but to
increase our particularized awareness of the assumptions about
poetry inherent in the words poets use.

If a reader turns to an eighteenth-century translation of the shipwreck passage, he will suffer a curious "shock of recognition":

The pow'rs, before most hostile, now conspir'd,
Fire and the sea, in ruin reconcil'd:
And in a night of tempest wild from Thrace
In all their fury rush'd the howling winds;
Tost by the forceful blasts ship against ship
In hideous conflict dash'd, or disappear'd
Driv'n at the boist'rous whirlwind's dreadful will.
But when the sun's fair light return'd, we see
Bodies of Grecians, and the wreck of ships

Float on the chaf'd foam of th' Aegean sea.
Us and our ship some God, the pow'r of man
Were all too weak, holding the helm preserv'd
Unhurt, or interceding for our safety;
And Fortune the deliverer steer'd our course
To shun the waves, that near the harbour's mouth
Boil high, or break upon the rocky shore.
Escap'd th' ingulfing sea, yet scarce secure
Of our escape, through the fair day we view
With sighs the recent sufferings of the host,
Cov'ring the sea with wrecks. If any breathe
This vital air, they deem us lost, as we
Think the same ruin theirs. Fair fall th' event!
But first and chief expect the Spartan king
T' arrive: if yet one ray of yon' bright sun
Beholds him living, through the care of Jove,
Who wills not to destroy that royal race,
Well may we hope to joy in his return.

The reader has been here before, but the landmarks have been redecorated. The first difference he notes is a uniformity of tone which is in sharp contrast with the variety of the original as seen in our basic version. It is a *royal* herald who speaks. He uses an idiom which belongs to the high converse of courts: "pow'rs conspir'd," "interceding for our safety," "the royal race," and so on. This is tragedy "in Scepter'd Pall." When the herald speaks of good luck, he expresses himself in words suitable to a Roman augur: "Fair fall th' event!" It is easy to see what the readers of this translation assumed as the proper level of tragic discourse.

This level is preserved even though as a result the storm—the subject of the oration—almost disappears. The omissions are more than curious: no mention of the bad waves, the rain (or spray), or the rattle of falling drops. The special character of Aeschylus' account of the storm is lost because the flock-shepherd metaphor is by-passed: for "butting with horns" there is "in hideous conflict dash'd"; for "whirled all ways by a wicked shepherd," we find "Driv'n at the bois'trous whirlwind's dreadful will." The dignity of tone is thus preserv'd; and there is no awkward mixing of sheep and holy alliances. The difference, not merely one of omission, but of substitution, is that Aeschylus' metaphors have been run through a generalizing machine which produces goods guaranteed to be free from inconvenient particulars. This process, obvious enough in the use of "hideous conflict" for "butting with horns," appears even in the rehandling of a very common metaphor:

> For they swore together, those inveterate enemies,
> Fire and sea, and proved their alliance, destroying
> The unhappy troops of Argos.

These acts, evidently too technical and too particular, are represented by:

> The pow'rs, before most hostile, now conspir'd,
> Fire and the sea, in ruin reconcil'd.

These metaphors offer more than a generalized version of the original; they explain and rationalize; they tell the audience what Aeschylus "really" meant. The most obvious example of this is the version of

> We saw the Aegean sea flowering with corpses
> Of Greek men and their ships' wreckage

which appears as:

> we see
> Bodies of Grecians, and the wreck of ships
> Float on the chaf'd foam of th' Aegean sea.

How Aeschylus came by this macabre talk of a sea blossoming with corpses is now clear: the foam tossed up by the stormy waves suggests floating plants or flowers. The reader is given the "facts" alone; the metaphor is simply omitted.

This combination of artful rationalizing with perfect elegance of tone effects a rather remarkable sea-change in the picture of Helen:

> To Ilion's tow'rs in wanton state
>   With speed she wings her easy way;
> Soft gales obedient round her wait,
>   And pant on the delighted sea.
>   Attendant on her side
> The richest ornaments of splendid pride:
>   The darts, whose golden points inspire,
> Shot from her eyes, the flames of soft desire;
>   The youthful bloom of rosy love,
> That fills with ecstasy the willing soul;
> With duteous zeal obey her sweet control.

We are not to suppose that Helen was "literally" referred to as "a notion of windless calm" or "delicate adornment of riches." The calm is the sea's; the ornaments adorn the lady (or are near her, or are ladies-in-waiting?). Again, the rationalizing directs us to the "real" facts. As in the "whirlwind's dreadful will" we were given a standard personification in place of Aeschylus' odd metaphor, so here we are offered the familiar tropes of pastoral poetry. The passage supplies a certain kind of eighteenth-century reader with the language of polite love, as that language was rendered in verse. Dr. Johnson, who was surely not a reader of this type, has a remark on Dryden which suits the author of this translation perfectly: "With the simple and elemental passions, as they spring separate in the mind, he seems not much acquainted." The words of our translator refer us mainly to the sensations which such language has aroused in similar poems and do not require us to go back of this ready-made literary response. The writer seems to have no experience—and so no language—which is any sort of equivalent for Aeschylus as we read him.

But his success in translating is very different when he renders the chorus on Justice.

> But Justice bids her ray divine
> E'en on the low-roof'd cottage shine;
> And beams her glories on the life,
> That knows not fraud, nor ruffian strife.
> The gorgeous glare of gold, obtain'd
> By foul polluted hands, disdain'd
> She leaves, and with averted eyes
> To humbler, holier mansions flies;
> And looking through the times to come
> Assigns each deed its righteous doom.

His language shows that he *is* "much acquainted" with certain forms of moral experience. The result is not simply "Aeschylus"; but at least the words make us re-think some of Aeschylus' thoughts (as we have defined them in our basic version). The language here does not offer us an irrelevant diversion.

That this re-thinking has its peculiarities is evident from "bids her ray divine/E'en on the low-roof'd cottage shine," and from "ruffian strife" and "humbler, holier mansions." The "low-roof'd cottage," lighted by a "ray divine" has a picturesque charm not found in Aeschylus' "smoky homes." For Aeschylus, Justice, Honest Dealing, can be seen as clearly in the smoke-stained house as in the golden mansion; she honors the just man without shedding a more kindly light over his house. Aeschylus has no adjective at all corresponding to "humbler." In the eighteenth-century version, the inference,

168

"humbler," therefore "holier," implies that Justice has a partiality for the poor—for the decent poor. Justice, who belongs to the aristocracy, does not give her blessing to "ruffian strife," to undecorous or revolutionary behavior. Here, as in the narrative, the dignified level of the discourse is more than a matter of style: it corresponds to the social status and values shared by translator and reader. But here as elsewhere in our analysis, we see how responsive the translator was to social and literary standards completely alien to Aeschylus. The sum of these responses composes a peculiar definition of the proper satisfactions of poetry.

To appreciate its peculiarity let us see what "poetry" looks like in an Elizabethan translation:

Then first a wynd with pipling puffes our launcing ships did dryve,
Which glyded downe upon our sayles the water beyng calme
With breath of westerne wynd so myld scant moved any walme . . .
The evening first did burnish bright, and paynt with starres the
    sky . . .
When cracking, ratling, rumbling noyse, rusht down with thundring
    sway
From top of hills, which greatter sturre doth threaten and bewraye.
With bellowings, and yellinges lowde, the shores do grunt and grone,
The craggy clyves and roaring rocks do howle in hollow stone,
The bubling waters swelles upreard before the wrastling wynd,
When sodaynly the lowring light of Mone is hid and blynd.
The glymsing starres do goe to glade, the surging seas are tost
Even to the skyes among the clowdes the light of heaven is lost
More nightes in one compacted are with shadow dim and blacke,
One shadow upon another doth more darknes heape and packe,
And every sparke of light consum'd the waves and skyes do meete,
The ruffling windes range on the seas, through every coast they flit . . .
But when the Gods (besought of us) began the rage to stay,
And Phoebus golden beames began a freshe to render lyght,
The dolefull day discried all the domage done by nyght.

This is not a translation of Aeschylus, but a translation of Seneca's adaptation. But to begin with, let us regard it as an Elizabethan reading of Greek tragedy, to see what the comparison tells us about the writer's definition of poetry. Later, we shall make a very brief comparison with the Senecan original to show where the Elizabethan writer's assumptions coincide with those of Seneca and his audience.

A reader of the narrative portion of this version will certainly not be inclined to speak of "restraint" or "generalizing quality." The essence of poetry here seems to be what Gray called "circumstance";

and "circumstance" at times means using two words where one will do. Of "circumstance" in a better sense there are some nice instances: "pipling puffes" (the soft whistling of a light breeze), "launching ships" (setting out to sea), the "glymsing starres" (glittering), the "ruffling windes." These phrases belong to speakers who know something about the sea; note, for instance, the observation in the last phrase of the wind spreading out across the water, curling up the waves. Aeschylus' language shows similar trueness of eye and ear; and Aeschylus, like the Elizabethan translator, heaps up images to create a super-storm. But the heaping in Aeschylus stops short of repetition. In reading the Elizabethan version it would be hard to say what "cracking" adds to our knowledge of the storm which isn't covered by "ratling"; or how "thundring sway" adds to "rumbling noyse"; and not even a medieval scholiast would try to tell us the difference between a "grunting" and a "groning" shore, or between "threaten" and "bewraye" or "heape" and "packe." The fury in these and similar words is not meteorological, but consonantal and alliterative. The "meaning" is in large part the immediate excitement of matched *r*'s and *g*'s, of assonance, and pairs of rhymed phrases. The smell of the open sea is blended with the smell of the lamp, of much reading in old and new verse.

More curious is the mixture of "literary" and "colloquial," of "high" and "low," to use eighteenth-century terms. This variety, which we noted also in the vocabulary of Aeschylus, appeared more incongruous and comic to readers of the eighteenth and nineteenth centuries than it does to us. For one thing we are more aware that the measure of colloquial quality in any text more than thirty years old is terribly uncertain. From citations in the Oxford Dictionary under "pipling" and "go to glade," it is very hard to decide whether either of these terms was for a contemporary primarily "colloquial" or primarily "literary." On the other hand, we can probably assume that words for such common acts as "grunt," "groan," and "yell," did not have literary associations. The real fact is that our eighteenth- and nineteenth-century categories did not exist for early Elizabethan writers (nor for Aeschylus). They were not so conscious of mixing "kinds" of words; they were using all the language as their needs required. We have to adjust ourselves to accepting seriously a translation in which "grunt" and "groan," "yellings" and "bellowings" are among the ways of talking in the narrative of tragic drama. And this plain speaking does not exclude a good deal of literary artifice. Similar statements might be made for Aeschylus, who, being unacquainted with modern handbooks, felt no obligation to write "classical" poetry and who accordingly put into the herald's speech some very rare compounds and surprising metaphors. But the Elizabethan writer offers more of everything; his readers wanted "the works" in poetry; and he gave it. In addition to the abundance of circumstantial detail and varied rhythmic devices, there are conventional literary tags—such as "burnish," "paynt," and "Phoebus golden beames"— the accumulation of hyperboles, and witty elaboration, such as appears in the "two-nights-in-one" paradox.

This translator did not always set out so rich a table, as a passage from the chorus will show:

> What Fortune doth advaunce and hysteth up on hye,
> Shee sets it up to fall agayne more greevously.
> The thinges of midle sort, and of a meane degree,
> Endure above the rest and longest dayes do see:
> The man of meane estate most happy is of all,
> Who pleased with the lot that doth to him befall,
> Doth sayle on silent shore with calme and quiet tide,
> And dreads with bruised barge on swelling Seas to ryde:
> Nor launcing to the depe where bottom none is found,
> May with its rudder search, and reach the shallow ground.

The vocabulary and idiom here are nearer to the Jonsonian standard of "such words as men do use," although the constant use of doublets and of alliteration belongs to the same literary strain which appears in the narrative. The middling quality of language and idea here has a literary ancestry too; it is Horatian and Roman. Nothing marks more clearly the line between the Aeschylean and the "classic" view of tragic fate than this smug Horatianism. Aeschylus does not recommend the "meane estate" because it is safe; he does not in fact recommend the mean estate; he is on the side of right action, in palaces or smoky houses. And the view of tragedy as simply the action of an arbitrary goddess of Fortune who raises men only to let them fall is very close to the older, simpler doctrine of *hybris* which Aeschylus corrects. These doctrines of the good life and the cause of tragedy, however un-Greek and commonplace, must be included in our full definition of poetry as it was unconsciously formulated by the Elizabethan translator and his audience.

Before reaching this point in the analysis every reader of Seneca has been itching to point out that we have been discussing a translation and that the last-mentioned like many other features of our definition is as much Senecan as Elizabethan. As this statement may be easily reversed, there is less cause for alarm. Since we are not tracing sources but are mainly interested in English translations for what they tell us about contemporary definitions of poetry, we need only point out the more obvious coincidences between the Senecan and

Elizabethan definitions. This can be done by comparison of Seneca's Latin with both the Greek original and the English version. We find that Seneca, like the Elizabethan poet, believes in giving a *full* account of the events:

> Nox prima caelum sparserat stellis, iacent
> deserta vento vela. tum murmur grave,
> maiora minitans, collibus summis cadit
> tractuque longo litus ac petrae gemunt;
> agitata ventis unda venturis tumet—
> cum subito luna conditur, stellae latent,
> in astra pontus tollitur, caelum perit.
> nec una nox est; densa tenebras obruit
> caligo et omni luce subducta fretum
> caelumque miscet.

The darkness of the night is systematically "covered," as compared with Aeschylus' brief "in the night." Of course the English writer outdoes Seneca in sheer repetition; and he adds the picture-epithets whose precision we have already noted. Poetry for the Senecan reader as for the Elizabethan is nothing if not literary: note, for example, the amazing amount of alliteration and the insistent hyperboles (*in astra pontus tollitur; caelum perit; fretum caelumque miscet*). Though Seneca is not the sole source of the alliteration in the Elizabethan version, he may have given an added classical sanction to the device. In Seneca we find the witty paradox which the Elizabethan poet clumsily imitates: *nec una nox est*. If we turn to the original of the chorus (lines 101–107), we shall find as in the translation the reduction of Agamemnon's tragedy to the play of Fortune; and we shall see the substitution of Horatian *mediocritas* for Aeschylus' moral rightness. But these attitudes are so diffused in Elizabethan literature as to be no more Senecan than Marlovian. The rhetorical devices which are common to Seneca and the translator are equally characteristic of many Elizabethan writers. The point to be stressed here is that poetry as it appeared in our analysis of the Elizabethan passages has on some sides a strong likeness to poetry as it was purveyed in the Silver Age.

The translation which follows is as far as possible from the literary conventions of the Elizabethan and Senecan translations:

> For they swore league, being arch-foes before that,
> Fire and the sea: and plighted troth approved they,
> Destroying the unhappy Argeian army.
> At night began the bad-wave-outbreak evils;

For, ships against each other Threkian breezes
Shattered: and these, butted at in a fury
By storm and typhoon, with surge rain-resounding,—
Off they went, vanished, thro' a bad herd's whirling.
And, when returned the brilliant light of Helios,
We view the Aigaian sea on flower with corpses
Of men Achaian and with naval ravage.
But us indeed, and ship, unhurt i' the hull too,
Either some one out-stole us or out-prayed us—
Some god—no man it was the tiller touching.
And Fortune, saviour, willing on our ship sat.
So as it neither had in harbor wave-surge
Nor ran aground against a shore all rocky.
And then, the water Hades having fled from
In the white day, not trusting to our fortune,
We chewed the cud in thoughts—this novel sorrow
O' the army laboring and badly pounded.
And now—of them if anyone is breathing—
They talk of us as having perished: why not?
And we—that they the same fate have, imagine.
May it be for the best! Meneleos, then,
Foremost and specially to come, expect thou!
If (that is) any ray o' the sun reports him
Living and seeing too—by Zeus' contrivings,
Not yet disposed to quite destroy the lineage—
Some hope is he shall come again to household.

This is a bluff and hearty, straight-from-the-shoulder, one-hundred-per-cent-Greek translation. (The date of publication is 1877.) No critic would be rash enough to suppose that a definition of poetry based on this version would hold for any large audience in the late nineteenth century. Nor will any reader suppose that this writer was seeking a translator's anonymity. Browning was never more Browning than when as here he was being intensely "Greek." His version represents an attempt to defy the first condition of all translating: the necessity for the translator to find within his own language and civilization some equivalents for what he has experienced through the language of the original.

The rather disastrous results of this defiance of the translator's law do not require much demonstration. One ironic result is that the English version is at times more difficult than the Greek. "Bad-wave-outbreak evils" hardly brings an English reader any nearer to grasping the manifold connotations of δυσκύμαντα. He needs a second translation to discover that "out-stole us or out-prayed us" means that some power (like a thief) snatched the ship from sinking or begged higher gods to save it. The reader finally reaches the limit in this kind of reverse-English with "We chewed the cud in thought." Pasturing leads to ruminating; and ruminating, to this!

Happily Browning had better qualities, some of which appear even in this translation: his hatred of poeticism and his desire to bring into poetry the language and rhythm of speech. Poetry, as it might be defined from this version, does not exclude such words as "butted" and "corpses." And among the monstrosities of literalism come lines that exactly reproduce the conversational tone of corresponding lines in Aeschylus:

> They talk of us as having perished: why not?

Browning does not shun the particularity in metaphor and observation which we find in Aeschylus and in the Elizabethan translation:

> ... these, butted at in a fury
> By storm and typhoon, with surge rain-resounding,—
> Off they went, vanished ...

All of these better qualities appear in the astonishingly good translation of the Helen chorus:

> At first, then, to the city of Ilion went
> A soul, as I might say, of windless calm—
> Wealth's quiet ornament,
> An eye's dart bearing balm,
> Love's spirit-biting flower.

"Balm" is the only concession to nineteenth-century prettiness, an incidental reminder that Browning was writing to an audience not entirely of his own creation. But in resisting such prettiness as he does elsewhere in this translation, Browning *was* "creating an audience," if by "creating" we mean anticipating the wants of readers not satisfied with popular Tennysonian poetry.

If we include in a definition of poetry the satisfaction of larger interests (such as those represented in the social and moral standards we spoke of at the beginning of this essay), we shall see that Browning's translation is in one respect what the mass of nineteenth-century readers wanted. It is a good example of Henry Adams' remark that "the whole of British literature in the nineteenth century was antiquarianism or anecdotage." Browning's translation is the nightmarish product of the nineteenth-century dream of reproducing the past "as it actually was." It is a Lay of Ancient Greece with the benefit of modern archaeology. The result, ironically, reminds us not of Greece but of Browning, who, as J. J. Chapman says, "established himself and his carpet-bag in comfortable lodgings on the Akropolis—which he spells with a *k* to show his intimate acquaintance with recent research."

After the "scientific forthrightness" of this 1877 translation, it is a shock to turn to a translation of 1920 and find that Browning's revolution had made almost no impression on the definition of poetry held by a large part of the literary public: (That this was a large audience is obvious from the wide sales of the author's translations).

> Two enemies most ancient, Fire and Sea,
> A sudden friendship swore, and proved their plight
> By war on us poor sailors through that night
> Of misery, when the horror of the wave
> Towered over us, and winds from Strymon drave
> Hull against hull, till good ships, by the horn
> Of the mad whirlwind gored and overborne,
> One here, one there, 'mid rain and blinding spray,
> Like sheep by a devil herded, passed away.
> And when the blessèd Sun upraised his head,
> We saw the Aegean waste a-foam with dead,
> Dead men, dead ships, and spars disasterful.
> Howbeit for us, our one unwounded hull
> Out of that wrath was stolen or begged free
> By some good spirit—sure no man was he!—
> Who guided clear our helm; and on till now
> Hath Saviour Fortune throned her on the prow,
> No surge to mar our mooring, and no floor
> Of rock to tear us when we made for shore.
> Till, fled from that sea-hell, with the clear sun
> Above us and all trust in fortune gone,
> We drove like sheep about our brain the thoughts
> Of that lost army, broken and scourged with knouts
> Of evil. And, methinks, if there is breath
> In them, they talk of us as gone to death—
> How else?—and so say we of them! For thee,
> Since Menelaüs thy first care must be,
> If by some word of Zeus, who wills not yet
> To leave the old house for ever desolate,
> Some ray of sunlight on a far-off sea
> Lights him, yet green and living . . . we may see
> His ship some day in the harbour!

We can get at the peculiarities of "poetry" here by noting the increments which the meaning has received as compared with that of our basic version. First, there is the addition of what we may crudely call the "sad-mad" meanings. There is, for example, the increased pathos of "us poor sailors" as compared with "unhappy [that is, unlucky] troops." "That night of misery" is offered for "in night." The "ships' wreckage" becomes in this version "spars distasteful." The "lineage" (the house of Atreus) is here "the old house" (!). The scene is horrible: "the horror of the wave;" and so it is easy to slip into a kind of dramatic dementia. Not the "big wind," but a "mad whirlwind" is blowing. With diabolical madness, too: "like sheep by a devil herded." Surprisingly enough, this mad dance of ships gets into the minds of the sailors:

> We drove like sheep about our brain the thoughts
> Of that lost army . . .

In the conclusion of the narrative madness disappears, and in its place appears a familiar note of wistfulness, of dreams of "old unhappy, far-off things";

> To leave the old house for ever desolate,
> Some ray of sunlight on a far-off sea . . .

The matter-of-fact supposition of the herald of Aeschylus has become sad reminiscence of

> Perilous seas, in faery lands forlorn.

The most surprising increment is what we might call the Biblical-Christian. In addition to the pseudo-archaic, "scriptural" idiom—drave, howbeit, throned her, wrath, hath, methinks—there is a collection of terms from which one could reconstruct much of the Christian myth: devil, blessed Sun, Saviour, hell, evil. The result is a rather sacrilegious miracle: the reader has the pleasant illusion of reading an old pagan author while indulging in all the familiar and approved emotions of Christianity. This "poetry" may be regarded as one of the cruder responses to Arnold's suggestion that poetry might offer the satisfactions of religion, that Christian religious literature might be read as poetry.

The full effect of this caricature of high-seriousness is seen in the lines on Justice:

> But Justice shineth in a house low-wrought
> With smoke-stained wall,

Seven Agamemnons

And honoureth him who filleth his own lot;
But the unclean hand upon the golden stair
With eyes averse she flieth, seeking where
     Things innocent are; and, recking not the power
Of wealth by man misgloried, guideth all
     To her own destined hour.

More curious than the Biblical piety of this strain is the obscurity; for the moral, which is all-important, is not clear in detail at two points: "who filleth his own lot" and "wealth by man misgloried." There may be some justification for the first on the grounds of a kind of literalness; but the literal meaning conceals from an English reader the point—that Justice honors the man who acts rightly. It would be hard to discover without a text or another translation that "misgloried" has some such meaning as "mis-stamped with approval."

The vagueness of "misgloried" for Aeschylus' peculiar counterfeiting metaphor is not untypical of this translation. Though much is added in the way of language which evokes a whole set of pathetic, strange, and pious-Christian feelings, much is taken away in the elimination of the sense particulars of Aeschylus' metaphors. The "sea flowering with corpses" has become

     ... the Aegean waste a-foam with dead,
     Dead men, dead ships, and spars disasterful.

This dead, dead sea—so potent in its suggestion—is not the bright fresh sea-field of the morning after the storm, incongruously alive and blooming with bodies of drowned men. The shock of Aeschylus' connection has disappeared in favor of an appropriate sadness. The supercharge of emotion produced by the vague metaphors of this translation comes with full force in the chorus on Helen:

     And how shall I call the thing that came
          At the first hour to Ilion city?
     Call it a dream of peace untold,
     A secret joy in a mist of gold,
     A woman's eye that was soft, like flame,
          A flower which ate a man's heart with pity.

The "windless calm" is a "dream of peace untold." Religiose, ineffable peace is—as so often—confused with the secrecy of passion, flame-like, and yet tender. This love is the nineteenth-century poet's stock-in-trade, corresponding to the elegant love of the eighteenth-

177

century poets. Both are irrelevant to Aeschylus, who is describing a "lively Idea" of Helen, an image balanced between Helen as "Calm Beauty" and Erinys and Helen as a woman who loved Paris. In looking over our analysis of this translation, it is not difficult to draw an outline picture of what a large part of the literary public during the early years of this century expected in "poetry." "Poetry" is emotion, if by emotion we mean an area of sad, strange, religiose, and dreamy-erotic feelings; and poetry is "high" language—the language of Shakespeare and the Bible.

If we now look back to our basic translation, we shall be struck at once with the revolution which has taken place in the last thirty years. But to state exactly the assumptions about poetry which are inherent in this contemporary version is not simple. One of the comforts of communicating with a contemporary lies in the fact that we do not have to state all that we assume. So it is easier to say in the present case what poetry is not than what it is. Poetry in this version (by MacNeice)[4] is not a recognizably poetic vocabulary; is is not confined to a particular area of feelings; it is not strictly confined to accepted metrical patterns. But these negatives carry positive implications. If we recall our original analysis of Aeschylus' metaphors and images, we can see that this translator enjoys a similar freedom in using the language of ordinary occupations and of less pleasant human experiences. In order and idiom alike, the herald's speech is nearer to a conversational norm than any of the other versions excepting a few lines of Browning's. Like Aeschylus he freely "abuses" language when necessary. He will also speak plainly, even if the result is clumsy and repetitious:

> And now if any of *them* still draw breath,
> They are thinking no doubt of us as being lost
> And we are thinking of them as being lost.

But the freedom results in an uncertainty as to tone which we never feel in reading Aeschylus. In the actual reading of Aeschylus,

4. Translations used, in order of quotation: Louis MacNeice, *The Agamemnon of Aeschylus* (London, 1936), pp. 35–36, 38, 39. Robert Potter (1721–1804), *The Works of the British Poets*, ed. Robert Walsh, Jun. (Boston, 1823), I, 43, 46, 47. The translation of Aeschylus was first published in 1777. John Studley, *Seneca his Tenne Tragedies*, ed. Thomas Newton anno 1581, The Tudor Translations (London, 1927), II, 118–123, 105. Seneca, *Seneca's Tragedies*, with an English translation by Frank Justus Miller, The Loeb Classical Library (London, 1907), II, 40–42, ll. 465–474. Robert Browning, *Agamemnon, La Saisiaz, Dramatic Idyls, and Jocoseria* (Boston, 1884), pp. 47–48, 50–51. Gilbert Murray, *The Agamemnon of Aeschylus* (New York, 1920), pp. 28–29, 33, 32.

as of Homer, we do not encounter the problem of "high" and "low" which disturbed the eighteenth-century translators. There is variety in language, as there was in heroic behavior; and the variety corresponds to the heroic form of society. As W. P. Ker has pointed out, "This aristocracy differs from that of later and more specialised forms of civilization . . . The art and pursuits of a gentleman in the heroic age are different from those of the churl, but not so far different as to keep them in different spheres. There is a community of prosaic interests. The great man is a good judge of cattle; he sails his own ship."[5]

The eighteenth-century translator, as we saw, solved his difficulty by elimination, by rejecting words and actions which would be at variance with the contemporary code of aristocratic behavior. The result was a uniformity of tone which the modern translator cannot achieve, for one reason because he has no corresponding assurance as to what constitutes aristocratic manners. He can only be honest in a blundering democratic way.

But this honesty pays some dividends. The reader's attention is directed primarily to what is going on, to what is happening. "Poetry," when so practiced, is concerned with the act, not the pure emotion. Like Aeschylus—we almost might say, like any writer who knows how language works—MacNeice defines the effect of the storm through telling what happens rather than by making an impossible attempt to "convey the emotion *directly*." By contrast, Murray, who translated the passages we have just been discussing, arouses plenty of feelings through obviously emotive language; but the feelings are, on inspection, largely irrelevant. Nor does MacNeice (any more than Aeschylus) give us those generalized summaries of the action and reflections on its meaning which we find in the eighteenth-century translator, Robert Potter. MacNeice is not *descriptive* in the manner of Potter's version, which is abloom with adjectives ("tempest wild," "forceful blasts," "hideous conflict," "dreadful will," "wanton state," "easy way," "rosy love," and so on). The reader —perhaps because of mere frequency—knows that so many adjectives cannot mean much; they are signals for a very tepid response compared with Murray's "sad, mad," and "far-off" expressions. But certainly the almost complete diversion of poetry, as in Murray, from the act to an exciting and even irrelevant penumbra begins historically with the eighteenth-century "describers." And a return to the "act" from the "feeling" is a good omen for the translation of Greek poets, especially of Aeschylus, whose six-footed epithets are hardly adjectives (in the sense of the term illustrated above), but whole

5. W. P. Ker, *Epic and Romance* (London, 1922), p. 7.

action-sentences which must be read with a sharp sense of the meaning of the separate roots: "desire that-eats-the-heart."

In the original discussion of MacNeice's translation we noted a good example of the modern translator's preference for the act to the abstraction: the translation of *dike* as "Honest Dealing." This phrase is an indication that in still another way this translation gives us "twentieth-century poetry." Justice is "social Justice." And though the category did not exist in fifth-century Athens, Aeschylus does seem in this passage to stress something like social justice in the sense of getting money without wronging other men. But "dealing" and "deals" carry the connotations of our world of "business" and "labor relations." Even more revealing than the use of such language is the avoidance of the traditional term. The possible "legal" or "moral" or "religious" varieties of justice are carefully excluded; whereas Aeschylus' term was more inclusive, not observing such sharp distinctions. A contemporary writer feels some inhibition against using these all-embracing abstractions which are the traditional value labels. He is less certain of what they stand for; and if he is honest, he must redefine them for himself and his contemporaries.

We have been indicating that MacNeice's translation, like the others, reflects the definition of approved poetic practice that was prevalent at the time it was written. We are of course less able to isolate modes of feeling and speaking which are so much a part of us. But the moral, as in the earlier translations, is essentially the same: the translation of poetry of the past is a translation into the poetry of the translator and his readers. The value to be drawn from noting this rather obvious truth is only in the analysis which it suggests; and the analysis will lead to a more particularized awareness of the definitions of poetry involved in the language-uses of the translators. Such analysis can also remind us of the kind of discounting necessary when we are reading any translation and of the sequel, that reading one translation means an obligation to read many and not merely those of our contemporaries. But the main interest here, as I pointed out at the beginning, is to show the usefulness of translations for ascertaining the various answers at various points in history to the questions "What is poetry?" and "What is a poem?"

INDEX

181

Index

Ovid (Publius Ovidius Naso), 10, 11, 36, 39, 121

Palmer, George Herbert, 96
Parry, Milman, 63–64, 67, 70
Pasternak, Boris, 13
Pater, Walter H., 125
Paul, St., 9
Pendlebury, B. J., 105
Petronius, Gaius, 15
Philips, Ambrose, 14
Philoctetes, 46–47
Pindar, 6, 11; analysis of metaphorical patterns of his odes, 46–54
Plato, 163
Pope, Alexander, 1, 12, 13, 15; and translation as parody, 4, 6; on Nature, 44; his translation of the *Iliad*, 55–76, 77–80, 82, 83, 160, 161; his *Rape of the Lock*, 81–89, 90, 94–95; and Jane Austen, 90–94, 95; satire of, compared with Dryden, 118; his mastery of poetry of irony, 156
Potter, Robert, 179
Pound, Ezra, 6, 15, 56
Poussin, Nicolas, 55
Putnam, Michael, 32

Racine, Jean Baptiste, 16, 155, 156
Raimondi, Marcantonio, 30–32, 34, 36
Ransom, John Crowe, 123
Raphael, 30
Rapin, René, 103
Richards, Ivor A., 125, 157
Rieu, E. V., 96, 97
Rosenberg, Jacob, 29, 35, 43
Rubens, Peter Paul, 12–13, 57, 76; his painting "Neptune Calming the Tempest" and Dryden's and Virgil's *Aeneid*, 17–20, 28–40, 41, 42, 43, 44
Rymer, Thomas, 85

Scaliger, Julius Caesar, 104
Scott, Robert, 163
Seneca, Lucius Annaeus, 10, 11, 129, 169, 171–172
Shakespeare, William, 1, 4, 15, 124, 178; *Love's Labor's Lost*, 10; *Julius Caesar*, 55, 151–157; plays of, mentioned, 56, 59, 65, 133; and Jane Austen, 92–93; *The Tempest*, 134–137; poetic and dramatic design in translations of,

139–158; *Hamlet*, 140–141, 146–151, 157–158; *Troilus and Cressida*, 142–146
Shaw, T. E., 96. *See* T. E. Lawrence.
Sherburn, George, 85
Simpson, Richard, 92–93
Sophocles, 12, 65, 124, 129
Spenser, Edmund, 12, 104
Stanyhurst, Richard, 11
Statius, Publius Papinius, 37
Stechow, Wolfgang, 13, 30
Sterne, Laurence, 93
Stevens, Wallace, 45, 148
Stoll, Elmer Edgar, 124
Studley, Thomas, 10
Swift, Jonathan, 67, 69, 94
Swinburne, Algernon Charles, 15

Tasso, Torquato, 105
Tassoni, Alessandro, 95
Tate, Nahum, 142
Tennyson, Alfred, Lord, 15
Theron of Agrigentum, 50
Thoreau, Henry David, his translation of Pindar, 46, 53
Thulden, T. van, 33
Tiepolo, Giambattista, 57–58, 71, 76
Tooke, Charles, 80
Trickett, Rachel, 91
Tyndale, William, 8

Valéry, Paul, 159
Verrall, Arthur W., 163, 164
Vida, Marco Girolamo, 104
Virgil (Publius Vergilius Maro), 2–3, 11, 12, 13, 79, 84; his *Aeneid*, Dryden's, and Ruben's painting "Neptune Calming the Tempest," 17–20, 24–28, 29–44 *passim*; and Pope's *Iliad*, 57, 58, 67, 68, 70, 75; Dryden's epic manner and, 103–122

Wade-Gery, H. T., 53
Warton, Joseph, 95
West, Gilbert, 51–52
Whibley, Charles, 3
Whitman, Cedric, 20, 77–78
Wilamowitz-Moellendorff, Ulrich von, 164
Wilbur, Richard, 13, 16
Wordsworth, William, 4, 5, 14, 26

Xenophon, 163

Yeats, William Butler, 13, 15, 56

Harvard Studies in Comparative Literature

* Out of print